Good and Comfortable Words

A page from John Pynchon's notes—January 26, 1640

Good and Comfortable Words

The Coded Sermon Notes of John Pynchon and the Frontier Preaching Ministry of George Moxon

DAVID M. POWERS

Foreword by Meredith M. Neuman

WIPF & STOCK · Eugene, Oregon

GOOD AND COMFORTABLE WORDS
The Coded Sermon Notes of John Pynchon and the Frontier Preaching Ministry of George Moxon

Copyright © 2017 David M. Powers. All rights reserved. Except for brief quotations in critical publications or reviews, no part of this book may be reproduced in any manner without prior written permission from the publisher. Write: Permissions, Wipf and Stock Publishers, 199 W. 8th Ave., Suite 3, Eugene, OR 97401.

Wipf & Stock
An Imprint of Wipf and Stock Publishers
199 W. 8th Ave., Suite 3
Eugene, OR 97401

www.wipfandstock.com

PAPERBACK ISBN: 978-1-5326-1800-0
HARDCOVER ISBN: 978-1-4982-4317-9
EBOOK ISBN: 978-1-4982-4316-2

Manufactured in the U.S.A.   AUGUST 28, 2017

To all those whose "good and comfortable words"
    have guided and strengthened me

Contents

Foreword by Meredith M. Neuman | *vii*
Acknowledgments | *xiii*
Abbreviations | *xiv*

Introduction | 1
    Mystifying Manuscripts
    George Moxon's Ministry and the Springfield Frontier
    Moxon as a Puritan Preacher
    Moxon's Message to Springfield
    A Refugee's Return

Notes on the Text | 41

THE SERMONS

1. January 26—March 16, 1640 | 45

    Lyman & Merrie Wood Museum of Springfield History
    Springfield, Massachusetts

        January 26, 1640—1 Peter 5:7
        February 2, 1640—1 Peter 5:7
        February 9, 1640—Psalm 32:5
        February 16, 1640—2 Thessalonians 2:17
        February 23, 1640—2 Thessalonians 2:17
        March 2, 1640—2 Thessalonians 2:17
        March 9, 1640—2 Thessalonians 2:17
        March 16, 1640—2 Thessalonians 2:17

2. December 6, 1640—January 3, 1641 | 91

    American Antiquarian Society
    Worcester, Massachusetts

        December 6, 1640—Malachi 4:2
        December 13, 1640—Malachi 4:2
        December 20, 1640—Malachi 4:2
        December 27, 1640—Malachi 4:2
        January 3, 1641—Malachi 4:2

3. April 1, 1649—December 2, 1649 | 117

    Gratz Collection—Pennsylvania Historical Society
    Philadelphia, Pennsylvania

        April 1, 1649—Romans 7:9
        April 8, 1649—Romans 7:9
        April 15, 1649—Romans 7:9
        April 22, 1649—Hebrews 4:1
        May 6, 1649—Hebrews 4:2
        May 13, 1649—Hebrews 4:2
        May 27, 1649—Hebrews 6:11
        June 3, 1649—Hebrews 6:12
        June 10, 1649—Hebrews 6:13,14
        June 24, 1649—Hebrews 6:15
        July 8, 1649—Hebrew 6:16
        July 15, 1649—Hebrews 6:17
        July 22, 1649—Hebrews 6:18
        July 29, 1649—Hebrews 6:18
        August 5, 1649—Hebrews 6:19
        August 12, 1649—Hebrews 6:20
        September 16, 1649—Job 31:1
        September 30, 1649—Job 31:3
        October 14, 1649—Psalm 86:11
        October 21, 1649—Psalm 86:11
        November 4, 1649—Matthew 15:22
        November 25, 1649—Matthew 15:24
        December 2, 1649—Matthew 15:25

Appendix: Sermon at Windsor, Connecticut by the Rev. George Moxon | *201*
Glossary of Archaic Words and Usages | *203*
List of Works Consulted | *207*
Index of Sermon Topics and Names | *211*

Foreword

Ten years ago, I had not imagined I would be lucky enough to be reading this book.

In my work with sermon notebooks kept by lay auditors as they listened to Puritan preaching in New England, I had encountered some handwriting that was relatively easy to puzzle out but much, much more that was extremely difficult—even impossible, it seemed—to decipher, including those notebooks that were full of what looked like shorthand notation. I found one coded notebook kept by fifteen-year-old John Pynchon ("John Pinch/Pyncheon?," as the name appears in the American Antiquarian Society catalog) that particularly tantalized me, with relatively legible letterforms mixed with so many unknown symbols that no single sentence was entirely decipherable. The fragmentary words and phrases that suggested a notetaker particularly skilled in capturing the very speech patterns of sermons spoken nearly four hundred years ago only whetted my desire to read the whole. When I chose an image from Pynchon's little book for the cover for my own monograph on notetaking and sermon culture, I thought that the interplay of legibility and illegibility was particularly illustrative of this intriguingly compelling, deeply challenging manuscript genre.

Coded manuscripts of the period are particularly difficult to decipher. Not only were a number of published "short writing" (i.e. shorthand) guides circulating simultaneously, but in practice it seems that most writers adapted these competing systems according to their own purposes and preferences. In some cases, symbol systems seemed to be entirely invented from scratch. Every individual code system, it appeared, was unique. A note dated 1829 in a different Puritan shorthand manuscript perfectly summarizes the frustration when the nineteenth-century antiquarian scholar concedes that

"After considerable labor I despair of being able to decipher the short hand minutes of the conference, without other help than this book alone affords" (Thomas Danforth notebook, 1662–66, Massachusetts Historical Society).

The idiosyncrasies of seventeenth-century codes have made transcription projects extremely rare. Francis Sypher (aptly named) was able to decipher the shorthand diary of Francis Willoughby because he identified the published system from which the Massachusetts governor adapted his own (*Proceedings of the American Antiquarian Society* 91:1, 1981). More recently, a team of undergraduates in mathematics, history, and American studies from Brown University used computer enabled techniques to crack a particularly stubborn system devised by Roger Williams and recover a previously undecipherable manuscript treatise (Linford D. Fisher, J. Stanley Lemons, and Lucan Mason-Brown, *Decoding Roger Williams: The Lost Essay of Rhode Island's Founding Father*, Baylor University Press, 2014). Until David M. Powers began his work on John Pynchon's notebooks, however, the only complete transcription of coded sermon notes was Douglas H. Shepard's valuable transcription of Henry Wolcott's shorthand notebook ("The Wolcott Shorthand Notebook Transcribed," Ph. D. diss., State University of Iowa, 1957). Powers's transcription of three entire notebooks by John Pynchon on the preaching of George Moxon is a major contribution, one that will enable many new discoveries and avenues of research.

The value of any modern edition of sermon notes—let alone a set of coded notes—cannot be overstated. The persistence of print sermons in conventional and now digital archives leads to a relative accessibility that misrepresents the seventeenth-century experience of preaching. Sermon culture proliferated early New England primarily via oral means—preaching on Sundays in the morning and the afternoon, Thursday lectures, and countless occasions for discussion of the minister's words within the family and amongst neighbors, based both on memory and on manuscript notes. The lived experience of Puritanism was simultaneously communal (centered both spiritually and politically on gathered churches) and individualistic (emphasizing the work of ceaseless self-examination in light of strong Calvinist doctrine). It was also intricately tied up with oral and aural engagement with scripture—from the minister's *ex tempore* performance in the pulpit, to subsequent discussions in the home, to private contemplation and prayer, to the offering of formal confessions of faith and even more frequent informal articulations of hopes and fears for one's spiritual estate.

For the modern reader, then, the fantasy of the lay sermon notebook is one of being a fly on the wall of the meetinghouse, as it were. Indeed, to read the notes of a skilled recorder such as Pynchon is to have an uncanny sense of time travel. Using shorthand allowed Pynchon to write faster, not only recording more detail but also capturing more of the sense of Moxon's specific phrasing than otherwise would have been possible. (Some notetakers recorded main ideas of the overall structure of sermons from memory once they returned home, but others managed to take notes in the meetinghouse as the minister was speaking.) In addition to gaining a fuller understanding of Moxon's theological perspective and the broader historical context of his sermons, the reader of Pynchon's notes is treated to moments when the style and cadences of the minister's preaching style break through. Impassioned sequences of rhetorical questions link plain style explication to pastoral exhortation. Particular words and phrases recur at key moments, like a leitmotif in a musical composition. Moxon's emphasis of the archaic verb "moider" and the transitive form of "tussle" in his January 26, 1640 sermon could fill in gaps in examples of seventeenth-century usage in the *Oxford English Dictionary*. Particularly charming, I think, is an apparently unusual moment when Moxon loses his place, and Pynchon records the minister's quick correction, "Only, by the way, one thing I forgot from what I said before . . . ", marking out the oral interruption with manuscript lines on the page (July 8, 1649).

For all that we can glimpse of Moxon's preaching style and the experience of the Springfield meetinghouse of the 1640s, it is also important to remind ourselves that the "fly on the wall" fantasy is, in fact, an aspirational exercise rather than a realistic outcome. That is to say, any attempt to record oral phenomena through acts of writing is an imperfect and highly mediated process. Accuracy is always in question. How, for example, do we determine whether or not a written account is accurate, and what do we think accuracy represents? In the few examples that I have found where two sets of notes exist for a single sermon delivery, the wording and details are never exactly the same. When reading any single record of a sermon, errors and lacunae are readily apparent through missing words that must be supplied, words that must be altered for the coherence of the sentence or that seem extraneous, phrases that are crossed out, and sentences that trail off. (I would not include scriptural citation errors in this category, as a good notetaker is likely accurate recording the minister's misattribution, a common phenomenon for Puritan clergy who often were preaching *ex tempore* and citing from memory, and one which challenges our notion of accuracy in the first place.)

Sermon notes record the minister's words with greater or lesser verbatim accuracy, but they also record, primarily, what the notetaker hears and thinks is most important to preserve. That is to say, this modern edition provides an encounter with Pynchon's experiential perception as much as with Moxon's ephemeral oral performance. The variety of ways that an individual auditor might engage with a sermon is vividly illustrated, for example, in Pynchon's notes on August 5 and November 25 of 1649. In both cases, Pynchon primarily records the sermon structure and summarizes the main points with only minimal sense of Moxon's oral delivery. In the afternoon, however, Pynchon returns to his more familiar style of (apparently) trying to get down Moxon's words verbatim and in full. While it is tempting to posit that a sleepy notetaker in the morning might revive by afternoon, in truth such attempts to reconstruct the subjectivity of the recording act are always highly speculative. Trailing off mid-sentence and leaving an entire passage incomplete might suggest inattention, but, as Powers rightly suggests, when Pynchon does so it seems to suggest that he is too absorbed by the oral performance to continue recording.

Then, too, the reader of any modern edition of a manuscript would do well to keep in mind all the mediation that is necessarily involved in transcribing a unique, handwritten textual artifact. Powers has accomplished the extraordinarily difficult task of making three complicated manuscripts accessible, coherent, and entirely compelling to read, and that labor is all the more apparent when one examines even a few pages of the original documents. While it is not feasible that every reader would also be able to travel to see the fragile manuscript sources archived in three separate New England institutions, recent digitization efforts have at least made some sample pages freely available. (As of the writing of this preface, the Congregational Library has made a nice selection available online, and it is to be hoped that the release of this edition increases interest in making available more images from this and other sermon notebooks.) Even without the visual field of Pynchon's manuscript page filled with its many perplexing symbols, the reader of this edition might profitably imagine the syntactic and orthographic irregularities that are typical of auditor sermon notes. Read any page in this volume and ignore all punctuation and even the missing words that Powers so helpfully supplies, and you will begin to get another sense of how a sermon notebook "reads." Embrace the odd and archaic spellings ("tearmes," "stablish," "togither"), the unfamiliar turns of phrase, the illogical pronoun choices, the incomplete sentences. These confusions, too, convey the sounds and experience of the meetinghouse, particularly the ongoing work in which notetakers attempted to fix ephemeral speech acts via ink and paper, to preserve the moments of warning and comfort, instruction and exhortation, doubt and faith in support of the likewise irregular course of spiritual sojourn.

To enter this book is to enter a uniquely collaborative realm of ministers and auditors, archivists and scholars, readers and interpreters. There are many new discoveries to be made thanks to this impressive contribution to our understanding of Puritan New England; local history and international Calvinism; sermon rhetoric, lived religion, and manuscript culture. Although the publication of this volume marks an extraordinary accomplishment in the recovery of what was essentially a "lost" series of texts, I expect and hope that it is also the beginning of many subsequent textual and scholarly ventures.

Meredith M. Neuman
Department of English
Clark University
Author, *Jeremiah's Scribes: Creating Sermon Literature in Puritan New England* (University of Pennsylvania Press, 2013)

Acknowledgments

For access to the primary documents on which I have based the text of this book I am indebted to the three institutions that hold those manuscripts: The Lyman and Merrie Wood Museum of Springfield History, in Springfield, Massachusetts; the American Antiquarian Society in Worcester, Massachusetts; and the Historical Society of Pennsylvania in Philadelphia, Pennsylvania.

I am very grateful to Meredith M. Neuman, whose pioneering work on sermon notetakers has informed and inspired me, for her foreword.

In addition to Maggie Humberston, Margaret Bendroth, and Kenneth Minkema for their words of endorsement, I want to express my gratitude to others whose advice made my work and this volume possible:

Ashley Cataldo, Assistant Curator of Manuscripts at the American Antiquarian Society in Worcester, Massachusetts;

Gloria Korsman, Research Librarian, Andover Harvard Library, Harvard Divinity School;

Cliff McCarthy, Archivist, Lyman and Merrie Wood Museum of Springfield History in Springfield, Massachusetts;

Alan W. Powers, Professor Emeritus of English, Bristol Community College, Fall River, Massachusetts, and my brother;

David D. Hall, Bartlett Professor of New England Church History, Harvard Divinity School;

and particularly Sally E. Norris, for her extraordinary support, gracious companionship, and most helpful suggestions, all of which have deeply enriched the hours I have spent on this venture, and for which I am very grateful.

Abbreviations

CCR	*The Public Records of the Colony of Connecticut*, J. Hammond Trumbull
MBCR	*Records of the Governor and Company of the Massachusetts Bay*, Nathaniel B. Shurtleff
ODNB	*Oxford Dictionary of National Biography*, H. C. G. Matthew and Brian Harrison
WP	*Winthrop Papers*, Allyn B. Forbes

Introduction

"I wonder how you can be cheerful, seeing you be a poor man and have so many children?"

This question was posed hypothetically as the words of an anonymous "man that cannot cast his care on God."[1] But when the Rev. George Moxon raised it on January 26, 1639/40, he was facing real people in the frontier settlement of Springfield, Massachusetts.

The minister was addressing a community which found itself in dismal circumstances in the course of a severe winter. The settlement was not even four years old. In those days before they built a meetinghouse the residents crowded together for worship and civic gatherings in the home of William Pynchon (1590–1662) who founded Springfield in 1636.[2] In the midst of the "Little Ice Age" the growing season was short, and insufficient for the traditional English crops they planted. The preacher was right: "you have so many afflictions." Food was scarce. Some of those in the congregation, he said, "have many children and . . . have got little for so many mouths." Margaret Wright and her thirty-four year old husband Deacon Samuel, who managed the sawmill, had eight children under the age of thirteen, one of whom was just one year old.[3] Forty-year old Jehu Burr, who served as the settlement's roofer, among other things, had four children under the age of fifteen with his wife, Elizabeth, plus another one on the way.

---

1. All quotations, unless otherwise identified, have been deciphered by the author from John Pynchon's coded sermon notes. Months and days are given as noted in the MSS; years are New Style. See also note 5.

2. For more information on William Pynchon, see Powers, *Damnable Heresy*, and *ODNB*, 45:642.

3. Barber, *Wright-Chamberlin Genealogy*, 9–10.

"Yet your spirit is cheerful," said Moxon's conjectural questioner. "I wonder at it." In response, said Moxon, "a believing heart [says], 'I have grounds enough to cheer up my heart. God does care for me and I can be cheerful enough. Though I have not a bit of bread for my children, yet God will care for them.'" Moxon maintained that those who despaired could do something about it. Regarding a man who says, "I am poor . . . and I have money to pay at such a time and I cannot tell how to pay," Moxon said, "You needlessly bring this grief upon yourself. And if you could but cast your care on God you would not be thus sorrowful." Faith could at least ease one's mind and improve one's point of view.

Records from the cold months of 1640 provide comparable perspectives on this topic from both the Springfield minister and a neighbor in the Connecticut River Valley. George Moxon's point of view is noticeably distinctive. On the very day Moxon spoke of hunger and need in Springfield, John Warham of Windsor, Connecticut urged his people not to pay too much attention to the harsh adversities they faced, because those were really blessings: "If thou be plagued, thou art plagued of purpose, so blessed," he said. "Studying plagues argues deep ill will. Studied plagues prove direful and unavoidable."[4] While Warham seemed to suggest that suffering is really a good thing, Moxon spoke unflinchingly to the pain and deprivation of his people.

MYSTIFYING MANUSCRIPTS

Moxon's comments emerge from a little sheaf of handwritten notes in Springfield, Massachusetts. I had seen them in 1966 when I first studied the Pynchon era. I asked to see them again forty years later, when the Museum was still in its original location in the Pynchon Memorial building on the Museum Quadrangle in Springfield. The staff could not find them at first; but after a little poking around they brought them out, and I took a quick look. Work responsibilities drew me in another direction, however, and it would be a couple of years before I could focus properly on the tiny, aged pages with their faded writing and all those arcane symbols.[5]

Where did this fragment of the 1600's come from? Its provenance is well known. John Pynchon (1625?–1703) was the only son of William and Ann Pynchon. John printed his name on one of the pages when he took

---

4. Shepard, "The Wolcott Shorthand Notebook Transcribed," 211–212.

5. The document is preserved at the Springfield History Library and Archives of the Lyman & Merrie Wood Museum of Springfield History, Springfield: ESM-05-06-02.

these notes as a teenager, fourteen or fifteen years old, in 1640. They are his record of sermons delivered to the residents of Pynchon's plantation on the Connecticut River. The occasion for John's Sunday labors may have been a homework assignment of sorts. As an apprentice leader of the community, John would have had to learn to listen carefully to others, to write fluently, and to speak convincingly in public settings, and this exercise would sharpen all those skills.

John would also need to understand the Puritan theological overview. The expectation in the Massachusetts Bay colony was that community leadership needed to be "godly;" that is, acquainted with the Scriptures, personally moved by the Christian Gospel, committed to Christian values, and an active member of the Church. John's father had followed that model in the previous generation of the Puritan enterprise. William Pynchon had been a churchwarden in All Saint's parish in Springfield, England. Unlike the churchwarden's role in subsequent eras, that office in Pynchon's time included responsibility for order and well-being in the area, and that required him to deal with such social concerns as unemployment, inadequate and overcrowded housing, and drunkenness and brawling. He then brought his experience with community leadership with him to New England when the Pynchons emigrated with the Winthrop fleet in 1630. In the new world he was a founder of two Congregational Churches, at Roxbury in 1631 and at Springfield in 1637. As one who was "to the manor born," his son John would clearly have been brought up to assume similar duties when his time would come; and in fact that is exactly what he did. The Worshipful Col. John Pynchon, as he eventually came to be known, was a prominent leader in western Massachusetts. He assisted in expanding the English immigrant community by acquiring land and developing towns. Like his father, he even preached on occasion at the Springfield Church. John was appropriately celebrated by the Rev. Solomon Stoddard in a funeral sermon for him, "God's Frown in the Death of Usefull Men."[6]

John's little set of youthful jottings has been studied in the past. The manuscript contains notes on six complete sermons, plus substantial parts of two more, dating from January 26 to March 16, 1640. The Springfield historian Harry Andrew Wright reported in 1945 that he had cracked the sermon code with the help of his daughter. Three boxes of files which Wright left behind, however, and which are now in the Springfield History Museum, contain not a trace of his efforts in this respect: no key to the symbols, no transcriptions, no explanations. If Wright could read the notes, he never explained how. Moreover, the snippets he did offer do not actually

---

6. Bridenbaugh, ed. *The Pynchon Papers*, 1:313-327

match the words John wrote. It remains a puzzle why Wright altered the clearly legible "Iohn Pinchon unfaithful & ungraci[ous]" to "John Pynchon is a disobedient and ungrateful boy."[7] In spite of Wright's efforts to unpack the Pynchon manuscript, I had nothing to go on as I began to examine it.

Recording sermon notes was a common Puritan practice. Keeping records of sermons was an important Puritan discipline, which Meredith M. Neuman has analyzed in her careful study of sermon notetakers, *Jeremiah's Scribes: Creating Sermon Literature in Puritan New England*. By recording what the ministers said, the hearers participated in a process of communication which connected Scripture and preacher and fellow worshippers. Their jottings became an aid for meditating on the preacher's message during the ensuing week, as well as a prompt for discussing the salient points with others. This conversation had its own give and take, sometimes explicitly, as when Ann Hutchinson gathered others at her house to discuss sermons given at First Church in Boston in the mid-1630's. But more often the sharing process was informal.

Yet, how to read those lines and angles and squiggles in the Springfield manuscript? I checked various volumes of the era which dealt with what was then called "short writing" to see if John followed an established protocol. Keeping verbatim records was a widespread fad towards the end of the sixteenth century and beginning of the seventeenth. That period marked the revival of shorthand, which was initiated in England by Timothie Bright's *Characterie; An Arte of shorte, swifte and secrete writing by Character* (1588). Several other systems soon emerged, some of them extraordinarily complicated. One developed by John Willis was called *The Art of Stenography* (1602); it was inspired by the principles of Ramistic philosophy, which divided everything into two. So, stenography consisted of abbreviations of 1. words or 2. sentences; sentences in turn could be simplified 1. wholly or 2. in part; when in part, it could be 1. by words, or 2. by clause. And so on. True to Peter Ramus's system of dyads, the volume itself included a second section on "Stegonographie," or "secret writing" in codes which others could not read.

The system which John's work most resembled, however, was invented by Thomas Shelton and described in his pamphlet entitled *Short-Writing, the Most Exact Methode* (1626). John did not actually follow the Shelton method. He adopted some of the symbols Shelton devised for common beginnings and endings for "long words," but John gave them his own meanings. And he seems to have simply made up many other signs.

---

7. Wright, *Meeting Houses of the First Church*, 11.

I realized that solving the mystery would require me to find repeated patterns among John's symbols.

The booklet consists of twenty sheets of paper, each of which measures about 18.5–19 cm. by 15.5 cm. (7 3/8 by 6 1/8 inches) before being folded in half. It was sewn in a couple of places along the fold, creating two fascicles of nested sheets. I photographed all eighty pages. However, because I was limited to using available light only, some images turned out to be fuzzy, which created even more questions about what the document said.

As I got started I remembered the comments of the noted historian Harry S. Stout, who is highly experienced working with sermon manuscripts. Indeed, his original research with ministers' notes led to a major reassessment of Puritan preaching, which he developed in his landmark study on *The New England Soul*. In remarks to the American Society of Church History he explained how he deciphered arcane handwriting. He advised starting with the Biblical text for the sermon; it is usually spelled out at the beginning of the notes, and the handwriting in question can be correlated with known wording. So I followed his suggestion.

The first sermon heading I found was on the seventh page. It stood out clearly, because John sketched elaborate headings for each Sunday's notes. The earliest was dated February 2, 1639—which by present reckoning would be 1640, since the old style Julian calendar then in use ended and began the year on March 25. But this heading, which featured 1 Peter 5:7, did not help because the text was recorded (though imperfectly) in carefully written complete words: "Cast all your . . . upon him for he careth for you."

Nevertheless, I was able to make out some words and ideas in the lines which followed the heading. And looking at lines on a previous page I was able to read: "and [unknown symbol here] as save as a ship riding att ancker w[ith] strong cables." Soon some of the most common symbols made sense because of the ways they fit the context, thereby creating complete sentences. So |, the unknown symbol mentioned above, means "is," \ means "not," and / represents "the" (and, as it turns out, "thee;" John worked by sounds, leading to a lot of homonyms).

As I leafed through its pages, I finally became confident that the code could be broken and the document read when I discovered a section that yielded more meanings and a solid sermon point:

> . . . God cars [=cares] for us & this is one
> thing that God poseth Job with 38 ch.
> 39 v. canst Z fill the appetitt of
> the Lion i can & v. 41 who provides for the
> ravens Job Z dost not i doe

Job 38:39 reads, "Wilt thou hunt the prey for the lion? or fill the appetite of the young lions . . ." So now I knew that Z means "thou." "Job, thou dost not; I do!"

I also discovered that the Rev. George Moxon, minister to the frontier settlement of Springfield, followed the practice of so many other Puritan preachers when it came to citing the Bible: he was content to paraphrase. Generally when Moxon actually quoted, he did so from the King James Bible of 1611; but he also sometimes echoed the classic Geneva Bible of 1560, which Puritans had sponsored and which enjoyed widespread approval among the godly. As communicator of the Word of God the minister was permitted a certain latitude in presenting what the Bible says. Proclaiming the Scripture powerfully and meaningfully was prized over reading word for word. So the preacher was free to intertwine the words of Scripture with their connotations. Lisa M. Gordis pointed out in her insightful study of the complicated role of the Bible in early New England, that Moxon's neighbor, the Rev. Thomas Hooker of Hartford (1586–1647), "treated the text as fluid, sometimes blurring the boundaries between the written text and the Word as he understood it."[8] Moxon did the same. To judge from John's notes, Moxon rarely recited Scripture exactly.

I found that I needed to view every photo in the most detailed format possible, many times actual size. Even the tiniest feature could potentially count. A period, for instance, or a seemingly random curved line might affect the reading. A dot over a horizontal line meant "that;" a dot under the identical line meant "might." Which marks were put there by John Pynchon, and which were due to the document's old age? What was simply an inkblot on the paper, and what was a significant symbol? As I made a transcription, page by page, I uncovered the meanings of over 120 symbols. Some few puzzles remain. It seems John might have changed the connotations of a couple of his symbols from their earliest uses—though after a point all of them seem quite consistent. And I confess that the meanings of other symbols, which occurred only once, are still elusive.

Another challenge required imagination as much as eyesight. What about symbols that are no longer there? I found myself trying to supply lost words where pieces of the sheet were torn away, often in the top or bottom lines at the edge of the page, or otherwise lost. And sometimes John skipped a beat in his hurry to capture Moxon's message, so an additional word or two are required for sense.[9]

---

8. Gordis, *Opening Scripture*, 74.

9. I have supplied the suggested words in italics within brackets.

Why did John encode his notes? Not for secrecy, though what he wrote would prove difficult for others to read. Rather, by using symbols he could write quickly and pack a longer text into a smaller space. He wrote in code not to conceal ideas, but to conserve paper. The following made-up sentence illustrates his system at work. Both the line of symbols and its transcription have an identical (though not particularly profound) meaning. The economy of John's code is obvious:

N ɔ b .s O | σ \ / R L >

"Now he sometimes says, 'How is this not the reason for sin?'"

The process of transcribing required careful concentration. In the case of many of John's symbols I posited tentative meanings, mere possibilities, which I replaced and refined as their usages became clearer. For instance, one pesky sign I named "opposite" until it became apparent that it meant "ungodly" (which of course *is* opposite, in a way.)

As I continued transcribing the notes, I found several puzzling breaks between pages. Sentences would end abruptly at the bottom of one page, while an altogether different subject would lead off the following page. Continuity collapsed. But then I noticed the same subject on widely separate pages. I decided some of the sheets must have been reversed. But which ones?

To solve this conundrum I very carefully checked every sheet of paper in the original to see which texts backed up to each other and connected across the sewn binding. I rearranged my transcription so that it physically replicated the original. Voilà! One sheet in the first fascicle and three in the second had been sewn in backwards by an unknown binder (whom I assume was not John, because I think he would have caught the mistake). New connections emerged. The texts made much more sense. Instead of the wildly uneven lengths I had found previously, the notes for all the sermons now turned out to be of similar extent.

During the time I was working on my transcription, meticulously analyzing the photos I had taken of the original, I became aware that the cover illustration for Meredith M. Neuman's important new resource was on the publisher's web site. Much to my surprise, it featured sermon notes by John Pynchon—but not any I had ever seen! Neuman revealed the source: a manuscript in the American Antiquarian Society in Worcester. So off I went to photograph another booklet.[10]

---

10. The notebook is identified as: "Sermon Notes; possibly those of John Pinch (1625–??)" in *Sermons Collection*, 1640–1875. Box 3, folder 26. Mss. boxes "s."

The Worcester manuscript has forty-two pages containing notes from all of three sermons and parts of two more, from December 6, 1640 to January 3, 1641. It is more closely bound and therefore more difficult to photograph. These notes had been given to the AAS by Deerfield Academy in March, 1855 and were subsequently (and curiously) identified as the work of "Pinch/ Pyncheon?, John," (1625–?). The shortened name had been deduced from a page where John tested his pen with a fragmentary signature. Concerning the dates in the label, it is well-established that John Pynchon died on January 17, 1703; but his birth year, while it probably was 1625, remains uncertain.

Still, there they were, all the old familiar symbols and their usages. Having additional text made it possible to clear up a few more meanings. One symbol which I had thought seemed to mean "blah, blah, blah" actually stood for "through" and "though" and "thorough," depending on the context.

In addition to the 1640 notes, I became aware, through an article by Michael P. Winship, of a third set of twenty-three Moxon sermons, dating from April 1 to December 2, 1649 and bound in a notebook at the Pennsylvania Historical Society in Philadelphia.[11] These notes, written in a more mature hand, lack almost all of John's original symbols. They are consequently far easier to read. They are also much shorter. While the 1640 notes, reshaped into English, average 2,460 words each for all the complete sermons (that is, those with both endings and beginnings), the 1649 notes (which are all in English to begin with) average only 1,590. The adult John Pynchon was more efficient at taking notes.

I was able to transcribe all three sets of notes in a format which imitated the original manuscripts in the number and length of lines per page. I retained John's words and original spelling, and sometimes even the relative size of his handwriting, but I turned his symbols into contemporary words. The images of the original pages of the Springfield and Worcester notes, as well as transcriptions, are available on-line at the Congregational Library and Archives "New England Hidden Histories."[12] But since those transcriptions are still challenging to read, I "translated" again, this time into sentences with modern punctuation, using contemporary spelling

---

11. Winship, "Contesting Control," 795–822. The notes are catalogued as John Pynchon, "Notes of the Rev. Mr. Moxon's Sermons by the Hon. John Pynchon of Springfield (1649)," unpublished manuscript, Simon Gratz Collection, Box 1, Historical Society of Pennsylvania, Philadelphia.

12. As of spring, 2017 they can be accessed at http://congregationallibrary.org/nehh/series2/PynchonJohn5127

while retaining the exact order of John Pynchon's original notes. That is the text in this volume.

There is a record of one other sermon beyond those in John Pynchon's notes. Henry Wolcott took down Moxon's October 21, 1638 sermon at Windsor, Connecticut, in shorthand notes. Wolcott was what Neuman calls a "content auditor," so he simply gave the text and summarized the points. The Moxon sermon which Wolcott recorded seems to have been preparatory to the celebration of communion. It was based on 1 Corinthians 11:28—"But let a man examine himself, and so let him eat of that bread, and drink of that cup." Wolcott's notes, as transcribed by Douglas H. Shepard, are given as Appendix I.[13]

Even though we possess many pages of John Pynchon's notes, a remaining question still intrigues me: are there any other sets of notes like these archived somewhere out there, hiding under a pseudonym or in plain sight, either in the Connecticut Valley or elsewhere?

Because John's notes exhibit what Neuman calls "aural auditing," they reveal a likely challenge which the first generation at Springfield faced in understanding one another: dialects and regional speech patterns abounded. William Pynchon and his children Anna, Mary, Margaret, and John came from Essex. His wife Frances and son-in-law Henry Smith came from Dorset. Several families and individuals, including Reese and Blanche Bedortha, Alexander Edwards, Morgan Jones, Timothy Merrick, Miles Morgan, and Hugh and Mary Parsons, were from Wales. And the preacher brought still another accent to the mix. Not only did he speak with a Yorkshire pronunciation—"Benjamean," "steeps" (for steps), "togither," "decleares," "tearmes" (terms)," "lood" (load); he also used North Country words, like "moidering," "slubbaring," and "gog."

John dutifully recorded all of these phonetically as he wrote down as much as he could of what he heard. He was focused on the sound and fullness of the speaker's language. He even included parenthetical observations, like "Only, by the way, one thing I forgot from what I said before . . . " His manuscripts reflect all the traits Neuman identifies with notes taken on site, at the time the sermon was delivered: "[s]loppy handwriting, the use of shorthand, numbered sections that run together in block paragraphs (rather than appearing each on a separate line), frequent cross-outs, skipped numbers, and incomplete sentences. . . . " As was the case with other "aural" auditors, John Pynchon was often able to "capture the rhythms of oral

---

13. Shepard, "The Wolcott Shorthand Notebook Transcribed," 1957.

delivery . . . even when a sense of the precise meaning of sentences is lost"—though most of his notes are complete and intelligible. His frequent use of the symbol E, probably for exhortation, suggests points of emphasis where Moxon may have stressed the claims he was making. John offers a good example of "the very idiosyncrasy" of the aural notetaker's methods which "makes it a particularly instructive style."[14]

And his notes reveal a teenager's distractions. At one point John repeatedly tested his pen in a series of "f"-shaped marks. At another time he practiced an elaborate alphabet of his own invention. And once he wrote a few symbols in such a shaky manner it seems he must have been trying to write with his non-dominant hand.

What can these relics from the seventeenth century offer today?

What began for John as a spiritual and educational exercise has become a valuable resource for understanding the past more deeply. When the clarifying question "Why are you telling me this now?" is addressed to points in Moxon's sermons, some of the topics he raised can be correlated with events in the community. The preacher's concerns can be analyzed in light of contemporary written records of the English legal and political institutions in Springfield and elsewhere. Reading backwards, so to speak, makes it possible to identify particular issues which claimed the minister's attention. So these little booklets offer a unique resource. They assist in accessing the issues, the questions, and the flavor of a long-lost community. Not only do they provide snippets of popular theological discourse at particular moments in the seventeenth century; they also point to the paramount issues of the day through the observations of a community leader charged with addressing a "word from the Lord" to his contemporaries.

The Pynchon sermon notes let us listen in on conversations which took place a long time ago. Add imagination, and these notes can provide a time-warp way to recover an hour spent in a social setting, as if one were seated on handmade benches in the midst of the worshipping congregation, witnessing a community experience from the seventeenth century. And read with care, these sermons can offer what has been called "detail—depth and contour" which can help us get inside the thought and word patterns of previous eras.[15] Thanks to John Pynchon, we can become virtually present in two different years in the seventeenth century.

---

14. Neuman, *Jeremiah's Scribes*, 30, 62, 65, 93, 92.
15. Francis, *Oxford Handbook of the British Sermon*, 613.

GEORGE MOXON'S MINISTRY AND
THE SPRINGFIELD FRONTIER

It is a long reach back to the first decades of the Massachusetts Bay Colony. But the data which survives from Springfield in that era offers us a helpful picture of the little frontier settlement and its minister. On all but two of the Sundays when John took notes on sermons, he heard and recorded the preaching of the plantation's minister, the Rev. George Moxon (1602–1687). William Pynchon had recruited Moxon from the Bay Colony, and convinced him to come to his remote community sometime in 1637. Magistrates and colony officers met as a Court of Assistants at Cambridge on September 7, 1637, probably at Pynchon's behest, and largely for the express purpose of giving Moxon a social status commensurate with his responsibilities by enrolling him and one other newcomer as freemen.[16]

Moxon came from Wakefield in the North Country of England.[17] Baptized on April 28, 1602, he graduated in 1624 from Sidney Sussex College at Cambridge, the school which Oliver Cromwell had attended. When Moxon was at the College, the moderate Calvinist Samuel Ward, one of the translators of the King James Bible, was Master; John Davenant was the University's Lady Margaret's Professor of Divinity. Moxon was reputed to be so skilled linguistically that he could imitate the Latin poetics of Horace[18] He was ordained to Christian ministry in 1626. After serving for a time as chaplain to Sir William Brereton of Handfort, Cheshire, he became a curate at St. Helen's in Lancashire.[19] But his service there was cut short when he intentionally omitted some *Book of Common Prayer* ceremonies, which irritated John Bridgman, the Bishop of Chester. Sometime early in 1637 Moxon found the Bishop's citation against him attached to the St. Helen's chapel door. He fled south in disguise to Bristol, where he and his family embarked as refugees for New England.

On arriving in the Bay Colony the Moxons went first to Dorchester; but within a matter of months they moved to Springfield. When Moxon arrived in the fall of 1637 Pynchon's plantation was only a little more than a year old. Beginning with eight settlers in 1636, by January 1638 there were perhaps twelve heads of family who were taxpayers resident in the village.

---

16. Shurtleff, *MBCR,* 1:202.
17. For more on George Moxon, see *ODNB*, 39:601–602.
18. Calamy, *An Account*, 128.
19. William Brereton (1604–1661) was a Puritan opponent of episcopacy and a successful military commander on the Parliamentary side in 1642–44, during the First Civil War. http://bcw-project.org/biography/sir-william-brereton (as of July, 2017).

The spring following their arrival in the Connecticut River Valley Moxon and his wife Ann moved into a just-built parsonage. Springfield residents voluntarily donated a little more than the £40 needed to build it.[20] This new home was located not far down the main street from Pynchon's own. It was built with some care: thirty-five by fifteen feet overall, four substantial rooms, and stairways which led to both the second floor bedrooms and the cellar, the walls of which were planked. A five by seven foot "porch" extended out from the south side, to provide space for an entryway at ground level as well as a small study on the second floor. Over the coming years four children would be born, including sons Union, baptized in 1641, Samuel, baptized in 1645, and daughters Martha and Rebecca. Eventually their eldest son, George, Jr., who had apparently remained in England, followed his father into the ministry.

Over the course of time Moxon acquired extensive property in Springfield. He received the house and lot on the main street in 1638. By 1643 he was granted eighteen acres for planting, perhaps north of the settlement, and eight acres of meadow in Agawam, plus four more acres somewhere on the western side of the Connecticut River. When land was taxed in 1647 to reimburse William Pynchon for the original purchase from the Natives, Moxon was rated for sixty-seven acres—no tax exemptions for clergy!—on which he paid 18s. 8d.

Financial support for ministers was a continuing topic in Massachusetts communities, as well as in the legislature. As the first item on the agenda at its very first meeting in Massachusetts, the Bay Company Court of Assistants set clergy salaries. They started out at a low rate, £20 or £30 per year. But compensation quickly rose. While some communities could afford only £40, most ranged from £60 to £70.[21]

Moxon's Springfield salary may have started lower, but by the mid-1640's he was given £55 per year, in semi-annual payments. He received these on March 25, which was then New Year's Day, and six months later on September 29, or Michaelmas, a day which played a role in the traditional English legal and academic systems. William Pynchon paid more than half of Moxon's maintenance expenses in 1640. As the plantation prospered and others joined the enterprise, the costs to Pynchon went down. Records in the earliest Pynchon Account Book show that by the end of the 1640's Pynchon's share amounted only to just under a quarter of the £55 sum. In 1649 Pynchon paid £13 16s. 8d., and in 1650 slightly less, £13 3s. 8d. Moxon

---

20. Specifications for the parsonage and financing details are in Burt, *First Century*, 1:160–161.

21. Shurtleff, *MBCR*, 1:73. Earle, *The Sabbath*, 292.

received Pynchon's contribution as credit at the company store. The long records of Moxon's account in Pynchon's day book show that he bought everything he needed there, from cloth to tobacco to bushels of wheat and corn to a 73-pound hog.²²

But some question arose regarding the financial arrangements between Moxon and the town. The controversy resulted in a vote in December, 1649 that the "Select Townsmen wth ye Deacons shall in behalf of the Towne draw up & send downe to ye Elders a letter desiring ym to explain ye cleere meaninge of our voates concerning mr moxons maintenance." The issue may have involved the adequacy of Moxon's pay. The relevant votes the Springfield authorities had to explain to the clergy in the Bay involved the annual renewal of Moxon's salary from 1645 onwards, always at the same £55—though in 1647 eighteen men agreed to add an additional £5 for his support. In any case, a year after the controversy, in January 1651 the town voted a substantial increase, to £70.²³

Still, Moxon's growing family seems to have created financial pressures. The minister, his family, and servants worked the land to some advantage. In his final year in Springfield Moxon earned £33 from 153 bushels of wheat which he harvested and John Pynchon exported. His profit equaled nearly half the stipend for his final year as minister.²⁴

Moxon participated fully in the civic life of Pynchon's plantation. He was the only college graduate in town, and the records, in keeping with Puritan practice, respectfully indicated his status by invariably calling him "Mr Moxon." His skills were useful whenever a trusted arbiter was needed. Pynchon relied on him as an advisor and witness at important moments. He made sure that Moxon was present for negotiations in 1638 when Pynchon was charged with failing to buy corn for Connecticut; Moxon also served as a witness at legal proceedings which followed. In April 1640 the town called upon him to use his persuasive and diplomatic capabilities to "restrayne ye Indians" from expanding their cultivated acreage onto land utilized by the colonists. On another occasion Moxon and Jehu Burr represented Springfield as its Committee (Delegates) at the Connecticut General Court. They were present at the session during which the Court admitted English responsibility for initiating the Pequot "War" of 1637. For the fifteen years

---

22. William and John Pynchon, "Account Book," manuscript volume, Forbes Library, Northampton, Massachusetts, vol. 1, 206, 209.

23. Burt, *First Century*, 1:161, 198, 192, 217.

24. Ibid., 1:171–173, 190. Bridenbaugh, ed. *Pynchon Papers*, 2:198. The amount was "pd to Mr Moxon by June 24th 1653," after Moxon had returned to England.

he was in Springfield, Moxon served as a close and valued collaborator of William Pynchon.[25]

In addition, Moxon's duties included some responsibility for the education of John Pynchon. He may have helped with John's penmanship, since John wrote more legibly, like Moxon, and not like his father. When William Pynchon was taught to write at the end of the sixteenth century, he learned a much earlier hand. He formed his "h's" upside-down, like a backwards "y" with a tail dangling below the line. There is almost none of that with John. And Moxon probably tutored John in Greek. A page in the December 1640 sermon notes provides evidence of John's efforts to learn the language. He struggled mightily with the comparative and superlative forms of some manly adjectives which (in spite of his problematic spelling) were intended to mean such things as "braver" and "more war-like" and "better, best." William had studied Greek in school in England, and no doubt wanted the same gentlemanly experience for his fifteen-year-old son and presumed successor.

A not yet fully charted frontier provided a demanding setting for Moxon's ministry. During its first few years Pynchon's community shared the name Agawam with the Native Americans of the area; but the English "Agawam" was an isolated island of a transplanted culture amid an ancient indigenous civilization. The Agawam Indians were what has come to be called a "segmentary tribe," consisting of several extended families, and numbering from 150 to 500, and possibly even more.[26] They lived from hunting and fishing, as well as crops such as maize, squash, and kidney beans which they cultivated, and other foods they gathered. The English settlement was rather close to their encampments. One Native village was on high ground overlooking Mill River, on the east side of the Connecticut and to the south of the English village, on what is now Longhill Street. Another was on the west side near the mouth of the Westfield River.

Before the English arrived in any significant numbers the Native peoples of the Valley had barely survived a devastating smallpox epidemic in 1633–34. The disease seems to have spread from the Massachuset and Pawtucket Indians westward through Connecticut. This tragedy decimated the Connecticut River watershed population to a mere fraction of the perhaps 12,000 Natives who had lived there previously. While largely independent, the Agawams shared an Algonquian language with other southern

---

25. Green, *Springfield*, 30. Burt, *First Century*, 1:166. Trumbull, ed., *CCR*, 1:17 (April 5, 1638).

26. Bruchac, "Revisiting Pocumtuck History in Deerfield: George Sheldon's Vanishing Indian Act," 36–38, citing Thomas, "Bridging the Cultural Gap: Indian/White Relations," 3.

New England Indians and occasionally formed alliances with neighboring communities in what has sometimes been called the Pocumtuck tribe. This federation occupied Connecticut Valley lands from northern Connecticut to northern Massachusetts, and connected a dozen villages, including Woronoco (Westfield), Nonotuck (Northampton), Squakheag (Northfield), and Pocumtuck (Deerfield). They collaborated with one another whenever it was mutually advantageous.[27]

Into this challenging environment the Pynchon venture sought to bring the institutions of English Puritan life.

The settlers began with a court of law. Soon after Moxon's arrival, and even before his house was built, the "Inhabitantes of Agaam uppon Quinnettecot" voted to "ordaine" William Pynchon to "execute the office of a magistrate." By this uncommon action—a popular election—the community itself explicitly empowered Pynchon to give oaths to constables and witnesses, take depositions, administer punishments (including incarceration), give direction to juries, and record verdicts. So Pynchon's authority derived from the consent of the governed.[28] This new court was relatively inactive for a while; but beginning November 1639 Pynchon's magistracy was deluged by charges of theft, failure to pay wages, and slander. The first recorded case involved a dispute between John Cable and John Woodcock. The circumstances are particularly curious, considering the fact that Cable had paid Woodcock's contribution for Moxon's new house in the spring of the previous year. In this case as in others the community was so small that twelve-man juries were impossible, and six became the norm for many years.[29]

Moxon was recorded as present at several sessions of Pynchon's court. Pynchon the magistrate used Moxon's good offices as guarantor of a legacy for the child John Searles when the widowed mother remarried in 1642. On two occasions Moxon himself became personally entangled in court cases. In early 1640 he became embroiled with John Woodcock in reciprocal suits for slander. Woodcock claimed that Moxon "tooke a false oath against him." After many mutual recriminations and much delay on Woodcock's part, Moxon won. It is unclear whether he ever collected the rather hefty sum of £6 13s. 4d. in damages from Woodcock. Another trial had a different outcome. In 1649 Moxon was a defendant in a suit regarding a team of oxen he co-owned with Thomas Cooper. Their team, along with seven others,

27. Thomas, "Bridging the Cultural Gap," 5–21, and "Contrastive Subsistence Strategies," 5–7. On the epidemic, see Karr, "Why Should You Be So Furious?," 895.
28. Powers, *Damnable Heresy*, 67–68.
29. Smith, *Colonial Justice*, especially 203–205.

had been left to roam on the western bank of the Connecticut after May 1, in violation of a town ordinance. All were found guilty, and Moxon and Cooper had to pay one and a half bushels of wheat in damages to Henry Burt.[30]

In addition to the first institution, the court, residents met periodically as the second institution, in town meeting. Only five months after its founding, on October 17, 1636, the plantation voted as its first by-law to prohibit the cutting of trees on any land that was intended for house lots. Subsequent meetings often dealt with property boundaries and land ownership, including strict rules for resale to "strangers." While Native peoples had a sense of territorial parameters, often consonant with natural features in the landscape, the English spent much time and energy in drawing more precise and abstract lines, and building fences to mark them out. The goal was to assure that every household had a variety of acreages. All settlers received house lots on the west side of what is now Main Street and wetlands on the other side of the road in the "muxie meddow," a hassock-filled marsh. They were also granted pasturage to the north of town, grassland south in the Long Meadow, and fields for planting and for orchards across the Connecticut in West Springfield and Agawam. From the beginning all inhabitants were involved in land distribution. By September 1644 the residents chose a Prudential Committee to help with a variety of necessary community functions, such as building and repairing roads, keeping the drainage ditch clear, getting rid of wolves, and the education of children; but the town still reserved to itself "ye liberty of disposing of their lands." Distribution of real estate to persons who may never have owned any land was a key innovation of the New England Puritans, and a vital contribution to community growth, especially in the earliest days. "Handing out land," noted historian David D. Hall, "was a practical means of keeping poverty at bay and caring for the disadvantaged."[31]

Rounding out these English community institutions was the church. Since the Springfield congregation's earliest records have been lost it is impossible to know when it was "gathered" as a body of self-acknowledged, intentionally believing, "godly" Christians. But the date is usually given as 1637, shortly after Moxon arrived. During the early years worship took place in the largest room of the Pynchon family's home. The weekly church schedule included two services on Sundays, at about 9:30 a.m. and in the afternoon, and a "Lecture" on Thursday mornings. While "Lectures" sound like one-way communication, they were actually mid-week services where

30. Ford, "Letters of William Pynchon," 43. Smith, *Colonial Justice*, 213, 205, 207–208, 220–221.

31. Burt, *First Century*, 1:227 (land distribution); 1:175–176 (Prudential Committee). Hall, *A Reforming People*, 63.

the message was generally more educational, more rigorously theological, and sometimes of an experimental nature.

For early New England Puritans the church in all its gatherings was an indispensable basic unit of society. It was the one setting which encompassed the widest range of people in any community. There men and women and children came together to experience community. There neighbors gathered to learn personal and public values, and exercise incipient democratic principles (church officers, including ministers, were elected). There they discussed issues while creating a warp and woof to sustain each other's lives. Church was as well the setting where consciences were shaped and right distinguished from wrong. Church was therefore vital for the very life of the community. As Moxon's comments made clear, not everybody came every time.[32] But weekly worship opportunities and experiences were thought to be essential rather than optional for the plantation's life, and Moxon played a key role in setting a conversational agenda on meaning and purpose for the entire settlement, and for the individuals in it.

In the spring of 1645 the plantation built a meetinghouse on what is now Court Square, and that became the site of town and church meetings. It was a simple structure, 25 or more by 40 feet, and located on the south side of the common. Built on stones for a foundation, with daubed half-timbered walls, it boasted a shingled roof rather than the more prevalent and flammable thatched roofs. Two larger windows on each side and smaller windows on each end provided light. There were two turrets, unusual for the times, one to accommodate a bell and the other a lookout for the nightwatch which every community was required to have. The main door was on the south side, facing what is today Elm Street. Another was on the east, facing Main Street. To help with its construction residents were expected to volunteer as unpaid laborers for up to twenty-eight days each, under the direction of Thomas Cooper, who served as the contractor. Much of the work was done in the slack winter days of March. In what must have been a building blitz, citizens erected the structure by March 26, 1645, six months ahead of schedule.[33]

The residents of Springfield generally got along peaceably with the surrounding Native peoples throughout the William Pynchon era, and even beyond. Unlike many of his contemporaries, Pynchon had extraordinarily positive relationships with Indians. He believed in treating Native peoples pragmatically, with caution and respect, and in taking all measures necessary to avoid escalating irritations into conflicts. Indeed, he even relocated

---

32. See sermons of June 3, 1649, and October 21, 1649.
33. Green, *Springfield*, 75–76 and Burt, *First Century*, 1:176–177, 184–185.

his settlement from the site he originally chose in Agawam "to avoid trespassing of" the Natives. In the deed to Springfield he included Algonquian words, the names of important women in the Agawams' matriarchal society, and specific rights the Indians requested—features which were distinctive to Pynchon, and which became hallmarks of deeds crafted by both William Pynchon and, later, his son John. So whether they liked it or not, the settlers were expected to avoid antagonizing Indians.[34]

Of course, there were occasional suspicions and accusations. Indians moved freely through the English community, and were subject to being blamed when things went missing.[35] Also, there was at least one intercultural troublemaker in Springfield. Thomas Miller was sued by Pynchon's translator Nippinsait for hitting him with the butt end of his gun. Miller lost. (In fact, Native Americans won the two cases they brought before Pynchon's court.) When Miller was granted land in Agawam near the "higher wigwam," he had to be explicitly warned against "any unwise Clashing with the Indians;" if he failed to behave he would forfeit that property. In a twist of fate Miller was one of only four or five Springfield residents to die in the so-called "King Philip's War" raid on October 5, 1675, when Metacom and his warriors attacked the settlement and burned most of it to the ground. Advanced warning sent from an Agawam living in Windsor helped to prepare the residents and keep them safe.[36]

Public records from the two years of extant Moxon sermons provide helpful background about the community to which Moxon addressed his preaching. On April 16, 1640 the isolated plantation assumed a new name, Springfield, after the locality near Chelmsford in Essex, England where William Pynchon had lived. That year the community acted to protect "Cannoe trees" from being felled without general approval, thus preserving a resource that could be hollowed and turned into boats needed for the river. In an effort to improve transportation and travel towards the east they decided to lay out the first stretch of a highway along the "Bay Path" which had been blazed over the centuries by the Indians. The beginnings of this route were a corduroy road of logs laid closely together, parallel to one another, which went across the "hassekey meddowe," up the hill, and along the route of State Street today. The year 1640 saw as well the arrival of several newcomers, one of whom, Elizur Holyoke, was to play a very important

---

34. Powers, *Damnable Heresy*, 36–58.

35. Forbes, *WP*, 3:267 (June 2, 1636). Hall, *Witch-Hunting*, 47–48.

36. Smith, *Colonial Justice*, 223. Burt, *First Century*, 1:224 (February 10, 1652). Remarks of Henry Morris in Green, *Springfield*, 381.

role in the Valley.³⁷ By December of that year he married Ann Pynchon, John's sister and William's daughter. Also in December, on Christmas Eve, the community distributed 176 rods of property, including a family-sized lot of ten rods for the newlyweds Elizur and Ann Holyoke—and a bigger lot of fourteen rods for the widow Horton, whose husband had died earlier that year, leaving her with two very young children.³⁸

By 1649 the community was larger and stronger. A tax list for 1646 named forty-two heads of household, three of them women. Nearly fifty men, some with families, came to the community between 1641 and the end of 1649.³⁹ That year saw the emergence of several issues. One was the problem of how to assure effective fencing in order to keep cattle from gardens in the Long Meadow. Another was the question of assigned seating in the meetinghouse to keep better order at town and church meetings.

And 1649 saw even more memorable developments as well. Suspicions of witchcraft directed towards Mary Parsons at the end of May created quite a stir in Springfield. Also in the same year William Pynchon finished writing a book on the Christian doctrine of the Atonement, entitled *The Meritorious Price of our Redemption, Iustification, &c. Cleering it from some common Errors*. This volume was destined to achieve a notorious reputation. In 1650, it became the first book banned—and burned—in British North America.⁴⁰

MOXON AS A PURITAN PREACHER

It is not surprising that Moxon's sermons all exemplify the conventional Puritan understanding of preaching. "The sermon was powerful," maintained Stout, "because it offered guidance in the all-encompassing search for salvation that could not be obtained in any other way."⁴¹ Moxon expressed the urgency involved in listening to sermons: "A man should hear as though his main work were to get to heaven by hearing, to escape hell by hearing, and

---

37. Elizur Holyoke (1624?–1676), with his brother-in-law John Pynchon, became the major authorities in Springfield when William Pynchon returned to England. Mt. Holyoke is named for him.

38. Burt, *First Century*, 1:166, 41–42, 166–168.

39. Ibid., 1:41–43, 190–191.

40. Powers, *Damnable Heresy*, especially 1–2, 103–108. Pynchon rejected the traditional claim that Christ suffered at God's behest; he maintained instead that Christ's obedience, rather than his suffering, accomplished humankind's reconciliation with God. Pynchon also maintained that Christ cannot take on human sin by "imputation," nor can Christ's sacrifice be imputed to benefit humankind.

41. Stout, *The New England Soul*, 32.

to do the work of God. You should hear for your life, hear as if heaven lay at stake." (May 13, 1649)

The Puritans called their manner of preaching "plain style." Neuman offers a useful definition: "straightforward scriptural explication that moves directly toward practical application and avoids rhetorical flourish for its own sake."[42] Plain style preachers represented an innovation over previous pulpit oratory, particularly in their intention to reach ordinary people. Simplicity was the hallmark. In plain style preaching, references to classical history and ancient mythological fables were excluded. So were elaborate allegories, moralistic anecdotes, and pious legends. Though Puritan preachers were trained in the theological writings of the Church fathers, plain style sermons generally lacked allusions to the great theologians of the past. Quoting was shunned.

But paradoxically, plain style simplicity required that sermons be carefully constructed. Conscientious preparation was deemed essential, so most Puritan preachers were university educated. A widely used textbook by William Perkins, *The Art of Prophecying* (1607), delineated what was involved in plain style preaching. Perkins urged ministers to apply theological "properties, divisions, and explications . . . [u]sing a gramaticall, rhetoricall, and logicall analysis and the helpe of the rest of the arts." Proper interpretation required "the opening of the words and sentences of the Scripture, that one entire and naturall sense may appeare. . . . There is one onelie sense," he said, "and the same is literall."[43]

Being "literal," however, should not be confused with being a literalist. Focusing on the "literal" sense of the text did not result in what would later be called "fundamentalism." It meant, rather, attention to letters, to what was written—with a strong preference for the most obvious meaning of a Scriptural phrase or sentence. It was considered crucially important to establish base-line meanings before figures of speech could be applied appropriately, or imaginative analogies developed correctly. The preacher was to avoid easy resort to the three other classical "senses" of scripture, namely, the allegorical (metaphorical, where one thing stands for something else), the tropological (ethically instructive, where morals are deduced and applied to everyday life), and the anagogical (mystical, where scripture is seen as a revelation of eternal life). As Perkins remarked, "An allegorie is onely a certaine manner of vttering the same [literal] sense. The Anagoge and Tropologie are waies, whereby the sense may be applied."[44] The literal style

---

42. Neuman, *Jeremiah's Scribes*, 4.
43. Perkins, *The Arte of Prophecying*, 26, 30, 31.
44. Ibid., 31.

resulted in much more conversational vocabulary and tone in comparison with other kinds of contemporary preaching.

On the basis of the Pynchon notes (the only record we have), it is difficult to identify printed resources Moxon may have used in background study for his sermons. John Pynchon named no Biblical commentators, probably because Moxon did not mention any. But it seems clear that he did make use of published authorities. While Moxon usually presented the circumstances of each text in a simple way, in a few cases his introductions can be loosely linked to volumes by classic commentators, such as Ainsworth and Calvin, which could have been available to him. I have suggested those links in footnotes to the sermon texts. Three other sources are clearer, however. He sometimes relied (as in his sermon of August 5, 1649, for example) on William Ames' magisterial compendium, *The Marrow of Sacred Divinity* (1638), which was translated from the Latin edition of 1634. In his August 12, 1649 sermon on Melchizedek he drew from Hugh Broughton's *A treatise of Melchisedek: proving him to be Sem.* (1591) And his parsing of Matthew 15:22, which he preached on November 4, 1649, can be correlated explicitly with points made in *Syrophænissa or, the Cananitish womans conflicts* (1601), a volume attributed to Robert Wilmot.

The pastor in Hartford, the Rev. Thomas Hooker, was a particularly well-known plain style preacher. Before emigrating to New England in 1633 he had served as the town Lecturer in Chelmsford, a post which was privately funded by Puritans. In that capacity he preached regularly at St. Mary the Virgin, the central parish church which eventually became the cathedral. His messages were tailored to the mercantile population in the community. That segment of society represented a strong source of the Puritan movement's energy. The final paragraph of his 1629 sermon on "The Poor Doubting Christian Drawn Unto Christ," for example, offered this example of plain style rhetoric:

> When men use to make a purchase they will reckon up all and say, "There is so much wood, worth so much, and so much stock, worth so much;" and then they offer for the whole, answerable to all the parcels. So there is item for an heavenly mind, that is worth thousands, and item for an humble heart, that is worth millions.[45]

Moxon composed his plain style sermons according to the customary Puritan schema, which has been extensively described by Perry Miller, Harry S. Stout, and others.[46] He began by commenting briefly on the cir-

---

45. Williams, ed., *Thomas Hooker-Writings in England and Holland*, 186.
46. For descriptions and assessments of the Puritan form for sermons see Miller,

cumstances of the text, which was invariably a single Bible verse that he would sometimes explicate as a *continua* for several weeks running. Such detailed explication of the Scriptures was standard for Puritan preachers. Painstaking attention to textual nuances was common; "[f]requently an entire doctrine within a sermon *continua* might turn on a single word of the scriptural verse."[47] Moxon's scrupulous focus resulted in sermons preached from verses in Hebrews 6:11-20 for ten consecutive weeks in the summer of 1649. Following his opening explication of the text Moxon next identified one or two Doctrines which could be extracted from it. Then he supported each doctrine by Reasons and usually other texts for Proofs. The "collation" of a string of proof texts juxtaposed verses drawn from various Scripture locations. The purpose was to reveal interconnections which served to make the meanings clearer.[48] Finally Moxon offered Uses or applications, which were generally of two kinds: either (1) to "inform" or to comfort and console the godly, the church people; or (2) to "reprove" the ungodly, those outside the church. Sometimes in connection with the Uses he offered more pointed Directions or Rules for his hearers to follow (he used those words interchangeably). In addition, Moxon occasionally raised hypothetical Questions and Objections which he then answered in a "rhetorical call-and-response," which made the sermon hearing experience more engaging and interactive.[49] All these components of Moxon's sermons were features commonly found throughout Puritan plain style preaching.

Also, as with other Puritans, Moxon developed his messages with a strong reliance on logic. Preachers understood that humans are rational, and must be convinced rationally. The Puritans felt that in effective persuasion "logic is always given a more valued position than emotions; it is not only more reliable, but ultimately the place of meaning."[50] So Puritans argued logically by constructing syllogisms in which the major premise (opening claim) was never supposed to be debatable, but rather so self-evident it had to be accepted. This was considered a much stronger form of presentation than mere rhetorical reliance on premises which the presenter hoped

---

The New England Mind: The Seventeenth Century, 332-333; Stout, *The New England Soul*, pp. 32-49; Gordis, *Opening Scripture*, 13-36; Neumann, *Jeremiah's Scribes*, 14-15; Herget, "Writing After the Ministers: The Significance of Sermon Notes," in Herget, ed., *Studies in New England Puritanism*, 118-120.

47. Neuman, *Jeremiah's Scribes*, 144.

48. On the practice of listing related proof texts, known as "collation," see Gordis, *Opening Scripture*, pp. 25-26, and Neuman, *Jeremiah's Scribes*, 150.

49. Neuman, *Jeremiah's Scribes*, 107.

50. Roberts Miller, *Voices*, 93.

hearers would accept.[51] While Moxon did not usually frame syllogisms in obvious ways, a few are explicit, such as, "[T]he Lord cares for all living things; man is a living [*thing*]; then God cares for us." (February 2, 1640)

The form of logic the Puritans most prized was developed by Peter Ramus (Pierre de la Ramée, 1515–1572) which became exceedingly popular among clergy who comprised the Puritan movement known in England as Independents and in New England, Congregationalists. Ramistic logic featured divisibility: everything was composed of two parts. As Walter Ong, S J, suggested, the effect is a yielding of more components "through a series of successive openings, like a Chinese puzzle."[52] At the time the Ramistic system seemed to be an exciting breakthrough from traditional Aristotelian logic. As applied in Moxon's sermons, we find the system focused around series of "branching points," usually into twos, which lead to ever more detailed explications. John Eusden characterized the result as "a kind of reverse tennis tournament chart."[53] It could be argued, however, that while the Ramist method provided a certain clarity, its starkly drawn bifurcations also furthered the unquestioning self-confidence and high relief contrasts found in Puritanism, and may well have contributed to the lack of malleability in Puritan thought, since everything must be either one thing or another. At a distance the method's uniqueness disappears, and within a relatively brief time the Ramist innovation itself and the certainty it engendered faded into oblivion.[54]

For those who expect to find only angry warnings and threatening "Jeremiads" in early New England sermons, Moxon's oratory reveals that Puritan preaching offered flexibility in tone and topic. While Moxon spoke in a carefully organized and reasoned plain style, particularly in his earlier efforts he rarely preached stereotypical "hellfire and brimstone" sermons. Puritans commonly reserved those for special occasions where the entire community was expected to be present, such as fast days or elections. The course of Moxon's Sunday sermons of 1640 exemplify his emphasis on hope. He stressed the power of God's forgiveness in a sermon on Psalm 32:5—"I said, I will confess my transgressions unto the Lord; and thou forgavest the iniquity of my sin." (February 9, 1640) For five Sundays late in 1640 he preached on the Bible's promise of health and growth, based on Malachi 4:2—"But unto you that fear my name shall the Sun of righteousness arise

51. Miller, *The New England Mind*, 292. Roberts-Miller, *Voices*, 52.

52. Ong, *Ramus*, 200.

53. Eusden, *The Marrow of Theology*, 41.

54. Roberts-Miller, *Voices*, 45–50, and 62: "Perhaps due to Ramistic dichotomies, many Puritan theories assume a binary opposition in terms of the positions available," such as elect vs. damned, order vs. sin, etc.

with healing in his wings; and ye shall go forth, and grow up as calves of the stall." He chose just as positive, encouraging texts for other Sundays, including January 26 and February 2, when he preached on 1 Peter 5:7—"[Cast] all your care upon him, for he careth for you," saying that God's mercies are "not like summer rivers that come a shower of rain and therefore in a drought [are] drawn dry, but God's more like the sea." (February 2, 1640) He went on to remark,

> And where it is said, "The eyes of the Lord run to and fro" [2 Chronicles 16:9], now to what end is it? Why do the Lord's eyes "run to and fro"? To spy out our faults? It is also to have him eyeing [?] providentially over us to exercise his goodness and to supply our wants, and not to behold all our faults; not only as a bystander to look on things. But the eyes of the Lord run to and fro to order the affairs of the world—to help all in their need that cast their care on him.

Even when his message called for repentance, Moxon consistently included a Use "for the comfort and consolation of all the godly." Clearly he intended to encourage the struggling community in the most constructive ways possible.

John's notes bear ample witness to Moxon's oratorical skills. His arguments were carefully organized. He often linked his points by parallel introductory phrases. He used synonyms judiciously. Sometimes he punctuated for emphasis by repeating brief, key sentences. While Moxon usually used the general plural "you," he switched to the more pointed singular "thou" to deliver particularly focused comments. His remarks on December 27, 1640 offer an example: "[M]ethinks it might make your very hearts to ache, that there should be so much in Christ, and thou hast none." He spoke with such verve, especially towards the end of some sermons, that sometimes Pynchon was able to take fragmentary notes only as he hastily recorded in broken sentences the passionate preaching of his minister.

MOXON'S MESSAGE TO SPRINGFIELD

Moxon's preaching was consistent with the messages of most other Puritans; he offered neither unusual Biblical interpretations nor theological innovations. But he did address a variety of local concerns in his frontier community. From Moxon's "uses" or applications it is possible to identify particular issues which claimed the minister's attention.

One was *hunger and poverty*. In the depths of the winter of 1640 Moxon told his congregation,

> Provide to live comfortably in a famine. Strengthen thyself against the day of adversity, when providences fail and all things do begin to slack: you be in want for food—then you will wish you have labored to live comfortably against such a day. It is your folly and sin that you do not prepare yourselves against such a day. And then how can you say, "The thing which I feared is come upon me?" Now prepare for such a day. Assure yourselves it will come upon you. (March 2, 1640)

This warning came some months ahead of a period of economic hardship in Massachusetts. In October, 1640, the Massachusetts General Court passed measures to address "a great stop in trade & comerce for want of money." Their solution was to permit payments in corn, cattle, fish, or other commodities.[55] By late 1641, serious financial distress led to a lowering of salaries in Springfield. In his study of the economic structure of seventeenth-century Springfield, *Labor in a New Land*, Stephen Innes noted that twelve of the twenty-two longer-term residents of the plantation "experience[d] serious indebtedness problems with the Pynchons."[56]

Moxon was also concerned with aspects of Springfield's *governance*. On July 8, 1649 he addressed the function of oaths. He considered oaths "a part of religious worship," as "lawful," as he put it, as praying or hearing God's Word:

> Every man, when he takes an oath though justly called to it, doth call God to witness that what he speaks is true, and to plague and punish him if he speak false—not only in general, but if he speak false on any particular.... [T]he use of an oath: it is for confirmation of something that is to be confirmed. Suppose one says, "Such a beast is mine." "No," says another, "It's mine." How shall this be decided now? Now must an oath be for confirmation one way or other.
>
> [*Another*] thing in an human oath: it is for the ending of a controversy ... [M]any times controversies among men cannot be ended without [an oath]. (July 8, 1649)

These comments came not more than a month after rumors of witchcraft began circulating in Springfield. Accusations by Mary Parsons ended in

---

55. Shurtleff, *MBCR*, 1:304
56. Burt, *First Century*, 1:168, 169, 171. Innes, *Labor in a New Land*, 10–11, 74–75.

her conviction for defaming the widow Marshfield. Squabbling over this very serious and frightening charge may have been behind Moxon's pointed aside, "I won't have men contentious in these oaths." (July 8, 1649) No doubt he meant women, too. Pynchon's Court Record reports that "solemn oaths" were used to determine the outcome of the Marshfield case.[57]

This first whisper of deviltry in Springfield seems to have grown out of a witchcraft scare in Connecticut which led to the execution of Alice Young of Windsor in 1647.[58] A second, much more serious incident, which also involved Mary Parsons, emerged in 1651. Both Mary and her husband Hugh Parsons came under suspicion of witchcraft. The Moxons' daughters Martha and Rebecca were drawn into the episode when they suffered from "fits." Unfortunately this happened at the very time Hugh was disputing with George Moxon about chimney work Parsons was supposed to do at the Moxons' home.[59] Mary, testifying against Hugh, repeated his threat that "if Mr. Moxon do force me to make bricks according to bargain I will be even with him or he shall get nothing by it." Hugh admitted that he had said, enigmatically, "[i]f [Moxon] would hold me to my bargain, I could puzzle him in the bargain." Moxon's own testimony claimed that Hugh softened his threat to merely stating that Moxon "could not in strictness hold him to the bargain[.]" "But," Moxon added, "this last threat doth not take of[f] the ill purpose of the former threatening." After a trial in Boston Hugh was released; but Mary died in prison. Lacking any further records we cannot know more of Moxon's views about witchcraft or the Parsons case.[60]

Moxon dealt with governance and respect for authority at a few other points as well, especially in later sermons. On September 16, 1649, for example, he reproved "all those that are loose spirited, that take no care of their thoughts and looks [= how they think and look at others], a carnal heart, so he can keep himself without [= outside] the compass of the magistrate." Community requires responsible citizens: "God is honored or dishonored according as you do duty or neglect it," he said. (May, 1649).

On more than one occasion, particularly in his later years in Springfield, Moxon addressed the *youth* of the community. He was worried about disorderly behavior that might disappoint parents and disrupt the

---

57. Smith, *Colonial Justice*, 220. Pynchon himself proposed oaths to resolve the corn controversy with Connecticut in which he became entangled in 1638; see Green, *Springfield*, 32.

58. Demos, *Entertaining Satan*, 301.

59. The work seems to have been completed and paid for by William Pynchon out of credit extended to Moxon at the Pynchon store. The bill came to £6 18s. 4d., which was 18s. less than the original estimate. Pynchon, "Account Book," vol. 1, 209.

60. Hall, *Witch Hunting*, 37–38; Powers, *Damnable Heresy*, 95–102.

community, perhaps similar to the young people breaking meetinghouse windows when playing in the churchyard in February, 1664.[61] He directly challenged the youth: "[I]t may be thou hast grieved thy parents and governors, broken their hearts, &c. And it may be thou hast been vild[62] against the godly, and such as thou shouldst have respected." He urged them to be responsible towards their parents, lest their own children in time fail to be responsible to them:

> Children, take heed of yourselves. If anything be amiss in you, it's your parents' sorrow. Therefore do you do your duty to your parents? Now you are grown up: if your aged parents need your help, requite them. If they be in any affliction, pity them. Help them. Make your parents' suffering your own, else it will be just with God, if ever you have children, to make them unnatural to you. And if you be helpful, and do lay to heart your parents' suffering, God may bless you in your children and make them as pity-full, as helpful, and as full of natural affection to you. (November 4, 1649)

He expected the same examination of conscience from the young as from adults, though he was clearly convinced that young people were not so self-aware and self-critical as the older generation: "And it might be young beginners in conversion take notice and confess some sins, such as they load on themselves, yet are not so apt of taking notice of other sins which by degrees God discovers,[63] as we do not take notice of breaking the rule. Yet now it might [be] God [will] discover it." (February 9, 1640) "It may be your governors tell you, 'You carry yourself stubbornly and disobediently.' Well go to the word and see when [an] inferior may be said to be disobedient—that says, 'Children, obey your parents in all things.'" (April 1, 1649) Moxon offered only one solution:

> Learn the Commandments. Here I mean the Commandments given on Mount Sinai which we call the Ten Commandments. It is very necessary that you should be well acquainted with them, and know the meaning and extent of them.... And therefore it's greatly to be bewailed that the younger sort are not better acquainted with the Commandments. This is the foundation of all: be well-acquainted with the Commandments. (April 1, 1649)

---

61. Burt, *First Century*, 1:314.
62. vile
63. uncovers, discloses

With this comment Moxon was addressing the paramount issue which challenged the Puritan enterprise over the course of time: how to continue the movement by replicating the experiences that gave it birth in those of subsequent generations.

The counterpart of children and youth were parents. Moxon expected of them the same sense of responsibility. He urged mutual sympathy. "Make the case of your children your own. If you can help your children, do. If you can prevent their sufferings, you should. Make their sufferings yours." (November 4, 1649) He understood (perhaps from personal experience?) that rearing children can be an ordeal, even for God's people: "[I]t sometimes falls out that the children of godly parents are as grievously vexed as any others. Sometimes God doth not spare the children of godly parents." (November 4, 1649)

Other themes appear less frequently in John's notes. One was a Puritan anxiety about *heresy*, which Moxon shared. He was particularly concerned about the specter of "Arminianism." The word can have various meanings, but Puritans used this label to criticize opposition to traditional Calvinist doctrine, and particularly the initiatives of William Laud (1573–1645). It was Laud's efforts as Archbishop of Canterbury from 1633 to 1640 that lead to Moxon's own exile in 1637. Arminianism took its name from the Dutch theologian Jacob Arminus (1560–1609), who claimed that human decisions and actions had as much to do with eternal salvation as the incontrovertible sovereign will of God. Whereas Calvinism centered on preaching and applied the dynamics of sin and salvation in an egalitarian way, exempting no one, Arminianism tended to be hierarchical and focused on ceremony and salvation through sacraments. To oversimplify, it could possibly be said that Arminians saw grey while Calvinists saw black and white. Moxon probably first became acquainted with Arminianism when he was at Sidney Sussex College at Cambridge. The commencement of 1622 witnessed a skirmish in the battle of Calvinists and Arminians as the preacher, William Lucy, lambasted Calvinist predestination.[64] In 1626 the King's proclamation forbade anyone to "raise any doubts, or publish or maintain any new inventions, or opinions, concerning religion," which had the effect of muzzling Calvinists. Archbishop William Laud oversaw the Arminian program during the 1630's. No more Calvinist bishops were appointed. Sacraments were emphasized over sermons. Altars at the east end of churches replaced communion tables.

And several stalwart preachers were compelled to resign, including Thomas Hooker, who was forced out of Chelmsford, and Thomas Shepard, who had to leave Earles Colne, both in Essex; and John Davenport, who left St. Stephens Coleman Street in London. In time all three emigrated to New England. Hooker became Moxon's neighbor in Hartford, Shepard the pastor in Cambridge, and Davenport in New Haven.[65] "Now when churches are not sound in doctrine," Moxon warned, "when the churches lose the truth and lose sound doctrine, so much more does anti-Christ creep in, and Arminianism has overspread churches." (March 9, 1640) He meant in the parishes of the Old England, not the congregations of the New. He was also concerned about atheism, which he defined as "not hoping in God and not resting on him." (February 2, 1640) To Moxon's mind, atheism was not so much a theoretical denial of the existence of God, which would have been unthinkable to him. Rather it was simply the practical result of unbelief: living as if there were no God. Treating God like some created being who does not "know the hearts of men" eviscerates God's power.

Another though less frequent theme was the new shape of *church life* which was then developing in New England, in comparison with traditional patterns in the old country. The subject arose in Moxon's preaching as early as just ten years after the Winthrop immigration. There were already signs of a gap between the more diverse practices in the mother country and the stricter standards in Massachusetts:

> [T]he practices of the churches of New England [*are*] not to admit none but them that are known to be saints. Now if you should go into Old England, you know not how your mind might be. And the practice of New England is not to baptize children without their parents be members. Now if you should go to old England you know not your mind. Be stablished in sound doctrine; you know not what you might be put upon. . . . We have not been trained up in our native country, and in his [= Christ's] prophetical [*office*]. We are not stable in teaching and instructing, and for these things we deserve to be reproved. If any of our own native country should come over and oppose this way, how can you answer? Now be stable in the truth. (March 9, 1640)

The New England Puritans, removed from their origins and at a considerable distance from their homeland's society, felt freer to shape their congregations according to more radical Reformation standards. Robert Browne's 1582 tract, *A Treatise of Reformation Without Tarrying for Anie*, expressed the radical Puritan intention: "[W]ee hold all those Preachers and

---

65. Ibid., 224, 187. On Davenport, see Bremer, *First Founders*, 147–168, and *Building a New Jerusalem*.

teachers accursed, which will not doe the duties of Pastors and teachers till the Magistrates doe force them thereto. They saye, the time is not yet come to builde the Lordes House, they must tarie for for the Magistrates and for Parliamentes to do it.... The Maguistrates doe hinder the Lordes building and kingdome...."[66] On the western shores of the Atlantic they were ready to build aright. For one thing, they set more demanding criteria for church membership, and that became the occasion for much trans-oceanic misunderstanding between divergent branches of the Puritan movement.[67] Moxon seems to have supported the stricter New England way. But he was aware that the times were changing. Commenting at one point on the increasing self-doubt he detected among his people, a flagging of their formerly robust beliefs now that they were in the new world, Moxon remarked, "This is not the way [in] the days of old." (March 9, 1640)

Moxon even commented obliquely on *relationships with Native peoples*. In spite of continuing contact between the Native American and English residents on the streets of Springfield and in Pynchon's warehouse in Agawam, there remained a considerable gulf between the two which was never bridged. A passing remark by George Moxon indicated that he shared the wariness that many English probably felt. Early in his time in Springfield Moxon is reported to have said to Pynchon, "An Indian promise is noe more then to have a pigg by the taile."[68] It is almost as if the Indians were simply a scarcely noticed feature of the landscape around the miniscule English community.

But even though Moxon never explicitly mentioned Indians in any context in the extant sermons covered by John Pynchon's notes, he did vividly retell the Acts 27-28 account of the shipwreck which cast St. Paul and his companions onto the wild shores of Malta, and he phrased the story in a way which may have reflected his own sense of indebtedness to the Agawams. He echoed an expression of appreciation for non-Christian natives in the Biblical text, using words from the Geneva Bible (Acts 28:2): "the barbarians kindled a fire and received them graciously." (February 26, 1640). And on November 4, 1649 Moxon commented on interreligious dialogue and communication with non-Christians. He noted that "where God hath a people it often falls out that other strangers that live among them receive something of that religion, if not the power of it to their effectual conversion." This sharing can happen through "godly conversation" on the

---

66. Browne, *A Treatise of Reformation*, C2v.

67. A case in point would be the 1646 challenge of Dr. Robert Child's "Remonstrance," which urged more laxity in church affairs. See *ODNB*, "Child, Robert," 11:433-434.

68. Green, *Springfield*, 1636-1886, 16.

part of Christians: living in a manner which expresses faith commitments, as well as willingness to discuss religious questions (Moxon said, "dispute about religion"). It can also happen through interest in Christianity on the part of non-Christians because of the good example of the conscientious lives they have seen. And it can even happen by deeper intercultural awareness through knowing one another's language. He said, "People of differing nations and languages conversing together come in some measure to be acquainted with one another's language and so, important matters of religion." Moxon's message at this point reflected the view expressed in the 1628 Bay Company Charter.[69]

But Moxon was especially concerned with his people's spiritual and emotional health. To counter the mood of discouragement in the face of adversities which many experienced while living in the Valley, Moxon urged a *positive frame of mind*. In February 1640 he said,

> God would have us live comfortably and rejoice. Now we should labor not to be so sad, because God will comfort our hearts. We should not make others sad when God would have them not so. When we have saddened our own hearts heretofore, now we should labor to reform. God would have us live comfortably, and truly the want of comfort puts you upon many distrusts of unbelief. When God affords you comfort, take it, lest you want beholding of God's providence, and want acquaintance with Christ. Never sadden your heart so needlessly and sinfully, seeing God would have you live comfortably. (February 23, 1640)

He was insistent that his people have a positive attitude even in their isolation on the frontier: "We in this wilderness here, what providences doth God give in outward conditions—clothing us, providing food for us, keeping us in health, increasing us, and the like. Also in regard of the ordinances in our inward spiritual condition—what precious providences! Many good meals, meat of the word. Now if these will not comfort us, then what will?" (March 2, 1640)

Moxon found sources for encouragement and hope in the grand themes of scripture, including those pertaining to the person of Jesus. He urged his people to find strength in identifying with Christ:

---

69. The charter expressed the hope that the colony "maie be soe religiously, peaceablie, and civilly governed, as their good life and orderlie conversacon maie wynn and incite the natives of country to the knowledg and obedience of the onlie true God and Savior of mankinde, and the Christian fayth, which, in our royall intencon and the adventurers free profession, is the principall ende of this plantacon." Shurtleff, *MBCR*, 1:17. Cogley, *John Eliot's Mission*, 5–9, calls this the "affective model" of evangelization.

> What is in Christ but in a sort it's said to be in believers. Is Christ dead? So are we. Is Christ risen? So we. Is Christ a King? So we. Doth Christ reign? So we. Romans 6:3 and 4. . . . Is Christ a King? We are Kings, too. Exodus 19:16. Peter has it, "a Kingly priesthood." Revelation 1:6—he has made us a Kingly priesthood. We are said to reign as Christ reigns. And doth Christ overcome? Then we overcome. Where Christ is there is liberty from sin. Has Christ a crown to set upon his head? So have believers crowns—crowns of pure gold. Revelation—"They threw down their crowns before thee." Yea, in a sort we have crowns here; Zechariah 6:10, 11, 12, 13, 14. (December 27, 1640)

Neighborliness was another motif in Moxon's preaching. He seems to have made it his aim to pull the community together by smoothing interpersonal friction and assuaging animosities. "[*We pray*] for others," he said, "in the Lord's prayer: 'Give us daily bread, deliver us from temptation.' It is not said, 'Give me bread, deliver me,' but us, implying others. So that as we are to pray for ourselves, so also for others; and then if we pray for our comfort, we must [*pray also*] for others." (March 2, 1640)

Beyond prayer came action. Community required compassionate concern for neighbors. The doctrine that we should pray for and procure the comfort of others, he said, "teacheth us, inasmuch as [*in*] us lies, to be tender of making other lives uncomfortable. Be tender over their natural lives. Your neighbors, put to [*them*] your helping hand to do what you can to make the natural lives of others comfortable—also their spiritual life; do not vex their spiritual lives." (March 2, 1640)

At the opposite pole of having a positive perspective, Moxon addressed the subject of *complaining*, which he found intolerable. In more than one sermon of December 1640 he complained of his people's complaining.

> [Y]ou are to be reproved for your complaining," he said, "as though there were no healing, in a sort complaining as [*to*] God and complaining as if he had provided no help for thee. . . . Shall a man complain for want of meat, and meat is before him? Shall a man complain of his sores, and yet he has a healing plaster provided for them? Yet this is his fault: he doth not apply it to the sores. Such is your case . . . Now examine your hearts and you shall find that when you most complain you do some way abstain from Jesus Christ. (December 6, 1640)

Actually, at the time Moxon himself had something to complain about. Throughout that year he had been dealing with the exasperating suits for slander which he and John Woodcock had brought against each other.

But most of Moxon's messages dealt with *struggles of the spirit*.

He preached on lust. "It's certain a man must be more than a man that can avoid committing of sin sometime or other, if he be not careful of his thoughts and looks [= how he thinks and looks]. And the truth is, if you will be loose, you do not know how far God may leave you. A man cannot always quench a fire when he please. The best is therefore to prevent or quench it in the beginning." (September 16, 1649) He spoke of confession and forgiveness: "[R]ight and sound confession of sins unto God will in the end bring pardon of them. . . . Confession of sin is the truest and rightest when we do confess our sin in particular. Yet indeed, if we know not particular sins, then to confess in the lump we are sinful." (February 9, 1640) He struggled with the question of hypocrisy: "A hypocrite may resemble the children of God, yet hath not really true comfort." He went on to say, "A hypocrite may seem to desire Christ, and therefore be content to fly to Christ. But here he fails; he mistakes his own heart in it. Therefore . . . a hypocrite cannot actually lay hold on Christ further than some fruits of temporary faith." (February 16, 1640 and July 29, 1649) He addressed the problem of unanswered prayer.

> Why doth God thus exercise the patience of his people? One reason, that they may the more prize the mercy and consequently be the more fitted for the mercy. . . . Expect that your patience will be tried. God will put his people upon delays and much try their patience, and the want of expecting this many times makes your patience mere impatience. . . . Always bear in mind that there is a great deal of difference to be made betwixt delays and denials, and that God ties not himself to times. (June 24, 1649)

Most of all, Moxon was particularly concerned with the corrosive and debilitating effect of *uncertainty*. He kept focusing on what Lisa M. Gordis has called "the problem of assurance that preoccupied Massachusetts Bay in the mid-1630s"—and probably a lot longer than that.[70]

To understand Moxon's problematical position as he stood before the people of Springfield, it is important to clarify his dual responsibility as both Minister to the community and Pastor to the church. Because of this two-fold obligation he needed to be aware that he was always addressing two audiences simultaneously. As a Puritan church, the Springfield congregation consisted of only those who had a conversion experience—those who could identify some way or ways in which God had acted upon them to drawn them onward in faith. On the other hand, those who gathered to hear Moxon's sermons consisted of everybody in town. So Moxon preached to encourage conversions, and according to William Pynchon, he did so with

---

70. Gordis, *Opening Scripture*, 90.

some accomplishment. A letter Pynchon wrote to Governor Winthrop in February 1644 reported his pastor's successful efforts: "The Lord has greatly blessed Mr. Moxon's ministry to the conversion of many souls that are lately added to our Church."[71]

Uncertainty was the crucible for the conversions the church needed, so Moxon preached both to exacerbate uncertainty and to assuage it. In his February 23, 1640, sermon he said,

> If you would draw comfort from the testimony of the spirit, then you must sum up the testimony of the spirit and the testimony of thy own conscience and see what it reaches to. Does it say, "I have the works of Christ. I have interest in him?" Or does it reach to this: "I hope I have grace. I might be the child of God," &c. Now sum up. Does it come to this, that "There is no more to be done to make me the child of God, and I have interest in Christ?" Now sum it up. Will the testimony of your conscience make your evidence clear? Or is it but hopes: "I might, hereafter," or the like? Now this is the reason that you have not drawn comfort, because you do not sum up the testimony of your conscience. (February 23, 1640)

For Moxon, uncertainty was an indispensable prerequisite: "Such of you as never saw yourselves undone and lost and in a miserable condition, labor to see yourself in a miserable condition, without God, Christ, and the hope of salvation." (August 5, 1649) A person had to hit bottom before transformation could happen.

Yet Moxon was impatient with anyone who dithered. His message was in effect, "Get over it!" "If you have the spirit," he said, "then you shall have it ever after, though you have not always the manifestation. If a man comes into his orchard in the winter and seeth trees have no fruit, shall he therefore think they will not bear in summer? . . . Now if once thou hast the spirit thou hast it still." (February 23, 1640) Two weeks later he said (in an image he used more than once),

> When God's people are always calling in question those comforts that sometimes they have had, so that God must always kiss them and be always dandling them on the knees or there can be no good done. Or as with little children, the nurse or the mother, if [she] does never so little go aside, then they cry for [her], so you must always see comfort and see your evidence of

---

71. Forbes, *WP,* 4:443. No doubt this church growth was affected by an influx of eleven men and their families which Springfield experienced in 1643, and which proved to have a tonic effect on the community.

grace. Or have you thought you have none? This sinful calling in question is to be reproved." (March 2, 1640; see also December 6, 1640)

In order to turn the ungodly from faithlessness to faith, Moxon kept urging everyone to "use the means." The "means" consist of anything that has the capacity to connect one with God, such as hearing God's word in worship, reading, prayer, meditation, and the like. Moxon accepted no excuses:

> You do not make use of this spiritual remedy. Now examine your hearts and you shall find that when you most complain you do some way abstain from Jesus Christ. Either you think you have tired him out, or else you think he will not hear you, or else you are lazy. Is the faith a hand? Now, then, if you have withered hands or if you have [any] hands, [you] have faith, and yet will not make use [of it]; this is your fault. Now, you stand complaining as [to] God. You stand pewling and wheeling, and yet you have a healing medicine if you would but be so much more urgent and pressing and laboring more for Christ. Indeed, a soul should as it were take Christ by violence; and you should lay hold on promises by violence. (December 6, 1640)

> A slothful person is apt to make excuses when work is to be done. Proverbs 26:13—"A lion is in the way." So Proverbs 22. Answerably in spiritual matters a slothful person makes excuses, will pretend this and that. "Why do you not pray?" "I have not a convenient place; children cry," &c. "Why do you not go to meeting on the Lord's Day?" "I want [= lack] a hat, want shoes, or the weather is cold, snowy, or rainy. I cannot conveniently go." "Why do you not read, meditate?" It's the slothfulness of your spirit. Sloth will make many excuses, and poor, slender excuses, as Matt. 25:26. (June 3, 1649)

In one sermon Moxon appears to have engaged in a dialogue of sorts with his patron. William Pynchon was a lay theologian in his own right. Their exchange occurred in the course of two sermons in 1649, the first by Moxon on August 12, the second by Pynchon the following Sunday. Moxon discoursed in some detail on the identity of the mysterious Genesis figure Melchizedek, whom he identified as Shem. This cannot possibly have been a hot topic in Springfield; but it was of concern to Pynchon, who ventured the very same opinion in his earliest writing, the anonymously published 1648 volume on *An Endevour After The reconcilement of that long debated and much lamented difference between the godly Presbyterians, and Independents,* as well as in one of his later writings.⁷² Pynchon's sermon on August 19 included among its final paragraphs an analysis of Christ's death which he restated as the conclusion of his then forthcoming book, so the topic was very much on his mind; his manuscript had probably just been sent off to the London printer.⁷³

Moreover, in his August 12 sermon, Moxon spoke of Christ as mediator, which was the very subject of Pynchon's book. Moxon's language did overlap with Pynchon's. He maintained that "Christ must offer a sacrifice, and that is himself. Hebrews 9:26. Christ as priest laid down his life. No man took it from him. He was offered to bear the sins of many; and Ephesians 5:2—'Christ hath given himself for us a sacrifice to God of a sweet smelling savor.' Christ was both the Altar priest and sacrifice. Revelation 8:3. Isaiah 53:4,5." (August 12, 1649) But Moxon's claims, though very general, do not seem to have been unorthodox in any way. Indeed, some of Moxon's points were echoed in the official 1653 volume by Pynchon's orthodox critic, John Norton.⁷⁴

Did Moxon's preaching change from 1640 to his sermons of nine years later? Yes. Moxon became crankier, crustier, crabbier with the passing years. For instance, in the thirteen sermons of 1640 he did not use the word "hell" even once, while Thomas Hooker's Hartford sermons from the early 1640s concerned "The Broken Heart" and the fires of hell.⁷⁵ But in nearly half—eleven out of twenty-three—of the sermons from 1649 he mentioned "hell" for a total of twenty-one times, including eight times in just one sermon. A few samples:

> So in spiritual things ordinary rewards will not carry on a slothful person; neither will ordinary fear make him do the Lord's work. But when God puts him upon the wrack, frights him with wrath, hell fire flashing about his ear . . . (June 3, 1649)

He did not need to finish the sentence!

---

72. Pynchon, *An Endevour*, 82. On this work see Winship, *Godly Republicanism*, 178. See also Pynchon, *The Covenant of Nature*, a1v, a2r.

73. *The Meritorious Price* was published "by J. M. for George Whittington and James Moxon, 1650." James the printer was probably a cousin of George the minister.

74. In *A Discussion of that Great Point in Divinity, the Sufferings of Christ* (London, 1653), John Norton maintained that "Christ was both Priest, Sacrifice, and Altar," 104; and that "He laid down his life of his own accord, otherwise there was no one could have taken it away, *Ioh*. 10.18." 154.

75. Hall, *The Faithful Shepherd*, 164–165.

> O tremble at the greatness and majesty of God! He can destroy both body and soul in hell. (June 10, 1649)

> Art thou fit to die, thinkest thou, when thou dost not know whether thou shalt go to heaven or hell? Do not delay time; time is precious. Till thou knowest thy state and condition thou canst not so honor God as otherwise thou might. Take heed lest through the just judgment of God thou be given over, &c. (July 15, 1649)

Moxon sometimes castigated his congregation. Clearly not all who lived in the godly community were saints:

> Some of you, whose wickedness is apparent to all—yet when I have come to speak with you I have found you persuaded that Christ was yours—you do not see your wickedness, and eternal destruction hanging over your head. Are there not among you such as live in lying, . . . workers of iniquity? Are there not among you disobedient to governors: proud persons, unchaste persons? If you should be asked particularly, "Do not you think you are workers of iniquity?," what could you answer? (September 30, 1649)

It is quite probable that pleas to the reprobate like this really functioned as not-so-subtle reassurances to the godly. As Priscilla Roberts-Miller remarked, "Given the sense that humans cannot change a sinner into a saint, it is most likely that the direct addresses serve the rhetorical function of apostrophe: appearing to speak to someone who is not actually the intended audience . . . [T]he saintly are confirmed in their godliness by participating in the minister's abuse and rejection of the opposition."[76]

Conscience was the tool for encouraging conversion, and two extraneous phrases in the 1640 notes reveal that the teenager John certainly had one. At the bottom of one page of a sermon about God's comfort John wrote, upside down and in the fanciest script he could muster, "proud men" (March 2, 1640); he signed his name at the bottom of another page, in a March 9, 1640 sermon on the need for sound doctrine.

At the end of Moxon's time in Springfield, a poetic tribute to him was composed for *Wonder-Working Providence,* a history of early New England which is generally attributed to Edward Johnson of Woburn. In keeping with the tendentious and polemical style of the book, this accolade suggests struggle, which may possibly be an allusion to the witchcraft scares which infected Springfield in 1649 and 1651:

---

76. Roberts-Miller, *Voices*, 66.

> As thou with strong and able parts art made,
> Thy person stout with toyl and labour shall
> With help of Christ through difficulties wade;
> Then spend for him, spare not thy self at all.
> When errors crowd close to thy self and friends,
> Take up truths sword, trifle not time, for why,
> Christ call'd his people hither for these ends,
> To tell the world that Babels fall is nigh;
> And that his Churches through the world shall spread,
> Maugre the might of wicked men and devils,
> Then Moxon thou need'st not at all to dread,
> But be aveng'd on Satan for his evils,
> Thy Lord Christ will under thy feet him tread.[77]

Was Moxon's person "stout" and made "of strong and able parts," as this rondel suggests? Some commentators have so concluded, but since no contemporary portraits remain, it is impossible to know.

A REFUGEE'S RETURN

William Pynchon departed for England by early 1652, following the General Court's condemnation of his book. But George Moxon stayed on in Springfield for a number of months. In mid-September 1652 the community arranged with Moxon to purchase his house and land so that their first pastor's property could "forever belong to ye ministry in Springfield." They raised £70 over the next two years to compensate him for the buy-back. Sometime before October 22, 1652, Moxon bought a pair of hinges from John Pynchon, possibly to be used for building a chest for the trip to England.[78]

The political situation after 1650 made return to the old country an attractive option. The decade of the forties had been hard on New England. With the Puritan movement thriving in its homeland, emigration to New England slowed to a trickle; the flow even reversed back across the Atlantic. Though exact figures are difficult to establish, it is likely that at least 1,500, and as many as 3,600 settlers, returned to England after 1640, out of a total immigrant population of 13,500 to 17,600 in New England. Included in that

---

77. Johnson, *History of New-England* ("Johnson's Wonder-Working Providence"), 199–200. For some unknown reason the entire account for Springfield is placed under the year 1645.

78. Burt, *First Century*, 222. Bridenbaugh, ed. *Pynchon Papers*, 2.31.

number were some of the major leaders of the Colony. One out of three of the clergy who had emigrated to New England returned after 1640. Half the graduates of Harvard College before 1660 ended their careers in the British Isles.[79] From the Puritan perspective Oliver Cromwell's regime had produced stability in England and Wales. Charles I was executed on January 30, 1649. Scots allied with the uncrowned Charles II were defeated at Dunbar on September 3, 1650. Things were looking up for the Puritan project.

Upon his return to Britain Moxon continued to serve in ministry. Some sources suggest that he may at some point have served as a naval chaplain, although the George Moxon in question may have been his son, who eventually served a congregation at Radwinter in Essex. In any case, it is clear that in time George, Sr. attained a position at Newbold Astbury with the help of his first patron, Sir William Brereton.[80]

Moxon's years in William Pynchon's Springfield probably left a lasting impact on his theology. Some commentators have concluded that Moxon shared Pynchon's heterodox views. But his sermonic response to Pynchon's views on the Atonement in the afternoon message of August 12, 1649, though not detailed, seems to have been perfectly orthodox. Twenty-five years later, however, a meeting of the "Messengers of the Associated Churches of Yorkshire, Lancashire and Cheshire" appointed a delegation to visit him to ask why he dissented from a Congregational / Independent statement "in certain points concerning the Satisfaction of Christ."[81] The Congregationalists / Independents had re-worked the Presbyterians' Westminister Confession into their own "Savoy Declaration" which they intended to encompass their theology in broad, widely acceptable terms. It was designed to be inclusive of all and offensive to none in their movement.

Why Moxon demurred is unclear. An arcane theological argument of the era may offer a possible explanation. The Savoy Declaration had inserted a phrase into the original Westminster section "Of Justification;" this addition concerned imputing "Christ's active obedience unto the whole Law, and passive obedience in his death for [the] whole and sole righteousness" of those whom God has called. William Pynchon, on the contrary, had attacked the very notion of "imputation." He claimed that God neither credited Christ's goodness to human beings, even though they do not deserve it,

---

79. Hardman Moore, *Pilgrims*, 53–56, 75, and Bailyn, *The Barbarous Years*, 473.

80. Hardman Moore, *Pilgrims*, 121. Another who endorsed him was the Welsh Congregationalist Walter Cradock. Regarding Moxon's (or possibly his son's?) service in the navy, see Capp, *Cromwell's Navy*, 313, 315.

81. Bremer, *Congregational Communion*, 225, citing notes from October 6, 1674 in *Congregational Historical Society Transactions*, "Remains of Thomas Jollie," 6 (1913–15):172–173.

nor that God punished Christ for the sin of humankind, even though he did not deserve it. In his banned book Pynchon had maintained that "Sinners are not made righteous by Christs passive Obedience Imputed." Perhaps Moxon agreed; though lacking further information it is impossible to say.[82]

At Astbury Moxon shared the pulpit and also the parsonage of St. Mary's Church with a Presbyterian pastor, the Rev. John Machin. Their unusual arrangement took seriously the proposals of the great Puritan Richard Baxter (1615–1691), who had championed Christian unity by urging collaboration among all Protestant Christians. Baxter's "Worcestershire Voluntary Association of Ministers," organized in 1652, gathered Independent / Congregational, Presbyterian, and even some Episcopal clergy to work together.[83] Moxon and Machin both preached every week, with each alternating between Astbury one week, and Rushton-Spencer, seven miles to the east, the next. This continued until 1660, when the impending collapse of the Puritan government saw the return of the pre-war Astbury incumbent. Moxon continued at Rushton until Charles II approved an "Act of Uniformity," which functioned as a clergy loyalty test; those Puritan preachers who would not conform, like Moxon, were ejected from their positions in 1662. By 1667, after "2 or 3 removes of his Habitation," he ended up at Congleton, where he gathered a Congregational church in his home near Dane Bridge. Because he was partially disabled by strokes he had to be assisted by Eliezer Birch from 1678 on. In 1687 the congregation constructed a new meetinghouse near his home. Sadly, the first service held there was George Moxon's funeral, shortly after he died on September 15, 1687 at the age of eighty-five.[84]

In the course of those pioneering years in Springfield the people of Pynchon's plantation were treated to George Moxon's engaging oratory as he presented the "sequence of salvation," which was intended to give shape to individual lives, as well as to the community. His carefully crafted messages, as recorded by John Pynchon, emphasized hope in the face of much uncertainty, and were sometimes directed towards community concerns, as he did his best to smooth the rough edges of life on the frontier.

---

82. Walker, *Creeds and Platforms*, 397. Pynchon, *Meritorious Price*, 136.
83. ODNB, 4:424–425.
84. Calamy, *An Account*, 129. Gordon, "Moxon, George," *Dictionary of National Biography*, 39:241.

Notes on the Text

In the texts which follow I have recast the transcriptions I made from John Pynchon's coded notes on the Rev. George Moxon's sermons into currently understandable English. My purpose has been to make these texts as readable as possible, with a minimum of editorial intrusions, while respecting conventions of documentary transcriptions. As there is very little punctuation in the original, particularly in the notes from 1640, I have supplied modern punctuation. Out of appreciation for John's vividness as an aural auditor, I have retained the exact word order of his notes throughout. I have also kept the original numbers used to distinguish the sermons' points, even when those are in a confusing order or incomplete.

I have silently changed many words by

- using contemporary spelling;
- reformatting most Scripture references into the pattern in current use;
- removing duplicates;
- aligning mismatched singulars and plurals;
- eliminating instances of the symbol "E" (presumably for "exhortation");
- clarifying some prepositions;
- adapting some verbal forms (particularly gerunds and past participles).

And I have included some explanatory footnotes to make the texts as accessible as possible. A very few footnotes indicate unnecessary extra words that might disrupt the meaning. Some indicate the sources of references cited in the text. Others offer alternative definitions to clarify obscure or archaic words.

Relying on the principles of *A Guide to Documentary Editing*, by Mary-Jo Kline (Baltimore, MD: Johns Hopkins, 1998), I have inserted the following:

Gaps in the manuscript and unfinished phrases and sentences are indicated by bracketed suspension points: [. . .] If they are missing because of a tear, that is indicated as [tear].

Suggested readings are sometimes supplied, followed by a question mark, where portions of the uncertain words can be discerned. Words or symbols which remain illegible or indecipherable are indicated by a question mark within brackets [?]. Words which have been crossed out while remaining legible are given as ~~word~~.

Words or letters supplied for clearer understanding are provided in *italics* within brackets [ ].

Words in the original which are mistaken are followed by a correction within brackets, labeled "sic-."

Days are given as recorded in Pynchon's notes; years are given in New Style (Gregorian calendar).

D.M.P.

The Sermons

1

January 26—March 16, 1640

*Lyman & Merrie Wood Museum
of Springfield History,
Springfield, Massachusetts*

JANUARY 26, 1640

1 Peter 5:7

Cast all your care upon him for he careth for you.

Use 1. We [must?] by necessity cast anything that is beyond the pale of man and they cannot attain unto but [*God*] must help them, whether it be the supply of what they want[1] or the taking away of that which troubles them, more particularly in affliction. Or when we be overcome with temptation, be it in case of outward wants, they be beyond your reach—and then cast your care on God. Or in other cases. It is a great work to weal a family. It is a great [*work*] for a magistrate to weal a Commonwealth. It is a great work for ministers to feed their people. Now cast your care on God.

Question: But you will say, "Doth no care belong to us? Must we be care-less?" Answer: First, if we would cast our care on God aright, as we should, we must be careful of something that God commands us. For the accomplishment of the end is the use of means that might accomplish the

---

1. lack

end; and though God promises blessing, yet it is in the use of means.[2] "I will be sought upon," as Paul, Acts 27.[3] When God [. . .] God doth not usually care for his people that neglect the means. Therefore the first thing is, use the means.

Though our Lord Christ says, "Care not for your selves, what ye eat or what ye drink,"[4] yet elsewhere Christ tells us that we must take up the broken fragments; "let nothing be lost."[5] And Solomon says that "ants in summer provide meat,"[6] and [?][7] says we must provide for [?]

Though God does promise things [tear] use the means.

2 What we are to do in [respect?] of ourselves, we must do it out of conscience because God [tear]

1. We must be conscious in the use [tear]

2. We must use faith. So much as a man [tear] faith on works,[8] so much he casts his care on God.

These things for direction, so that we must use means for conscience sake and with faith.

Now for reasons:

First reason: we are bound to cast our care on God, because otherwise it will bring abundance of trouble and inconvenience unto us. It exposes us to temptation, as in [the] case of afflictions and suffering. A man's heart will ever be ready to lash out into impatience under them if a man's heart be not bottomed on God. Secondly, it will be apt [to] make the mind to use unlawful means to accomplish that that, if they would put to God, he would bring things comfortably to pass. The heart of man, except he cast his care on God, will not only be full of sorrows and trouble, but also will use indirect and sinful means to accomplish its end.

Second reason: God commands us to cast our care upon him. This duty must be done; commands must be obeyed, else there will be breach of rule, and such a man will be left under guilt. A man must cast his care on God because it is commanded us so to do. It is our duty to do it.

[Third] reason: because on our part there lies a kind of necessity that we should cast our care upon God. Or there is a necessity that we should

---

2. Exercises and experiences for growing closer to God, such as sermons, sacraments, reading the scriptures, etc.

3. Possibly Acts 17:27

4. Matthew 6:25

5. John 6:12

6. Proverbs 6:6, 30:25

7. 1 Timothy 5:8—"But if any provide not for his own, and specially for those of his own house, he hath denied the faith."

8. set faith at work

seek [else?] where to such as are worse, because we cannot accomplish things beyond our reach. God can. Therefore seeing we cannot do it, we must look to [the] help of those that can. Only God can provide food, raiment, and remove afflictions. Man cannot.

Use for reproof to those that are so cast [down] in the times and cases of their necessity. The heart of man is apt to be filled with abundance of care, nothing but contrivency.⁹ The heart seeks help from man, and God is forsaken—all this while as in outward things, when there are wants, a man is not able to bear it. He supposes he should want such a thing; then what is there to get it? And in such cases the heart of man is marvelous sad, as is sometimes seen in your countenances, as Jonadab seeth it in Amnon,¹⁰ sometimes by your very looks. It appears in your talk many times, and so unfit for conference, nay possibly unfit for prayer, and that worst of all. It might be, unfit for sleep. And this is a judgment, that which the Psalmist [says], "thou always hold mine eyes open."¹¹ Now some of you might confess that sometimes you have been in this case unfit for sleep. "And I cannot tell what to think of myself." For truly, this is for want of eyeing God's providence.

And this proceeds from want of faith, and secondly, from judging of God's dealings by the present apprehensions. As you see what God accomplisheth, so you work accordingly. You look not at what God does behind the curtains, saying "I know not yet what God is doing for me." But you judge according to appearances. God lets not man always find what he is doing. The heart must go on in the use of means, and wait God's time of deliverance. It was the wretched speech of the King of Syria, "Wherefore shall I wait?"¹²

The root is naught and the branches cannot be good, for we sin in it: 1. against God, and 2. against our own selves.

Against God:

1. Against his gracious promises. Is there no promise that might stay thy heart? Look well. Is it for outward things? Those that fear the Lord shall not lack.¹³ Also, "I will not leave nor forsake thee."¹⁴ You now sin against God's promises. You must have a pawn¹⁵ or else you will not believe God. All

---

9. scheming
10. 2 Samuel 13:4
11. Psalm 77:4
12. 2 Kings 6:33—"What should I wait for the LORD any longer?"
13. See Psalm 34:9
14. Hebrews 13:5
15. surety

the promises of God in Christ are yea and amen.[16] And the mediator of the covenant is made none account with us. We cannot believe God's promises: "they that fear the Lord shall want nothing," &c.[17] Now we cannot take God's word, and this is to make God a liar.

2. We sin against God in sinning against his providence, as though God could not bring these things to pass which he would not. God does all things that he does good. Now our moidering[18] care cannot thus believe God but thinks he is not working and rather sitting idle in heaven. Though God works all things for all men, yet we do not [credit?] it. We do not believe it, whether does man live by bread or by his contrivencies; or is it that [man] lives by every word that proceeds from the mouth of God? Who is it feeds the ravens, all the beasts of the field? It is the Lord; and we do not conceive it. We do, as it were, blame God that he doth but weakly and deals imperfectly and does not make thorough work of it. We in a sort think God has turned man into the world to scramble and shift and takes no care for him. ~~Now as we~~

3. We sin against God in turning him out of his place. We take his office out of his hand, as much as in us lies. We [think] God either not able or not fit to govern the world, but we will contrive things for ourselves and tussle God out of his chair. Says the unbeliever, "Seeing God will not order things, I will do it." And thus we take that upon us which does not properly belong unto us. Philippians 4:8[19]—"Be careful in nothing; but make your request known unto God."

Now say our sinful, moidering hearts, "We might pray—but what of that? When we have done, God is so slow that he will not work that which we would not have worked—or at least not soon enough." Now thus we take God's office out of his [hands] and tussle him out of his seat; and these ways we sin against God.

Now secondly, we sin against ourselves,

1. By making our life uncomfortable by needless fears and grievous want of casting our hearts upon God. And there is such a difference between the soul that holds to God and [one] that does not. He that casts his soul on God is like Mount Zion and is as safe as a ship riding at anchor with strong cables. Says David, "God will keep me." Now says a man that cannot cast his care on God, "I wonder how you can be cheerful, seeing you be a poor man and have so many children besides? You have so many afflictions, yet your

---

16. 2 Corinthians 1:20
17. See Psalm 34:10
18. bothering, bewildering
19. Philippians 4:6

spirit is cheerful. I wonder at it." Now says a believing heart, "I have grounds enough to cheer up my heart. God does care for me and I can be cheerful enough, though I have not a bit of bread for my children—yet God will care for them." Now says a heart that did not cast his care on God, "I am poor and I have many children and I have got little for so many mouths, and I have money to pay at such a time and I cannot tell how to pay, and I have prayed and I can find no answer to my prayer and I am but a man of sorrow." I say, "You needlessly bring this grief upon yourself. And if you could but cast your care on God you would not be thus sorrowful.

Also you find you have temptation and you cannot tell what to do. "Nay," says he, "I shall one day prove an apostate, and so never a quiet day, but I shall be a wretch. One day I shall be so, and so bring an ill name upon the gospel." Now this proceeds from want of casting your care on God. You must consider you are in Christ's arms, and he will do as he pleases with you, and it is not in our power. We by our moidering cares sin against God; thus we sin against our selves, and against God also, by filling our head with such thoughts.

2. We sin against ourselves in making our souls fit subjects for Satan to work upon. And truly that heart that is so full of moidering cares is never without the devil's company. But you shall find the devil still carrying him on in temptation. When men have come to some moidering cares, the child of God will see that then the devil has power over him, because thus mistrusting God does weaken our faith. And when faith is weakened, the devil cannot have a better object to work upon. Through this distrust the soul is apt to give Satan a world of passages. And the further the soul goeth from God the more it lies open to Satan, and his own corruptions hath the more power.

3. You sin against yourself, and so against God, in hindering your soul for better things. You are not fit for that God calls you unto. Christ says you must give an account for every idle word, because then you might say a better word. So while you are in such moidering care you must give an account, because then you might have been about better things than mistrusting God, for also it hinders the exercise[20] of better things. The thoughts of man should be holy, carried to God. And this hinders better things, when your minds are how to contrive matters, and you tussle [better?] [?] [and cast?] this out [?] when he of your heart.[21] Man's heart will be doing something. It will never be idle. And then it is apt to fall upon those things that are most

---

20. performance

21. At this point John Pynchon seems to have written over notes taken by an older person.

vain and frothy. Thou complainest many times: thou hath but weak gifts and thou hast a bad memory, now that thou hast brought this upon thyself by needless, frothy cares. Your own hearts will tell you that you might have had more gifts but that other moidering cares drive them out of your mind; and thus you hinder better things.

4. You sin against yourselves in depriving yourselves of that help that you might have if you would leave things unto God. He would help you, and he would carry on things for you. God says, "Care thou for nothing. I will care for thee." Now it is a marvelous ungrateful part of man to say to God, "I will not be beholden to thee; I will care for thy [sic-*my*] self;" and truly thus he puts God out of office. And if there were no one to help us, then [*a*] poor man would be glad that there were a God to take care for him.

And thus to fill the head with such cares, the sin is the greater because man has had so many experiences. And truly God does, as it were, say to man, "I will let thee have help from me: and see how I deal with thee. And if thou likest my help, then let me have more of thy custom." This is an earnest penny for to draw us to rest on God.

Also, it is further aggravated[22] considering how far God is dishonored by thy moidering cares. Make the best you can of it, and you set up the creature of the wit and shifts of men instead of God. Here is the ground of repentance, that you [sic-*we*] do thus sin against God and ourselves.

Second use for instruction: to teach us what we are to do when anything troubles the mind, heart's communion with God—and let God care for us.

FEBRUARY 2, 1640

1 PETER 5:7

Cast all your [. . .] upon him for he careth for you.

It is the duty of God's people in all necessities to cast their care upon him. Reasons have been made:

First, because else it will be a great inconveniency—will expose us unto temptation.

Second reason: because it is God's command.

Third reason: there is a necessity to cast our care on God because he will accomplish things that be out of our reach.

22. exacerbated, made more serious

The first use is for reproof to them that are so cast down in times of their necessity, which proceeds from want of faith and by judging God's dealings according to present apprehensions; and thus do we sin against God and against ourselves. And for these things we must be reproved. These things were then largely opened—now reopened:

Second use: for instruction, to teach and direct what to do in all difficult cases for supply of all we want, for removing that which troubles us.

It many a time is our case to fill our head with thoughts, "What to do?" Yet still we are driven to a nonplus;[23] and this teaches us to cast our care on God. And we must be careful on our part to use means, and that we be in God's way, and then cast your care on God. Use the means, and leave the success unto God. For when a man has done what he can in contrivencies, yet we can do nothing, though we care never so much. As Christ says in another case, "Which of you can add one cubit to his stature?"[24] And thus when we have done what we can do, at last we cast our care on God. It should teach us so to do at first. And truly if we would but cast our care on God we should have a deal of benefits. These benefits:

First, it will acquaint our hearts more with God, and we in the consequence will be more drawn from atheism, and it will make us more to subdue not hoping in God and not resting on him, which is atheism.

Second benefit that it will bring is, it will empty our heads of abundance of sinful thoughts—how to know the events of things—and our heads would be abundantly emptied of such contrivency of our own.

Third, it will make us more experienced with God's dealing goodness and mercy toward us. For these evils come by neglecting to cast our cares on God.

First, though God helps us, yet we cannot look at God's hand in helping us. Our eyes do not believe it because we think our own care has done it. So much as we see of our care we tussle God.

Second [?]: our sinful care binds God's blessings that he is not so liberal to us as he would [be]. Can we look that God should thrust mercy upon us? Now God's children that are exercised[25] in casting our cares on God tell by experience of abundance of God's helping them.

And another thing would flow from this, that we should take mercy more kindly if we did but cast our care on God. Yea, this thing would follow also: we should more train up ourselves with the dependence upon God in his providence. Now in all cases and in all necessities we must cast our

23. inability to proceed
24. Matthew 6:27; Luke 12:25
25. practiced

care on God, and we should have the benefit by it. Man is apt to forsake God, trust to himself, to forsake the fountain of living water and dig broken cisterns[26]—a double evil. In all necessity cast your care on God. Thus much for this doctrine.

Second doctrine: from the words, "God cares for you." Note doctrine that God cares for his people in their needs. God cares for them in their affliction, in supplying or in removing that troubles them. God does care for his people in all their needs. The text says, Psalm 8, then "thou art mindful of man."[27] The prophets do admire that God should ever be so mindful of man; so Isaiah 9. "He forgets not the cry of the humble."[28] Now if he did not care for them, he would forget them. So that God is mindful of his people, and so mindful that he never fails; Psalm 9:10—"Thou neither fails nor forsakes them."[29] All the men in the world cannot instance[30] one time that God did ever fail his people.

And I will show this further by reasons:

One reason is from man: he is apt to care for himself and [*not*] to care for others. As Paul's instance how: Philippians 2:20—"mind." [sic-*like-minded*] 1 Timothy—"Take heed unto thyself" of your state;[31] and Philippians 4:10—of the Philippians care of him; and 2 Corinthians 7:12—he tells of his care of the church of Corinth; and he lays it down[32] as a duty for members to be like [sic-*likewise*] careful, one of another. Men are apt to care for themselves, and apt to care for others. Parents are apt to care for their children, sometimes religiously. Now a double inference and duty I would reason, thus: that that care which is from man and is based in God, it comes from God and it's but a drop of the bucket—the principle that God puts in us. And it comes from him. Now if we care for ourselves and for others, much more will God care for us from whence our care comes. Are we merciful? Much more is God merciful, because it is he makes us merciful. It comes from him. Now might we reason, "Do my parents care for [*me*] and do I care for myself? Much more will [?] God care for me because care [comes?] from him, and it is God makes us to care, for all care is from God. He is the ocean." Thus Isaiah 49:14, 15. Isaiah reasons, when thou complainest, "God

---

26. Jeremiah 2:13
27. Psalm 8:4
28. Psalm 9:12
29. See also Deuteronomy 31:6, 8; Hebrews 13:6 (Geneva Bible)
30. give an example of
31. 1 Timothy 4:16; see also Philippians 2:20
32. emphasize; stress

cares not for me," says God, "Can a woman forget the son of her womb?"[33] Now this is possible, not probable. Yet says he, "God does not forget; it is impossible for God to forget."

2. Inference or deduction:

Seeing man is careful one of another, if God should not be careful, this were absurd. And can we think that friends will care more for us than God will care for us? Parents help their children, and will care for them. Now does God care no more? Yes, and this is but a drop of care; for God is the ocean. This is the first reason drawn from the verse.

Second reason: God cares for all his creatures, [*the one*] whom is worst, and he [sic-*him*] that he is bound to love less than man. And this: Matthew 26, Luke 12:24—"Consider the ravens that spin not, neither have barns nor storehouses" to lay up for another time. So [*the*] Psalm—"He gives food to the beast and to the young ravens that cry; and so the eyes of all wait upon thee, and thou satisfies the eye of all living things."[34] Now the Lord cares for all living things; man is a living [*thing*]; then God cares for us. And this is one thing that God poseth Job with, chapter 38, v. 39—"Canst thou fill the appetite of the lion? I can." And v. 41—"Who provides for the ravens? Job, thou dost not; I do." And the Apostle says, 1 Corinthians 1:9[35]—"[*God*] doth care for oxen." Now if God cares for oxen, much more for man. As God thus cares for the lion and the ravens (for when do you find them that have died for hunger?), now much more will God care for us.

Third reason: it were unreasonable that God should leave things to us to care for that are beyond our reach. It is true that Adam has forfeited all our interest and helps. Yet by Christ it is restored.

Fourth reason is drawn on the contrary, that if man has no help and no one to care for him, but he must care for himself, then he is worse than other creatures, for they have help. Or if man should have no one to supply wants, but he must do it himself, then of all creatures he is the most miserable, for God will help them. Or if thou say that God does care for man in some things, but not in others, then what means this argument: "Fear not, it is your Father's will to give you a Kingdom"?[36] That God does take care for the souls and will care for the soul of man, that is enough.

Further, if God did not care for people, what use were there, then, of prayer? What? Are we the ne'er to pray? "I pray unto a God that turns his deaf ear unto us and will not hear." And if God did not care for us, of what

---

33. Isaiah 49:15
34. See Psalm 147:9
35. 1 Corinthians 9:9
36. Luke 12:32

use is that argument, "Your heavenly father knows that you have need of all these things."[37] And where it is said, "The eyes of the Lord run to and fro,"[38] now to what end is it? Why do the Lord's eyes run to and fro? To spy out our faults? It is also to have him eyeing [?] *providentially* over us to exercise[39] his goodness and to supply our wants, and not to behold all our faults; not only as a bystander to look on things. But the eyes of the Lord run to and fro to order the affairs of the world—to help all in their need that cast their care on him. Now have not these arguments sufficient ground to move us to cast our care upon God? And moreover if God care not for his people, whence come all these helps and kindness that we have? Do they, as it is said of Adam, rise out of the dust? Do they not come from—heaven?

Now for uses:

First use: does God care for his people? Believe this. Have this grounded in you as a truth.

It might be you can say, "Fear not, neighbor; God will care for you." But when it is your case, then you fly from him. Then you will not hold yourself. All the while a man's hand is full of all necessaries, then he will say, "God does care and he will supply." But when barns and houses and pockets and cupboards all be empty, then he cannot think God will provide. Then his heart begins to doubt when it comes to his case. Then he cannot think so.

Labor to have this engraven, that God does always care for his people. Now if any scruple should come into your mind, what wherein does God care for his people? If a man could but instance the text you should see how the servant of God hath said in this, "God hath cared for me." David could say, when he hath been oppressed with enemies, "God hath cared for me;" and so in all want his psalms will with [...]

Now what? Then believe that God will care for you. But now has [sic-does] something stick[40] still? What [is] that? That God will not care for me in all times. Yet God will always only take those limitations that the text gives, and he will save at all times. Now believe it as a truth.

And that you might better believe it, I will give you these grounds of faith for your elbow to lean upon, that God does care for his [own].

First ground: from the goodness of God's nature. Texts will instance of God's goodness. Psalm 119:38[41]—"Thou art good and doest good." Thou art not good in thy self, but thou doest good to others. Psalm 104:24, 28—"The

---

37. Matthew 6:32
38. 2 Chronicles 16:9
39. perform
40. cause to linger, be unable to make progress
41. Psalm 119:68

earth is full of thy riches," and "thou openest thy hand and fillest them." And so Acts—seeing thou givest "life and breath and all things."[42] Christ tells by Matthew 5:44, 45, Christ does good to all, good and bad, and when he calls us to works of mercy, he says that "Ye be like your heavenly father." Why? In doing good! Wherein does God not do good?

Second ~~ground~~: from the graciousness of God. Psalm 116—"Gracious is the Lord," and Psalm 145:8—"The Lord is gracious and full of compassion." Graciousness is that whereby the Lord out of his free love doth give [to] us.

Thirdly, God's nature is good, [from] which [it] appears that ~~2 ground~~ God is "bountiful"—Psalm 13:6. "Because he hath dealt bountifully with me"—Psalm 116:7. He hath a liberal hand.

Fourth, God's mercy shows the goodness of God's nature. 2 Corinthians 1:3—he is called the Father of Mercy, and if so, then abundance of mercy. He is to deal with his children, and if the children want anything, God will supply. Psalm 145:9—The Lord is "tender" in mercy; he hath abundance of mercy. Psalm 86—"Thou, Lord, art good and plenteous in mercy" to all them that come unto thee.[43] The mercies of God are not like summer rivers that come a shower of rain, but then in a drought drawn dry, but God's more like the sea. 1 Chronicles 21:13—David said to God, "I am in a great strait; let me fall into the hand of the Lord, for manifold are his mercies." And Nehemiah tells concerning abundance of God's mercy. Now how can it be that God should be so merciful, except he cares for his people? Psalm 54:4—"God is my helper." If God be a helper, and if he doth help, then he cannot choose but to care for his people.

[A] ground for faith to rest upon is the providence of God. He orders all the creatures he has made for the praise of his glory. A sparrow does not fall to the ground without God's providence. In Luke 6[44] [it] is said that not one of them is forgotten of God. Now if God does [value?] two sparrows, much more does [he value?] his people. Now from God's very providence we have enough grounds that God cares for his people.

Third ground: if, from the promise of God's presence, if we be in his way. How oft does the text say, "I am with thee? I am with thee to deliver; I am with thee to supply thee." When Abraham went to Mesopotamia, "I am with thee." Aye, that was for supply of what he wanted. And so says God to Moses, "I am with thee;" and so to Joseph, "I will not leave thee nor forsake thee;" and David, "No man shall lay hands on thee to hurt thee."

---

42. Acts 17:25
43. Psalm 86:15
44. Luke 12:6

Deuteronomy 31:6—Moses hath this encouragement of God: "He will go with thee, he will not fail thee nor forsake thee." So 1 Chronicles 28:20—when David speaks to Solomon concerning building the temple, "It is a great [*work*], yet God will be with thee and he will not fail, not fail thee, till thou hast finished all thy work."[45] Now Moses, he instances this promise. So David takes up the same, and the Apostle a third time takes up the same providence. He hath said, "I will not leave thee nor forsake thee." Now God does go a long way with his people and is present for supply for deliverance. And God's people—when does enter in Christ Jesus—God promises them, "I will be your God." "I am God all-sufficient;"[46] this implies that God will care for you.

Fourth ground: for the use of prayer. God bids you pray. Philippians—"In all things make your request unto God."[47] Now God would never bid us pray if he would not supply. He would not send us to the throne of grace to spend our breath for nothing, but that he will care for us. Now these are grounds that faith might have strong consolation. And a Christian is not worth a straw without he will set faith on works.

Fifth ground is taken from the Kingdom of Christ, and it is own [sic-*one*] part of Christ's Kingly office to care for his people. "I will not leave you." And that is the office of King, to care for the good of their subjects. It is but a sorry King that will sit still and never make laws for their subjects. The Lord Christ would be but a sorry King if he would not care for his people in case temptation lies upon us. It is part of Christ's Kingly office to rescue us from our enemies. Now if we did but know Christ's Kingly office aright we have grounds enough.

Now having these grounds, believe that God will care for us. Let God order all affairs in point of ordering the world; let God, alone. Set faith on work. You will not come to be glorious Christians till you set up God in the soul.

Use for comfort and consolation to all that cast their care on God: some might see [sic-*say*], "You bid us set faith on works and cast our care on God. What then, are we the better?" Truly, then, if you do set your faith on works you might write upon[48] it that God will care for you. Use the means and set faith on works and you will never be looser by it. My heart fails me, and my own contrivencies and my wit fail me. But God never fails me; if he does, it [*is*] for want of faith. Set up God and you will find him to help and

---

45. 1 Chronicles 28:20
46. Genesis 17:1, 35:11 (Geneva Bible)
47. Philippians 4:6
48. make a record of

to work graciously for you. And you may, seeing God cares for you, make this use so much to condemn your souls as you have cared for your selves. God will care for you, and in all necessities. Then what need have you to care for yourself? Now labor to have it graven upon your heart, that God doth care for you.

Thus much for this time and text.
FINIS

FEBRUARY 9, 1640

Psalm 32:5

I acknowledged my sin unto thee, and mine iniquity have I not hid.
I said I will confess my transgressions unto the Lord
& thou forgavest my sin.

There is difference among expositors wherefore the occasion of this psalm is.[49] But that which I do rather think is that [*it is*] from the 51st Psalm. When David committed the sin of adultery and murder upon that occasion, now this psalm is penned; for David says, "while I held my peace."[50] That is, he confessed sin; but it was so overly[51] that now God has opened his eyes. He seeth that all his confession was as if he hath held a peace.

Now he seeing that all his confession hitherto hath been as nothing and hath brought no comfortable issue, now he will thoroughly confess. And for the psalm itself, David first of all propounds this divine proposition, "Blessed is the man whose sin is forgiven and in whose heart there is no guile."[52] Now David did prove this by his own experience that he might have rested sooner if [*it*] had not been for his guilt. So that he proves it partly [*by*] his own terror and sorrow while he hath sin, and partly by his own [*sin*] that he was not apprehensive off. For when he comes to the fifth verse, he says,

---

49. Moxon sided with Antoine de Chandieu, *Moste excellent Meditations vppon the xxxii. Psalme* (London: 1579), 6, and Samuel Hieron on Psalm 51, *Davids Penitentiall Psalme Opened* (Cambridge, 1617), 7, in identifying the occasion for Psalm 32 as David's adultery and manslaughter, and not with Thomas Taylor, *Davids Learning, or the Way to True Happinesse: In a Commentarie vpon the XXXII. Psalme* (London, 1618), 108, who felt David's sin was "very foolishly . . . numbering the people."

50. Psalm 39:2

51. haughtily, superciliously, slightingly

52. Psalm 32:2

when he did acknowledge sin, then he found rest. Says he, "Blessed are they that have not guile."

There are two doctrines especially in these words:

One doctrine: the godly are apt to lie a long time in sin before their own hearts will bring them to confess it aright. I lay it down,[53] the godly; for so was David, and therefore it certainly holds true in others. But this now take along, that in some particular sins David twelve months lay in this sin until Nathan came to him 'fore the child was born. And Joseph's brethren—Genesis 42—lie in the sin of selling their brother twenty years before they confessed.[54]

First reason: conviction must go before thorough confession, because it's long ere the godly be convicted of some sins. Two things in conviction:

1. of the fact;
2. of the sin.

In the fact, God's children lie under sin, not convicted, for certain grounds.

One ground: because though acts be sinful, yet if they appear not so, they pass as not blameworthy. Conscience is not touched because the judgment is not informed. Something there is in that action of the church of Corinth. 1 Corinthians—"It is reported there is fornication among you,"[55] and such fornication as is not once named among the gentiles. And they are puffed up; they do not take notice of it, so far that they make themselves guilty of communication [sic-*contumation*?]. They do not see it is sin. But when the Apostle thoroughly convinces them of it, then they do reform, as you see if you compare this place with 2 Corinthians 7. Such a sin they see, and reform.

Second grounds why men are apt to forget such actions as are sinful, yet do not appear so unto them: because memory, being but sanctified in part, is apt to forget that it should [. . .] Memory is tempted, letting through that which is naught. We are apt to justify ourselves in many sinful acts. It is hard to convince the heart of sin.

Second reason: because after conviction of sin, the heart is apt to lie a long time under legal terror, or but formal confession.

The law is a "schoolmaster to bring us to Christ,"[56] and the law must have its work; and the heart is apt to lie a long time under legal terror before

---

53. emphasize, stress
54. Genesis 37:23–27; Genesis 45:4–5
55. 1 Corinthians 5:1
56. Galatians 3:24

it be brought to a kindly work. Now the heart is apt, after legal terrors, to lie in formal confession.

What mean you by "formal confession?"

1. when it wants due aggravation[57] of our sins, want of condemning ourselves for sin;

2. want of due sense of God's honor;

3. want of closing with Christ the Lord, Son of God, in promises.

Now when it wants any of these I call it formal confession—much more when it wants all these.

1. When it wants due aggravating of sin it is formal confession, while God does some way or other make us to aggravate our sin so far as we do condemn ourselves. What think you of Job when he was so impatient, and his friends charged him to be an ungodly? He did justify himself. Now God takes him in hand and about the 41 chapter he says, "I abhor myself, and I have spoken once, yea twice, yet will I speak no more."[58] Now it is a difficult thing before a man is brought thoroughly to conviction in himself; and it might be a man might confess to God that he is to blame. Yet when God brings him thoroughly to conviction, then he can aggravate his sin with such a world of circumstances. As one of the ancients, Austin—he says how that he hath robbed [an] orchard to get apples,[59] not for any need he had, but to give them [to] the swine—what tricks he had done to his neighbor. And when God brings him to true confession of sin then says he, "These things have I done. What a heart have I!" So you might see that when God does bring us to a thorough confession, what complaining and condemning ourselves, and "What a heart have I, Lord! What shall I do?"

2. If confession is but formal when it is not touched with thorough apprehensions of sins, dishonor before our confessions be right. We cannot come to say law is broken, Gospel is dishonored, and the Lord Jesus Christ is dishonored. Formal confession cannot say thus; but when thorough confession is [made], then the working of the Gospel does mark us so to condemn ourselves; "I'm ashamed to look up to heaven for God's dishonor." Thus was the publican.[60]

3. It is but formal confession if [it] so be we do not close unto Christ and look up unto really closing with him in a promise. That which does make the child of God to look up to Christ for pardon is hope of a promise.

---

57. exacerbation

58. Job 42:6; 40:5

59. The story is in Augustine's *Confessions*, 2. 4.9, where the fruit was identified as coming from a pear tree.

60. Luke 18:13

Says the child of God, "God hath promised, and I will press after him and at length he will perform." Yet at first he begins, "Lord, I believe; help mine unbelief."[61] Thus, while we come to close with God's promises and look at them as the best treasure in the world to get salvation, it is not faith we want, this, but formal confession.

[*First*] use, for information: it shows what bunglers we are in the things of God—weaklings—and with what little skill and weak confession we have confession of sin. How apt are we to miss it! If our skill fail us, methinks it should fail in other things and not so much in this. Yet take notice of it. How we miss in this duty! Hast thou ever been so oft at the throne and yet do not confess sin? And yet you should. Now here let us lay [*a*] load[62] upon ourselves and take it as our shame that we are so unskillful in right confessing. I believe you are as unskilled in other duties as well as this. You itt[63] might lie a whole year in overly confession before you come to confess aright. Now take note of this: as you sin, and the greater your sins, the more is your humiliation.

Second use, for direction: try[64] now whether you have not been thus overly in confession. Do you not lie in overly confession many months before you confess aright? And it might be young beginners in conversion take notice and confess some sins, such as they load on themselves, yet are not so apt of taking notice of other sins which by degrees God discovers,[65] as we do not take notice of breaking the rule. Yet now it might [*be*] God [*will*] discover it.

Examine whether God does not discover many sins now that he never discovered before. Then try whether the sin that God does discover unto you, it might be you confess, but it is overly. Now your sin, if you have missed in your confession, yet labor to amend and confess so as God might accept of you another day. And so far as your confession has been overly, let it humble you.

So much for this doctrine.

A second doctrine to be gathered from the words is that right and sound confession of sins unto God will in the end bring pardon of them.

You must confess sin as God doth require it. He will pardon. This I speak especially unto the godly. This you might see of David when he

---

61. Mark 9:24
62. "lood"
63. unnecessary extra word
64. test
65. reveals

confessed unto Nathan. And, says Nathan, "thy sin is pardoned."[66] And the publican, when he did but say, "Lord, be merciful unto me a sinner," the text says he went away justified rather than the other.[67] So Jeremiah 13:12, 13—he calls upon Israel to confess their backsliding and thereupon promises mercy.

Now for reasons:

[*First*] reason: true confession hath the promise of pardon. "He that confesseth and forsaketh shall obtain mercy"—Proverbs 28:13. So 1 John 1:9—he is just and ready to forgive. So Ezekiel—if they return unto [sic-*turn from*] the evils of their ways God will blot out all their iniquity.[68]

Now God is a God of justice to perform these promises. It is an act of God's justice to those [*who*] confess sin aright to obtain pardon.

1. God is a God of justice (Deuteronomy), and therefore, if so, it is injustice, seeing Christ hath redeemed us and got pardon to come upon us; this is injustice.

2. It is an act of God's justice also in this respect, as it is kindness and mercy to promise us. Yet now, seeing through his mercy he hath promised, now it is justice to fulfill his promise.

A second reason is that confession of sin is a part of prayer. But prayer in the several parts of it must be heard; there is a promise so. And besides, a third reason:

Third reason: if that true confession of sin will not bring pardon, therefore wherefore did Christ [*die*]? Christ's death was in vain; and then you will take away the mercy of God and the redemption that is spoken of concerning Christ. And then it will follow that believers are in no better circumstances than very reprobates. For reprobates do confess sin and to no purpose. Now if God's people should confess and be sent empty handed, then they were worse than reprobates. And it will follow then that the Elect are most miserable of all. And the truth is, if they cannot have pardon of sin upon right confession and closing with Christ in promises, then there were no means, and then also it will follow that all the scriptures were lies, which were wretched blasphemy.

Thus for reasons. Uses:

First use: instruction upon what terms[69] we might have our sin pardoned: namely, if we do but confess sin aright.

How shall I know when I confess sin aright, and when it is counterfeit?

---

66. 2 Samuel 12:13
67. Luke 18:10–14
68. Ezekiel 18:30
69. "tearmes;" so spelled throughout these notes.

1. Confession of sin is the truest and rightest when we do confess our sin in particular. Yet indeed, if we know not particular sins, then to confess in the lump we are sinful—we are vild, full of temptation, nothing but sin—and aggravate it. Now how can you yet expect that God should pardon your sins, and you will not once name them? You confess in the lump and do not name particulars. Now then how can you expect pardon? How oft have you known sound repentance to be without confessing particular sins? And then does not this necessarily follow, that when the heart doth repent there must needs be particular sin confessed? When confession is sound, it makes a man confess particular sins unto God.

2. Confession of sin, when it is right, is always accompanied with a godly endeavor to break off the course of sin. It [sic-*He*] does not only confess that sin he is convinced of, but watches over his own heart against all, whereas the spirit of God says, "If I regard iniquity in my heart the Lord will not hear me."[70] I make no question but that a flattering heart will tell a man that he doth forsake sin when he doth not. I advise you to labor to know whether you do confess your sin aright. And the next thing must be that we must forsake; and now, do you truly forsake? We must be sure that we forsake them—sins that we confess, all others, not allowing ourselves[71] in any sin whatsoever.

3. True confession comes from an inward spiritual principal. If it be fear of [the devil?] or for self ends or afraid of punishment that we confess sin, this is not from an inward principle. Says the soul that doth truly confess sin, "I will hail God at the throne of grace. How bad I am, and what a condition I am in!" As David heretofore, "I said, 'I will confess my sin; thou forgavest mine iniquity.'"[72]

4. Confession of sin is true and sound first when it hath those spiritual affections that should accompany in prayer, as fervency of spirit, earnestness with God, urging him to forgive.

Now, for your information: let [*it*] inform what to do and how you confess sin aright.

Second use, for information: to inform us the cause why so many good—and bad—go on a long time in their sin. The reason is because you do not confess. The fault is your own. If thy sin be not pardoned, I should rather impute it that you have not gone in God's way.

---

70. Psalm 66:18
71. making allowances for ourselves
72. Psalm 32:5

Third use: I would now persuade you to believe this to be a truth, that they that do confess sin should find pardon. We do oft think God will pardon little sins, and not great.

Let these considerations be as so many arguments of faith.

1. Consider that sound confession will confess sin with sighs and groans. These confessions God will hear. He always hears the sighs and groans of his spirit, wheresoever it be.

2. Thou hast a good mediator of the covenant, Jesus Christ, which hath made full satisfaction for all believers. And then what virtue is there in these words, "It is finished," but that Christ has truly finished the work of redemption?

3. Consider what a dangerous soul-damning sin it is for thee to question whether thou shall have sin pardoned or not. And thou questionest Christ's satisfaction and makest Christ naught [*more*] to thee than to the damned. Now all these things consider. See what grounds we have of faith in Christ, and that there is enough righteousness in him.

Thus much for this text.

FEBRUARY 16, 1640

2 Thessalonians 2:17

Comfort your hearts and stablish you in every good word and work.

These words are imperfect[73] and are to be made up by the former verses: "Now our Lord Jesus Christ comfort you," &c. The words are a prayer wherein Paul doth entreat that God and Christ would comfort their hearts.

And why doth he pray to God to comfort their hearts? The reason is in the first chapter, 3 and 4: "for your patience and faith" in all their persecutions.[74] And the Apostle prays for them, being in a troubled, persecuted condition for Christ's sake, that God would comfort their hearts. The words need no explication. Two things are prayed for:

1. Comfort of heart;
2. Settledness or stableness in well doing.

From the first observe:

Doctrine: God doth comfort his people.

---

73. not complete
74. 2 Thessalonians 1:4

For proof: Isaiah 51:12—"I am he that comforts you." 52:9—the Lord comforts his [*people*]. 2 Corinthians 1:3, 4—"Blessed be God," &c. "The God of all comfort, who comforts in all tribulations," &c. So Romans 15:5—"Now the God of patience and consolation." He is called the God of comfort.

For explication:

1. God doth comfort his people inwardly;

2. Outwardly.

1. Inwardly by:

1. the spirit of God

2. by our own consciences or by the spirit of God witnessing in our consciences.

John 14:16, 26—the spirit is called "the Comforter." Galatians 5:22—Joy is a fruit of the spirit. Acts 9:31—It is called "the comfort of the Holy Ghost." Now our own consciences comfort us when on just grounds they witness pardon of God, justification, and interest in Christ. The Apostle says, "being justified by faith." And he that hath peace of conscience hath "a continual feast."[75]

2 Corinthians 1:12—This is our rejoicing, "the testimony of a good conscience." Romans 2:15—"their own consciences in the mean time accusing or excusing." Now a man's own conscience, clearing him and saying [*he is*] guiltless, affords abundance of comfort. Thus much for inward comfort.

2. God comforts his people outwardly by the ministry of the word. 1 Corinthians 14:31—but if all prophesy, "ye may all prophesy one by one so that all may learn, and if all learn, all may be comforted." Psalm 119:50—"This is my comfort, that thy word hast quickened me," comforted me.

2. As we have comfort from the word, so also from God's people: in the society of God's people, and from the communication of their gifts and graces.

1. From Christ's gift and graces of God's people, so far as we get God and are helped forward by them. Now this affords comfort, and it is comfort to live amongst God's people. Romans 1:12—Paul hopes that he [sic-*they*] shall get God by their faith and that they should get God by his gifts. Colossians 4:11—"These are my fellow workers which have been a comfort unto me." 1 Thessalonians 4:18, the Apostle lays it down as a rule, "Comfort ye one another," "comfort ye the feebleminded,"[76] so that God's people might be great comforts and help to one another in respect of their graces.

---

75. Proverbs 15:15

76. 1 Thessalonians 5:14

2. God's people might be helped in regard of their obedience. Says Paul to Philemon, verse 7—that I might [*be*] "comforted in thy obedience;"[77] 2 Corinthians 7:6—"Nevertheless, God that comforteth those that be cast down comforts us by Titus."

How doth Titus comfort Paul? Partly because he was comforted "in you." And partly because the good that was wrought. Paul, seeing such a warm-hearted church of Corinth, was comforted. Bringing news to Paul, he was comforted also. So Isaiah 66:13—"you shall be comforted" in regard of the flourishing of the churches. God comforts Jerusalem in regard of the spiritual welfare of the church. It does pitifully vex with men to see the church flourish; yet it doth exceeding make the godly rejoice.

3. God doth comfort his people by the comfort of this life, by what the world affords. And this is by removing the evils that lie upon them. Isaiah 40:1—"Comfort ye, comfort ye my people, says the Lord. Cry unto her that her welfare is accomplished and she hath received of the Lord double for her sins," &c. Job 42—God doth exercise[78] Job in comfort. God restores outward things unto him doubly. God's goodness doth exceedingly appear.

2. God doth comfort his people by supporting them under affliction. "This is my consolation under my affliction."[79] 2 Corinthians 1:4, 5—"comfort us in all our tribulations." Though God doth exercise his people many times under many sad trials, yet he leaves them not in them. 2 Corinthians 4:8, 9—"We are troubled on every side yet not distressed; cast down, yet not destroyed." Under many trials God doth exercise his people. Yet all is for their good. And what comfort hath Paul? God hath delivered and will deliver. It is a wonder to see that the affliction as [sic-*of*] some of God's people is as no affliction at all. It is God that strengthens and enables to bear. Thus God supports them.

Lastly, God doth comfort his people in providing graciously for them, giving them many good things according to their straits. And when Paul and his company were in the ship that [*was*] cast away, and the season cold, yet they were forced some to swim, some to get upon planks, and all came to shore yet wet and cold. Now God provided for them, that the barbarians kindled a fire and received them graciously.[80] Thus God provided for them. God doth give us daily bread; and when that is spent, more. God doth feed us. And Genesis 24—Isaac was comforted in the death of his mother. He

---

77. Philemon 1:7—"we have great joy and consolation in thy love;" also 1:21.
78. train
79. See 1 Thessalonians 3:7
80. Acts 27:43—28:2

hath sad afflictions for her, yet God provided a good wife for him which comforted him under sad affliction.

Now for reasons:

First reason. God doth comfort his people because he seeth they have need of it, both of inward comfort and outward comfort. God seeth that his people have need of great consolation. The spirit of a man is not able to sustain his own infirmity. There is need of [a great] deal of comfort in want. The heart of man is not able to bear sickness, sorrows. Says a man, "Is any man's sorrow and aggravation like mine?"[81]

Second reason. God doth comfort his people because he would have them in a comfortable condition. God would have them to walk so, and God would let the world know that he keeps a good house. He oft tells them that he will rejoice over them to do them good; see Deuteronomy 28:3 and Isaiah 62:5. "Rejoice evermore, again I say, rejoice."[82] For spiritual joy all the hours of a life, a man must rejoice. God speaks comfort to his people and answers with good and comfortable words, and how oft: "Daughter, be of good cheer! Let not your hearts be sad." It is for the honor of God that his flock must fear well and live [in] comfort.

Third reason. Christ hath purchased comfort enough for his people, and there is enough in Christ of comfort. Philippians. 2:1—"If there be any consolation in Christ"—not questioning it. Hebrews 6:18—God "confirmed it by an oath" that through Christ we might under "two immutable witnesses" have "strong consolation."

Objection: you say God comforts his people. But doth he not also comfort those that are not his people? What? Doth he not all? Answer: In a sort God doth comfort them; in a sort, not. In some regards God doth comfort and in some regards he doth not.

I cannot deny but that he gives them inward with outward comfort. Yet there is a plain and ready difference between one and the other:

1. They might have inward comfort, abundance of joy, inward joy. They might take themselves to be God's people. They might think they are the children of God and take the children's bread. They conceive themselves to have interest in Christ, and that they do for his sake cleanse themselves from secret sins and love the brethren. Now accordingly they take joy in the promises.

2. Again, men might have abundance of outward comfort, as removals from evil, support under troubles and persecution. And the Apostle says a man that gives his body to be burned and yet have not love in communication

---

81. See Lamentations 1:12

82. Philippians 4:4

of gifts,[83] a man might have a deal of society with God's people. Yet all does not reach so far as the godly. They might be seeming grounds unto that [*which*] God's people might have—and yet not the same.

For now a second question will follow: what difference is there between the comforts of God's people and the ungodly? Answer: There is abundance of difference. They differ in regard of ground work, in regard of the origin from where they proceed.

The comfort of God's people is grounded in a promise according to the tenor and condition. And Christ does not use to comfort but in his way; and his way is to perform the condition of the promise. Now God's people, they look at this, namely, at the condition of the promise.

But now the ungodly's comfort is grounded upon his interest in Christ applied in a promise, but contrary or at least differing to the condition of the promise.

To sum up, all the children of God do try and search what he is willing, not take his [sic-*one's*] own judgment, and makes his case known to the godly, to those that have the tongue of the learned, the ministers, and will have a judgment, and is shy in taking others' judgment. Now those that be but a shadow and blossom [*do*] not come to the perfection. Now the ungodly takes these blossoms and so has but a common work, such as might be without grace. And so he takes comfort to himself upon those grounds that the spirit of God never bade him.

2. They differ in respect of the fruit that does accompany the one and the other. The fruits that accompany the godly are these (more than these, but such like):

Sanctified walking.
Love to the brethren.
Love to God.
Self denial.
Self abhorring.
Sanctified purposes and a resolution of better obedience.
Closing more with Christ.
Desiring more to be found in Christ.
Being brought more out of the love of himself.
Admiring the goodness of God, that has other spiritual fruit accompanying;

and these fruits (such like) are in God's children always. So then the children of God: "Who am I that such fruit should be bestowed upon me—his loving kindness? Now what shall I render unto him? I will be more

---

83. 1 Corinthians 13:3

humble and honor him," &c. And still the soul lays burden on itself. "Oh, that I should give so little to God! I can never do enough." And the soul still labors to be more humble, more base.

Now for the comfort and joy of an ungodly, this temper you shall find him in (if he have joy):

Full of admiration.
Ravishing his affections.
Filling himself with raptures of joy.
Thinking full of himself.
Blessing himself and speaking well [*of himself*].

And then what does follow? Self flattery, abundance of self-justification. Abundance of self depends [sic-*dependency*]. Want of self-denial.

Third difference: The godly and the ungodly differ in their inward comfort because the comfort of God's people does carry the soul so much more in acquaintance with Christ, setting up his honor, having dependence on Christ, and bottoming himself on Christ for comfort. Now an ungodly doth not set up Christ, but sets up himself, depends on himself, bottoms his comfort on himself, and the like.

Now by these things you might find whether your comfort be of God's people or the ungodly's comfort.

2. They differ one from the other in outward grounds. First, they differ because the godly, when [*they*] have comfort, look at God giving [*it to*] them and behold the love of God more than the mercy or the blessing. God's people look at Christ in all. Now the ungodly looks at corn and wine and oil; it is for that he looks. We used to say that a penny from a friend, we take it more kindly than the worth. They look at the love of the friend; so do God's people. But the ungodly look at the worth, &c.

Also God sends rain upon the just and unjust.[84] Now here is outward comfort, and really to the godly, but not so to the ungodly. And truly the bitterest things are comfort to God's people. Excommunication out of the church is comfort; God makes it so to his people. Yet the ungodly, all the comfort that ever they have, they have an adder's sting along with their bitings of a guilty conscience—going along with a comfort that they receive after they have the comfort of God's people, yet not the kernel. A hypocrite may resemble the children of God, yet hath not really true comfort.

Now to apply this:

First use: is it so that God does comfort the hearts of his people? Then we should labor to draw comfort from God's mercy, those things wherein God does afford comfort unto us. Both in regard of inward comfort and outward comfort there is enough to be had. Now we should take that God allots unto us.

Question: How shall we be able to draw comfort from God aright? Answer: If you would be able to draw comfort aright from God,

1. Be sure that you have right [to] comfort. And also take comfort upon Christ's terms, upon the assurance of that spiritual work which Christ hath wrought, either in general or particular. A man can never take comfort inwardly but it must be done in relation to Christ. We must do this with reference to Christ, as bottoming ourselves upon him. I say, be sure you go in Christ's way. If we do not observe the condition we can never take promises aright.

2. If you would draw comfort from God then you must be careful to watch against whatever might hinder your comfort. Whatever particular sin it is that does damp the comfort of God's people, disquiet the conscience, there must be watch over. If you will have true comfort you must watch over what sin it is that hinders it. You see David; all the while he did not confess, could not have true [comfort].

3. Believe if the soul would have comfort aright, it must draw it from the fountain of comfort who is Christ. The soul must still set up Christ and act with Christ. Labor to know Christ to be king, priest, and prophet to teach us and the like; for if you want gifts, resort unto the kingly office to trample Satan under his foot, for there is obtaining of inward comfort. And if sin does overcome you and trouble you look to the priesthood of Christ. And if ignorance troubles, go to his prophetical office to teach and instruct you. Plead with Christ for these things. Amen.

FEBRUARY 23, 1640

2 THESSALONIANS 2:17

Comfort your hearts and stablish you in every good word and work.

These words are to be made up by the former verses, "Now the Lord Jesus Christ himself [and] God our Father which have loved us, and given everlasting consolation, comfort your hearts," &c.

Doctrine: God has comforted his people inwardly and outwardly. This has been proved; this has been given. And objection has been made: the Lord comforted his people, but does he not comfort them that are not? In some sort [he does], and in some not. He does comfort them, yet not as the godly. Then was it was objected, where lies the difference? And those differences I have showed. Then I came to a use: if it be so that God comforts the heart of his [own], then we should draw comfort from God.

Then was a question: How should we who comfort by the spirit our own consciences and outwardly by the [actions?] by his people, be able to draw comfort from God aright? The answer was made:

1. We must be sure to have right to comfort;
2. You must be careful to watch against what might hinder comfort;
3. If the soul would have comfort it must draw it from the fountain.

The soul is to set up Christ's offices of king, priest, and prophet. We should go to Christ's kingly offices for to trample Satan under foot; we should go to his priestly office to subdue sin; and to his prophetical office to teach us. If we take these rules we should draw comfort from God aright. This was last Lord's day; now to proceed.

Now to give some directions how we might draw comfort from these things—from the spirit, from the promises, from the word by God's providence. And this I will do by way of Questions and Exhortations.

First Question: How [sic-*What*] shall I do to draw comfort from the spirit or from my conscience witnessing in the spirit? For answer:

First direction: Be sure you have the spirit of God as God's people have. [*The*] ungodly might have the spirit, but not in the sanctified operation; this only have the children of God. Now you must pitch upon[85] this: what do you find of the spirit of God working in thee that an ungodly might not have? What work have you that an ungodly has not? Now be sure thou findest something in thee that an ungodly cannot have and judge right. Go upon good ground, and then thou shalt have comfort.

Now, have you this comfort? An ungodly cannot have it. If you have, then, &c. Now be sure you have the spirit of God and that which an ungodly cannot have. Pitch upon this, and then you might draw comfort aright. If the soul can say, "I have that comfort which an ungodly cannot have," then I dare write upon it. Be sure you have the spirit and that you find such a work of God on your soul as no ungodly can have.

Second direction: if once thou hast found the evidence of the spirit and the testimony of a good conscience upon such grounds as will hold water, then justify the same. You must not be off and on, but if once you have the work, write upon [*it*], tell Christ that you have such and such principles which beget sanctified affection, praising Christ and abasing and humbling myself. Now hold this, and there is no ungodly in the world can have this. And this is the way to get comfort. Now write upon this; and though you be (it may be) somewhat unsettled, the water is stirred, it will grow clear. And therefore, "I am the child of God." Now be not off and on, but hold to it. When you have the spirit, hold to it forever. And that is the way to get comfort.

God does sometimes withdraw his spirit and then you be off and on: "I have no grace," &c. This is not the way [in] the days of old. And if you have the spirit, then you shall have it ever after, though you have not always the manifestation. If a man comes into his orchard not[86] in the winter and seeth trees have no fruit, shall he therefore think they will not bear in summer? Yet these things might decay, but the Spirit [. . .] Now if once thou hast the Spirit thou hast it still.

Third direction: if you would draw comfort from the testimony of the Spirit then you must sum up the testimony of the Spirit and the testimony of thy own conscience and see what it reaches to. Does it say, "I have the works of Christ. I have interest in him"? Or does it reach to this: "I hope I have grace. I might be the child of God," &c. Now sum up. Does it come to this, that "There is no more to be done to make me the child of God, and I have interest in Christ"? Now sum it up. Will the testimony of your conscience make your evidence clear? Or is it but hopes: "I might, hereafter," or the like? Now this is the reason that you have not drawn comfort, because you do not sum up the testimony of your conscience. Now when your testimony is the clearest, then is the time to sum it up. Now, is the testimony of the Spirit clear? Then you might draw comfort from it. First, ways we might draw comfort from the Spirit.

Now secondly, how might we draw comfort from the promises?

Direction 1: Be sure thou hast right to them and be sure thou art a child of comfort. You cannot tell whether you be an ungodly or what you are? You cannot tell whether promises belong to you? Now, then, promises will be as uncertain. But yet assure yourself that if you be not a child of comfort, you do not have comfort in the promises. The one thing is, to be sure to know yourself to be a child of comfort.

Direction 2: Find thyself if thou wilt have comfort; then find thyself to have necessity of it. Sometimes God indeed gives [people] a greater increase of comfort when they have comfort already. But God does not always do such. Now unbottom thyself of thy own righteousness, and see nothing to comfort thy heart. Then a soul is fittest for comfort, when it is thus brokenhearted and empty. Isaiah 61:1, 2, 3. Who are those to whom comfort is promised? To the brokenhearted and them that mourn. Now those that are thus in heaviness for sins, [there] is comfort to them. Then they are fittest for

---

86. unnecessary extra word

comfort, and then does Christ most give comfort. Find thyself to have need of comfort. While you are so whole-hearted and so full of justification and self-flattery, your own heart tells you that you are full, &c. 1 Peter 5:6—God gives grace to the humble.

Rule and Direction 3: Labor to see what it is that God speaks unto you in a promise and what you might challenge[87] from God by virtue of a promise. You must not haul a promise further than it will reach. If God promises comfort, then it is at his time. You must not stretch his promise to have comfort when you will but when he will—else you will not have comfort.

Now when[88] we will stretch promises that are but for common things unto spiritual mercy. But the way is for a soul to go and open all promises. Break them open as the promises that Christ makes with them that are to enter into church condition. Now we do not understand it. We should break it open and see what it means, &c. The soul must suck the comfort that is in a promise as the child sucks the milk from its mother's breast: it will have all, be it more or less. So take all the comfort that is in a promise. Now the less comfort, the less exercise of faith.

Rule 4: In the promises be sure that you look unto Christ beyond the promises. It is Christ that gives comforts. If you look unto the promises without Christ, they will do little good. All the promises in Christ are yea and amen. And from Christ they [are] enough. God makes promises first with Christ the head of the Covenant: "This is my well-beloved son in whom I am well pleased."[89] In all the promises behold Christ. As, suppose it be a promise for pardon of sin. You must look beyond the promise and look up to Christ for pardon. Now look beyond promises and close with Christ, as this promise: "We have an advocate, Jesus Christ."[90] Now we must not look at the promise, but Christ. 1 Peter 1:8; so 2 Peter 1:3[91]—the promises are "exceeding great and precious." Now how is it so, but in Christ?

Ephesians 3:8—"I should preach the unsearchable riches." Wherein do these Christian riches consist but in a promise Christ promised? Look at Christ in the promises. Now look beyond the promises to Christ in them.

Helps that accompany this word—and they are the seals of the covenant whereby God conveys comfort to his: sacraments, as in Canticles—"stay me

87. lay claim to
88. unnecessary extra word
89. Matthew 3:17
90. 1 John 2:1
91. 1 Peter 1:4

with flagons."[92] The more seals, the more faith, and the more faith, the more comfort. As means [of] comforting our faith, draw comfort from the seals of the covenant.

~

Now the next thing wherein God does comfort his people is in outward providences, as removal of evil, supply of want.

Question: How shall a soul be able draw comfort from God's outward providence? Answer: We have many comforts. God comforts us when we have many blessings from the good providence of God. Now how shall I draw comfort from these?

First rule and direction: Make the right and true exposition of the providence. For what providences do befall thee? The first thing thou shouldst look unto is what God doth speak by his providence. Truly it is marvelous to know God's providence. John 13:7—"What I did thou knowest not now, but shall hereafter." Now in God's providence we do not know, yet might know now what should we do. Therefore it directs:

1. To pray to God

2. Ponder them in our heart, as Mary did her child's soul. And Genesis 37:11—Jacob pondered Joseph's dream. So that first we must pray to God what his providence is. Ponder it now.

3. We must exercise our patience till God's mind appear. Joseph, when his brethren sold him, might [have] said, "what should become of me?" Yet he waited. God gave a comfortable issue. He [= Joseph] waited [for] God's providence.

Now Job did with patience bear God's providence. Says James 4, "Let patience have its work."[93] So say I, let providence have its work. Now make such exposition of providence as God doth intend. If David should, when Saul was exercising[94] [him], should say, "I shall one day die by the hand of Saul," this is an unsound exposition. Now if we make not right exposition of God's providence we should hinder abundance of comfort.

Now I say, take these two things:

One, [the] command to "rejoice evermore; I say rejoice."[95]

Two, "all things work for the good of those that fear God."[96]

Now labor to make a right exposition of providence.

92. Song of Songs 2:5
93. James 1:4
94. testing
95. Philippians 4:4
96. Romans 8:28

Second rule: take this providence:

1. As fruit of promises. Behold God's promise in his providence.
2. Take God's providences as fruit of prayer.
3. Take them as fruit of covenant.

Now, first find out promises and then set the providence with them; and then here is comfort in providences. This is that which makes you such [*an*] atheist under providence. Take this providence as fruits of promise; and this is comfort.

Second, take providences as fruits of prayer. Does anything befall thee? Answer: First thou hast begged it of God, either in particular or general. Now take this providence as fruit of prayer. God doth now exercise by providences. As [*for example*], it might be thou hast prayed that God would mortify thy heart. He seeth the word will not do it. He afflicts to mortify thee. Thou prayest that God would wean thy heart from the world. Now he takes away some of thy cattle or thy house or the like. Now these are God's providence as fruits of prayer.

Third, thou art to take these outward things as fruits of the covenant that God does make with his people through Christ. God says he will make a covenant with the beasts.[97] But now the restoring of creatures is that which God has promised. "And I will be thy God."[98] This is a fruit of the covenant. And [*in*] these providences we are to behold the mediator of the covenant. In them we have merciful passages in this kind and in that kind. Now all these things we are to behold as fruit of the covenant.

Truly God does afford many precious providences to us, and if we could but believe God in his providences we might have as much comfort as the world can afford.

Third Rule: Labor to behold God and Christ in these providences. Look beyond the providence. And in believing God and Christ the soul should fall upon a double act:

1. In meditation concerning God and Christ in these providences. A wise God has many providences. How much wisdom is in God in ordering things as according to his providence; and a faithful God, merciful, just, &c. Now what providences do befall but we might believe some act of the providences of Christ. In revealing his word to you [sic-*us*] we might behold his prophetical office. And in the very growing of herbs we might behold Christ's providence.

2. We might behold God as in meditating concerning him. So also we might believe God and Christ in spiritualities, in concluding spiritually

---

97. Genesis 9:12–16
98. Exodus 6:7; Leviticus 26:12

concerning God and Christ. David concludes, "The Lord hath led me into green pasture and spread my table;" now he concludes, "I shall dwell forever in the house of God."[99] Now will not this comfort the heart, when we that make a special use thus of God's providence as, firstly, to meditate of God and then secondly, to conclude spiritually of God?

Now here is for consolation:

Now first, if we make a right exposition of God's providences, and secondly, [if we] will take them as fruit of promises, prayer and covenant and then to behold Christ in these providences—out of these things arises abundance of comfort.

Use to exhort us: seeing God comforts his people, what we should do, what courses we should take.

God would have us live comfortably and rejoice. Now we should labor not to be so sad, because God would comfort our hearts. We should not make others sad when God would have them not so. When we have saddened our own hearts heretofore, now we should labor to reform. God would have us live comfortably, and truly the want of comfort puts you upon many distrusts of unbelief. When God affords you comfort, take it, lest you want beholding of God's providence, and want acquaintance with Christ. Don't sadden your heart so needlessly and sinfully, seeing God would have you live comfortably.

Thus much for this time.

MARCH 2, 1640

2 THESSALONIANS 2:17

Now our Lord, &c. comfort your hearts
establish you in every good word and work.

God comforts his people. Reasons have been given and I have made uses:

1. How should we draw comfort from God? The spirit, our own consciences, the promises, and providence. Also there was a use of exhortation, that we might comfort our hearts; but more of that anon. Now to proceed.

Third use, for reproof to those that do not make a right use—that do not draw comfort from those things that God would have used unto God's people, for whom comfort is mainly intended. Now the children of God do

---

99. Psalm 23

deprive themselves from abundance of comfort; in terms of their spiritual condition they deprive themselves of comfort:

1. Because they are uncertain whether comfort be sound or no, and such as they might lay hold of. When you are first beginning the work of God in your soul, then to deprive yourself of comfort, it is the better to be borne with. But now you have had many manifestations of God's spirit, yet cannot lay no more hold of comfort, the more blameworthy you are. You are to be blamed now because you do not lay hold of these manifestations of the spirit and so challenge comfort.

Those also are more to be blamed that have laid hold of the manifestations of the spirit and have examined whether they have them and have found God, as it were, to seal unto their soul that they have the spirit of God, yet are ever and anon calling in question whether they can challenge comfort aright. These are to be reproved.

And also those having thus examined, yet think what unworthy creatures they are. And while they are thinking thus, God answers and their consciences tell them that they are not so unworthy, but Christ accepts, and they have interest; and it might be, have been answered by the ministry of the word that Christ accepts of an unworthy. Yet [thou] are still questioning thy interest in Christ.

And also it might be you have been in a secure situation and so might challenge interest in Christ; yet both the spirit [and] the Lord tell thee that for all that thou hast interest in Christ, yet thou callest in question whether thou hast true grace or no. And the spirit and he [= *Christ*] both have oft beat thee off of this; yet thou think thou hast no interest in Christ. Also you have [?] temptation in, it might be, and so think you have no interest in Christ. Yet the spirit of God does evidence unto you that that condition which thou art in, [have] striven against, and have labored to amend, will stand with the truth of grace. Yet presently you are in the same temper. You cannot see that you have grace.

These that are diversely calling in question their interest in Christ after some evidences of it, they are mightily to be reproved. These questions, whether you have grace, these objections—what good get you by them that you are so loath to part with them? Now when thou dost ever and anon call into question their [sic-*your*] former conditions, [*you*] are to be reproved. When God's people are always calling in question those comforts that sometimes they have had, so that God must always kiss them and be always dandling them on the knees or there can be no good done.[100] Or as with little children, the nurse or the mother, if it [sic-*she*] does never so little

---

100. See December 6, 1640.

go aside, then they cry for it [sic-*her*], so you must always see comfort and see your evidence of grace. Or have you thought you have none? This sinful calling in question is to be reproved. Mourn for it, for the devil does labor to catch you. He brings you to distrust of your interest in Christ and so make the soul to fear that it should even is [sic-*be*] reject [sic-*rejected*]. Thus Satan works and tosses the soul to and fro.

Further I add, you sin against God because that God, which [sic-*who*] keeps a good table and will comfort you with his good cheer, now you scarce will taste of them [?]—comforts of the Gospel you refuse. You do not admire the grace of God in this condition. Now while the soul doth thus distrust its interest in Christ, hath not the devil got thee into this temptation? Now thou distrustest; for hast thou not confessed to God of thy grace? Hast not thou confessed to God at the throne of grace of thy interest in Christ? Now the devil has got you into this sinful hold, when you refuse that comfort that Christ affords. How far are you guilty of sinful humility, such as was Peter's; he would not let Christ wash his feet. So John the Baptist—"I have need to be baptized of thee, and comest thou to me?"[101] Now you are t̶o̶ reproved o̶f̶ for your sinful distrust, whether you love Christ or no. Now be humbled and mourn greatly for this.

Now another sort that are to be reproved are those that cannot make use of God's providences. We in this wilderness here, what providences doth God give in outward conditions—clothing us, providing food for us, keeping us in health, increasing us, and the like. Also in respect of the ordinances[102] in our inward spiritual condition—what precious providences! Many good meals, meat of the word. Now if these will not comfort us, then what will?

Also those are to be blamed that if they [sic-*we*] have changes of providence which we like not, as if we be merry, then presently God brings such a providence as crosses, then how sad [*we are*], because not any comfort is in us. But when we have no loss, no dispraise, then we be comfortable enough. But when we are disgraced or have any dispraise or loss, then how comfortless are we! Where was David's comfort when he said one day, "I shall perish by the hand of Saul"?[103] Now let it serve as a use of reproof, seeing God affords some comfort, that we are so comfortless. J̶e̶s̶u̶s̶ Christ is the savior of them that be his people. Varieties of providence we have.

Use for exhortation: you are exhorted here to live comfortably. Provide to live comfortably in a famine. Strengthen thyself against the day of adversity, when providences fail and all things do begin to slack, you be in

---

101. Matthew 3:14
102. Means of growing closer to God in public and private worship.
103. 1 Samuel 27:1

want for food—and then you will wish you have labored to live comfortably against such a day. It is your folly and sin that you do not prepare yourselves against such a day. And then how can you say, "The thing which I feared is come upon me?"[104] Now prepare for such a day. Assure yourselves it will come upon you. Suck out what comfort God affords.

Only one caveat: beware that men be not too greedy of comfort afore God would have you thus. An ungodly cannot be content without comfort; they be exceeding ready of comfort. Be not too greedy of comfort. Seek comfort in those things that God has afforded, but not otherwise. Truly comfort when it is sanctified and joy when it is sanctified might be a kind of help. God's dear people, so far as they be strengthened by rewards, might carry on the work of grace without comfort, so that comfort is not simply necessary. A man might be godly and yet be without this comfort. Yet sanctified comfort would be better.

Sum up all, and then take comfort where God affords it. And if God doth not afford you comfort do not go wheeling and pining for want of comfort. Sum up all. See what the exhortation comes unto, that sanctified comfort should be labored for.

Thus much for this doctrine: that God comforts his people. "The Lord God comforts your hearts." Take these words as a prayer that the Apostle Paul puts up to God for comfort of the Thessalonians. Whence observe:

Doctrine: it is our duty to pray for and procure, inasmuch as in us lies, the comfort of others. Comfort is twofold:

1. in the large, from apprehension of things;
2. natural comforts;

1. For inward comfort, further it in others and also advance their natural [. . .].

[*"proud men"*][105]

We are to pray for other men's comfort. Thus we are to pray for others; that is called upon. Then if we are to pray for others we must pray for that which is needful and necessary for them. Such is comfort. We must pray for comfort [*for them*] as we pray for ourselves. [*We pray*] for others in the Lord's prayer: "Give us daily bread, deliver us from temptation." It is not said, "Give me bread, deliver me," but us, implying others. So that as we are to pray for ourselves, so also for others; and then if we pray for our comfort, we must [*pray also*] for others. 2 Corinthians 1:7[106]—that we might

---

104. Job 3:25
105. These words are written upside-down.
106. 2 Corinthians 1:4

be able to comfort others that are in trouble. Oft says the Apostle, "comfort the feebleminded."[107]

The Apostle bids, Galatians 6, "restore such a man;"[108] then we must comfort him if we restore him. We cannot otherwise choose. Those but do [?] He will have them afterward to confirm their love toward them. The Apostle did use to comfort the hearts of the hearers, and the Jews did used to comfort one another.

Now for the uses of this point:

First use. If we must labor to comfort others, then it will follow that we must comfort ourselves. Here is another argument, for love must first begin at home. Then if we be commanded to comfort others, then ourselves also.

Second use: to reprove those that are so slack in praying for the comforting of others. We pray for others, but are very short in prayer. It also reproves those that do not pray for the welfare of others. If we do not [*pray for*] their conditions we shall be marvelous unmerciful.

Third use: to reprove those that are so far from comforting others that they do discomfort them by their jangling and do not agree. These are to be reproved; also those that discomfort others by their sins, by being scandalous unto others. By your scandal "you have made the heart of the righteous sad whom I have not have made sad."[109] 2 Corinthians 10:32—"give no offence neither to the Jews nor gentiles nor to the church of God." Now by your sins you bring scandals. Such are offensive to the church of God.

Use: therefore it teacheth us, inasmuch as [*in*] us lies, to be tender of making other lives uncomfortable. Be tender over their natural lives. Your neighbors, put to [*them*] your helping hand to do what you can to make the natural lives of others comfortable—also their spiritual life; do not vex their spiritual lives. Tell them that they have no grace and that they be not the child of God, but comfort their lives and pray to God to comfort them.

Thus much for this time

---

107. 1 Thessalonians 5:14
108. Galatians 6:1
109. Ezekiel 13:22

MARCH 9, 1640

2 Thessalonians 2:17

The Lord Jesus Christ comfort our hearts
stablish them in every good word and work.

I have spoken of the former part of this verse; now will [*speak of*] the latter: "And stablish you in every good word and work." The Apostle does now also in this part pray to God to stablish them in God as well as to comfort. Also the Apostle does exhort them to stableness and to stand steadfast in the faith. In the former chapter he speaks of the delusion of anti-Christ so that they must be stable in doctrine.

Out of the words, three things:
1. Paul would have the Thessalonians established in doctrine;
2. God and Christ would establish them;
3. the Apostle Paul doth pray for it.

Of the first, note this doctrine: Christians or the churches of Christ must be settled and grounded in sound doctrine.

For providing the doctrine: [?] Ephesians 4:14—"be not like children tossed to and fro." The Apostle would not have them be like children—any things will [*make*] their [*heads*] turn—but be sound. Hebrews—"Hold the profession of the faith without wavering."[110]

The doctrine is clear. For explication of "sound doctrine," what is it?

Sound doctrine is reduced by the Spirit of God into two heads, Acts 20:21—repentance toward God and faith in Christ, such as concerns:
1. in point of judgment;
2. in point of practice.[111]

Some truth to be [?] held in judgments that are not concerning practice, and many things concerning practice also. A man must be grounded in judgment, that it be not erroneous. So also in practice: both are to be in churches and members. Titus 1:9—Elders or Bishops that have the care of the church must "hold fast sound doctrine," being able "to exhort and convince." They must be apt to teach, and willing also.

Secondly, they must have gifts, and exercise them for the good of the churches. Also they must exercise their abilities as church officers. So also

---

110. Hebrews 10:23

111. Moxon here employs the Ramistic dichotomies cited by William Ames in his instruction on preaching in *The Marrow of Sacred Divinity* (London, 1639), I, xxv, 36: "This use either pertaines to the judgment, or to practice, 2 Tim. 3:16." p. 158. See Dowden, *The Marrow of Theology*, 193.

church members, they must be well-settled in sound doctrine. And it is the truth, because sometimes they might have occasion to exercise gifts; and it is not enough for them that their officers be well-grounded, but they must not be ignorant. Yet a man is not so to be settled in an opinion that he will not alter, be it false or what it will. But be stable in God, and be not apt to change opinion but upon good deliberations.

First reason why Christians should be settled in good doctrine is because the Christians and churches of Christ are the persons to whom sound doctrine is delivered, safely to be kept. The churches of Christ, being [*created*] to deal for Christ, are fittest to keep sound doctrine. 1 Timothy 3:15—the church is "the ground and pillar of truth." The churches of Christ are fittest for sound doctrine, and it is one part of their legacy. This is the first point.

Second reason: there is a necessity that we should be settled in sound doctrine in regard of posterity. If we be unsettled and have not sound doctrine our posterity will be like to follow our traditions. In the days of popery—woeful experiences. And truly if the father should be bad he would train up the children like him; and if that churches should not hold sound doctrine their posterity would not have sound doctrine, and so they would be unsettled in the faith. What benefit is it that sound doctrine should be witnessed, those truths that Adam communicated to his children!

Now in regard of posterity, we must be marvelous careful to be grounded in the truth. And indeed we in New England should be stable so [?] far as it concerns judgment and so far as practice, either in their [sic-*our*] personal walking or ecclesiastical, so that we might leave a legacy to posterity.

Third reason: it is necessary because sound doctrine and knowledge is an excellent thing in itself—excellent to us also. Philippians 3:8—"all things I count but dung and dross for Christ in regard of his excellent knowledge." This is life eternal, to know God and Christ, to know our selves, and to know the means of salvation. It is excellent; it is an excellent privilege to have it. "I will give them teachers after mine own heart. Knowledge shall fill the earth."[112] This is great mercy, and on the contrary a great judgment. When God takes away the candle [*so*] that we cannot see, when we have no means to know Christ, now the children of God themselves count it a great privilege. Paul himself—Galatians 2—Paul stood stiffly for it, that the truth of the [?] doctrine might be steadfast. Paul stands for the defense of the truth and chides them that are so unsettled in the truth, as the Galatians. He

---

112. Isaiah 11:9, Habbakuk 2:14

marvels, chapter 6,[113] that they are removed from the truth.[114] So Jude bids us contend for the faith.[115] And all God's people do count sound doctrine to be of precious use for themselves. Witness so much trading for the means. ["Many a mill in foul weather . . . "][116] Yea, Christians do expose themselves to the rage of wicked men, rather than to lose the faith.

[upside-down: *"Iohn Pinchon unfaithful & ungracious"*][117]

The experience of the Apostles and martyrs will witness it. It is marvelous needful for the churches of Christ. If officers have not this sound doctrine, what can they do? Make the best, they will be but blind leading blinder. Members need it in regard of their covenant; their covenant is to walk according to the ways of Christ. Now if they be not grounded in sounded doctrine how can they perform their covenant with God? Many things that they know, they want strength to practice. But how will you practice when you know not what to practice, when you are not settled in knowledge? This is—it must be—a light to our feet and a lantern to our paths.[118]

Fourth reason: if a Christian or if the churches be not well established in sound doctrine, then they will be so much more exposed to temptation both in judgment and in practice. "Establish you in every good word and work,"[119] he speaks concerning anti-Christ. Now when churches are not sound in doctrine, when the churches lose the truth and lose sound doctrine, so much more does anti-Christ creep in, and Arminianism has overspread churches. And the reason is want of God's doctrine. And what is the reason the churches in our own native country are so pestered with erroneous doctrine? The reason is because they be not established in the truth.

Now the way to prevent all this and to be sound in judgment is to be stablished in sound doctrine. Now if churches be not well-grounded they will be more licentious and subject to temptation in practice. They will be loose concerning the honor of Christ. But if sound [in] doctrine, then more exact in holiness. 1 Peter 2:6—Peter speaking of Paul's epistle says those unlearned, unstable and unsettled take that along. These pervert many things to their own destruction.

---

113. chapter 5
114. Galatians 5:7
115. Jude 1:3
116. These words seem to be part of an incomplete saying from an undetermined source.
117. Written here at the bottom of a page of notes.
118. Psalm 119:105
119. 2 Thessalonians 2:17

Thus much for reasons. Now for uses, and to apply the doctrine.

The first use is for information: if churches must be settled and grounded in sound doctrine then they must abound in knowledge and must have knowledge so that they can be stablished in the Apostle. While they were exceeding ignorant concerning Christ, at that time they were not grounded in sound doctrine. So Nicodemus, while he was a sinner. You might say then that he was established in sound doctrine and was settled concerning repentance and the state of a sinner. Come to an ignorant man, &c. Ask him concerning Church affairs, what covenant he has made? Or ask him why he doth read in his family? He might tell you, but he will be at a stand. Now this man is not established. Now if we would be established in sound doctrine, first we must have it.

The second use, for reproof: it reproves that unstablesness in point [*of judgment*]. Christians are too apt to it, are apt to be too moveable, and novelties are apt to carry away the mind. We are apt to turn as the wind and to be unstable, and there is too great an aptitude in man this way. If we but instance in the practices of the churches of New England not to admit none but them that are known to be saints; now if you should go into Old England, you know not how your mind might be. And the practice of New England is not to baptize children without their parents be members; now if you should go to old England you know not your mind. Be stablished in sound doctrine. You know not what you might be put upon. You know not whether, &c. So, in churches, it is good to be established in the gathering of churches.

Two ways we are to serve God in regard of personal service: we must serve God spiritually. We are to be reproached that we are so unstable in these things in regard of the kingly office of Christ. We have not been trained up in our native country, and in his prophetical [*office*]. We are not stable in teaching and instructing and for these things we deserve to be reproved. If any of our own native country should come over and oppose this way, how can you answer? Now be stable in the truth. It is our sin that we are no more stable in these things.

And truly for my part the churches of Christ losing the truth is the reason of so much popery and of so much of anti-Christ in the world. Now the churches being not established in these truths is that which makes so many erroneous judgments. Now let it reprove them that are so unestablished in these things. You do not know many things, whether they be sin or not. Many of God's people are established in sound doctrine concerning the education of the family, training up a child. Now a profane heart is not thus established.

Now what is the reason we are so unstable in sound doctrine and knowledge?

First reason is, the light esteem you have of the love of it. 2d reason You do not highly prize that light that God has communicated unto [us]. We do not highly prize sound doctrine and knowledge. We do not see that we are apt to fall into such profaneness [of] heart. It might be thought it [sic-*you*] can keep up good conscience, with knowledge or without as well. And you do not highly prize knowledge. People can make a shift to be without [it]. You do not set a high price upon wholesome doctrine and sound truth, things that you care not for. You cannot set a high price upon [them]. In the public ministry you do not set a high price upon that which is revealed; you do not treasure up these things as you ought to do. You do not set a price upon the means. God's own people that are dear unto him, for their sakes God communicates knowledge publicly to make[120] take, if they will. But it is communicated for God's people, and they lay up some. And indeed it is a sin they lay [up] so little.

A second reason why you are unsettled in sound doctrine is because you have not walked in that light that God hath communicated. God communicates light and you smother it up. Your lust will not let you walk according to the light. Again, it can never be expected that God should bless means to them that will make no use [of them].

A third thing, and reason why men are unstable in sound doctrine, is because you take the truth of God in regard of persons. Such a man is a worthy, and so is his opinion, and thou followest it without knowing his reasons. This makes a man unstable. Also it may be another man holds as [sic-*an*] opinion and it is a truth; he gives reason why it is so, and texts to prove it. Yet thou dost not greatly affect the person, and so yield not to his truth. This makes unsoundness in doctrine, that you receive truth from the reverence that you have to some person; and others, you do not esteem them, [and so] not their doctrine. These things are to be reproved in you.

Third use: We have great cause of humiliation for this unsettledness in sound doctrine. If God should but put us upon trial in point of errors, [in] what would we be settled, in doctrine? Truly we are exceedingly ignorant in sound doctrine, in any truth. Let us take it and bewail it as our burthen.

Fourth use: For exhortation to settledness and stableness in sound doctrine.

1. Consider if once thou hast the truth and art settled in sound doctrine and fallest from it again, thou fallest into an error.

---

120. unnecessary extra word

2. Consider that God affords many means and helps. We should labor to be settled in sound doctrine considering what means and helps God affords us. We have no plea for our unstableness.

3. Consider there is no truth that God doth reveal unto you but one day you will have need. Every day, sermons that you have lost you will find that you have need of and you will be in the issue less able to keep a good conscience. Now let these considerations exhort you to be settled in well-doing and to be stable in sound doctrine

MARCH 16, 1640

2 Thessalonians 2:17

The Lord stablish you in every good word and work.

Last Lord's Day, out of these words I noted three things:
    1. Paul would have the Thessalonians stable in sound doctrine.
    2. God and Christ must do it.
    3. The Apostle prays for it.
    Concerning the first, last Lord's Day I noted:
    Doctrine: churches must be stable in sound doctrine and knowledge. I have proved it by scripture, given reasons, and have made uses. Now to proceed on.
    From the first things note this doctrine also:
    Second doctrine: the duty [of] Christian Churches to be established in every good work.
    For proof: James 5:8—"stablish your hearts;" 1 Corinthians 15:58—"Be ye steadfast and unmovable," established in the work concerning the Lord. Ephesians 6:10—"Be strong in the Lord, and in the power of his might." 2 Timothy 2:1.
    Two things in the doctrine:
    1. The act [by] which it is established;
    2. The object wherein [it is established]—in every good work.
    1. Of establishing the text [sic-*work*]—carrying it on. Hold your profession to the end. Be established in particular duties. And the text calls, to be established to the end. Many might make a shift to get to heaven, yet have an unconstant spirit in many particular duties. A man might be strong to his dying day, yet have many fits of sickness, [as] a traveler [on] a ship, &c.

Secondly, the text extends it to those [*in whom*] God works—Hebrews 13:21. So is it that Christ did. John 8:29—"I did always those things that please him," for it was in stableness in every good word and work. Christians should always do that which is pleasing [*to God, for*] which they must be stable in every good work. Truly there is no work that God commands but it is a Christian duty, and he [= *a Christian*] does not well omit any good work that God commands. He will dishonor God if he neglect it.

God does not only command a Christian to be constant in hearing, stable in reading; this is not every good work, and he must be stable in every good work, else he will be but half a Christian.

Reasons:

1. [A] man must be thus stablished if he does regard the difficulty that they [sic-*he*] shall meet.

2. In regard of the work, we have to do what is required.

3. Consider ourselves, what need we have to be stable.

First, men must be thus stablished. If he [= *a man*] does regard the trials a Christian will meet with, a world of trials, abundance of temptations—if a Christian does not know this, he knows himself not their [sic-*his*] own heart. Ephesians 6—the Apostle is speaking to them to "Put on the whole armor."[121] Why? Because we shall meet with great tribulations. Christians might [?] be tempted in everything they do: in unkindness from others, in the fruit in your basket.[122] And [*this*] shows that you might trust too much in them. In the very holy things you have temptations. Now what is the life of a Christian? Nothing but to fall down and get up again.[123] Truly if we mourn for sin we cannot choose but see the temptations that draw them to [sic-*us to them*]. These many temptations should make us the more stable.

Second reason, in terms of the work that we have to do. There is reason enough for us to be stable if there were no work to do but on a Sabbath hear sermons and then repeat them. Is this all? Truly this were hard enough for our spirit. But this is not half the work that God requires. Hebrews—"The Lord make you perfect to do his will."[124] We cannot do half God wills without we be more stable.

Third reason: if we do but consider ourselves, we would be stable. First, because we are weak. Does not the Apostle tell of weak graces, weak faith, etc.? 1 Corinthians—the Apostle tells of weak conscience.[125] Ezekiel

---

121. Ephesians 6:11
122. See Deuteronomy 26:2
123. Proverbs 24:16
124. Hebrews 13:21
125. 1 Corinthians 8:10

16:30—"How weak is thine heart, O Jerusalem." So that weak faith, weak graces, weak gifts, weak conscience, weak heart and affection—all weak. The inward man is weak. Hebrews 12:12—"Lift up the hands that hang down and the feeble knees." This might be meant of the inward man. The text does oft calls upon officer [*and*] member to support the weak, comfort the feeble. "Support the weak."[126]

Now if we must support others that be weak, much more ourselves. Now as we are weak, so add in the second place: what groaning and wearied spirit have you for want of stablenesss?

Fourth. I add a fourth reason: that God commands us to be stable. It is a good thing, the spirit of God says, and also bids [*us*] have a strong and stable spirit. And now if the breach of God's command is a sin in other things, so also in this. Let God's command have authority to make thee stable. "The God of peace stablish you in every good work."

Four uses:

First use, this: it informs us what secret, close duty that be marvelous necessary, yet we little take notice. This "establishing"—how little do we take notice that we are unstable and inconstant! God's people might be too much guilty that he does [sic-*we do*] so little look at these close secret duties which do concern the inward man.

Second use: try now whether you have not unstable spirits so. [Have?] you not unconstant minds?

First, for direction: whence are those many convictions, and then resolutions of better obedience? You are convinced of your sin, so begin to abhor yourself, and you say, "I will look a little better. I will keep a better watch." So [*you*] set to confession of sin and humiliation, for a fit.[127] But it lasts not. Thou, art thou thus? Then thou art unstable in thy purposes. Or it may be thou thinkest thou hast some misgivings whether thou art a child of God, whether thou wilt know the spiritual labor. "What mettle I am made of?" Within a while these purposes fall. Or says another, "I have been unprofitable in my family. Will [*I be so*] ever after? I will labor to drop wholesome instruction into my family." Yet within a while these purposes fall. Or says another, "I am overcome with temptations; they overbear me. Will I have so much temptation that I will strive against it and get power?" Yet still the same temptation dogs thee. Now canst thou not behold an unconstant spirit in all these things? Now this is [*thine*] own ground of conviction: so much as thou let these holy purposes fall, so much unconstancy.

---

126. 1 Thessalonians 5:14
127. for a while

Second, for conviction: whence is it that those scandals of yours come? Whence are those froward passions and unjust dealings? Consider what affections sometimes thou hast had: warm affections, strictness [in] watchfulness over thine own; also what little affection, no mind at all to duty. [Try?] if thy spirit hath been constant: then thou [torn]

[torn] watchful and in as good affection [torn]
[torn] much unconstancy. Now [torn]
[torn] this conviction: thou hast an unconstant spirit [torn]
[torn] conviction, whence is so little
[torn] [th?] in grace but from the
[torn] unconstancy [?] your spirit
[torn] Now be convinced thou hast an unconstant spirit. ([*An*] unconstant spirit is a curse.) What begets this unconstancy?
[torn] [ly?] thy temptation, corruption not
[torn] yet [torn]

2. I would look at this unconstancy as a spiritual judgment. So Adam in his innocency was unconstant and thou are driven now to the root to see whence thou first proceeded. Thou tookest this from Adam.

3. Thou art unconstant in the use of means, unconstant in fruit. Sometimes thou useth the means, other times not. As with fruit, take away the sun and rain or take away the mold and they cannot live without they be constant. So it is with thee.

Second use: heart humiliation, that our spirits are so unconstant in every good word

[torn] is a very bad consequence [torn]
[torn] [ott?] with God and judgment [torn]
many texts to prove it in [torn]
to be constant by [?] [torn]
James 8—"Be stable." Corinthians—"Be steadfast" [?]
than any to be unconstant [torn]
[torn] [?] this [?] sin to be unconstant, a judgment to be unstable, unconstant. Now be humbled for this, and for [f?] [torn]

humiliation see what this unconstancy of spirit does expose [*you*] unto?

1. Unto [?]

John Pynchon's notes-December 27, 1640

2

December 6, 1640—January 3, 1641
American Antiquarian Society, Worcester, Massachusetts

DECEMBER 6, 1640

MALACHI 4:2

But to you that fear my name the Sun of righteousness shall rise with healing in his wings and ye shall go out and grow up as calves of the stall.

A child of God cannot damn himself [. . .] were not every child miserable had [father?] or mother to tend them better than and [?] tend them selves. Such would become of us poor creatures. [Here?] is our happiness, that we have such healing laid up for us. God doth as it were write upon this child as soon as he comes into the world, a Vessel of Mercy. Yet how many weaknesses doth he betray to his dying day? Now then God [?] is his healing. What a happiness is this for him! Oh, that we did but know our happiness.

    Second use for reproof to the godly that lie so much under complaints: if your complaints were but aggravation of sin to humiliate you! You are from time to time complaining of sin as if Christ could not pardon. They complain so much as though they had no means at all to recover themselves, and this is it: you are to be reproved for your complaining, as though there were no healing, in a sort complaining as [*to*] God and complaining as if he had provided no help for thee.

"It's true I do complain and cannot but complain and all God's people do complain." Then what is the reason that all God's [people] do thus complain, as if [a man] should complain he is hungry and has [?]? Why do God's people thus complain for these reasons?

You do not make use of these means that God has propounded for your healing. Shall a man complain for want of meat, and meat is before them [sic-*him*]? Shall a man complain of his sores, and yet he has a healing plaster provided for them? Yet this is his fault: he doth not apply it to the sores. Such is your case. You do not make use of this spiritual remedy. Now examine your hearts and you shall find that when you most complain you do some way abstain from Jesus Christ. Either you think you have tired him out, or else you think he will not hear you, or else you are lazy. Is the faith a hand? Now then if you have withered hands, or if you have [*any*] hands, [*you*] have faith, and yet will not make use [*of it*]. This is your fault.

Now, you stand complaining as [*to*] God. You stand pewling and wheeling, and yet you have a healing medicine if you would but be so much more urgent and pressing and laboring more for Christ. Indeed, a soul should as it were take Christ by violence; and you should lay hold on promises by violence.

As in humiliation, a man should make himself as bad, as vild [*a*] man, sinful as might be. But when acting of faith comes you must put away this making yourself mean and think yourself accepted in God's eyes. And you should think yourself as happy as ever. Yet you do as a man loath to go to a friends' house, because he has been in there much afore—yet his friend wishes him to come. Thus it's with you. Christ wishes you to come and spreads out his hands for you. Yet you are loath to trouble him. Christ would not have you so. He calls, "Thou art fair, my love, thou art fair; thou hast doves' eyes."[1] Christ would have you come.

Now put on a holy violence. Did not Jacob wrestle with the angel by prayer? And why not by faith? Now then do you wrestle by faith and not needlessly absent yourselves from Christ, but be fervent and Jacob-like. Depart not with [sic-*without*] a blessing. Why are you so mannerly? Be not so. The text would not have you so.

It might be you do not find right qualifications in yourself that your [*hearts be*] warm and that you are not yet deeply humbled for your sins. Now how oft shall I tell you that you are all times alike accepted with Christ? "You are not so close [*to*] God [*as*] you oft [*were*], and not today;" but if ever, then today! Now I say you will not take healing. You depart from Christ. Before he cast you off, you cast yourselves off, for you find ever how it has

---

1. Song of Solomon 1:15.

been with you formerly. Thou hast had many rich experiences beyond expectation. Thou wilt make the estate of the children of God not worth a straw. What do you make of Christ? Now what do you make of him but an idol? You do not make use of the remedy Christ has propounded. How oft doth the text make use of Christ's freeness and readiness to pardon sin, and thou givest the lie unto all these. Thou art a deal worse to thy self than thou needest [be], like a willful patient. He will not take the course that the physician prescribes for his healing.

Second reason why God's people go under some complaining for all there is such healing medicines propounded, is because you will not stay the time of healing. Some diseases will not be cured without a course of taking physic. Some will be cured by once or twice taking physic. Now [you] will take physic once, and if it heal not you will be tired, except Jesus Christ take you and dandle you in his lap, and kiss you with the kisses of his mouth and heal you at the first clap.[2] You are ever tired. You think you cannot be healed. Such wretched surmises! Thou fillest thy head—for with that they will be your utter undoing. You will have things in your own time; even your spirits are tired out waiting how the Lord will hear you in the issue. You cannot, though you are bidden stand fast in the faith—"Quit you like men"—and bid to wait on the Lord. Isaiah 40:31—and then you "shall renew your strength." Whoever waited upon the Lord and was ashamed? Yet you cannot wait. This is the reason you are so full of needless complaining.

Third reason is because you do not make use of form [sic-*former*] experience. A man might say it's pity you should have any more experiences and cannot be taught by them. When we see the ground covered with snow should we not be apt to say we should never have grass more, but that for experiences? We see that snow lasts not always. Now will experience do nothing unto you? The Lord has delivered Christ; he will deliver. And why cannot you make it a help unto your faith? You might help yourselves against these needless complainings if you had but made use of former experience.

Third use for comfort to all God's people that have need of comfort, and to say [to] those hearts that are ready to sink and to faint: to whom doth healing belong? For you say Christ doth forbid, and you have no right to this healing. How dost thou prove it? Art thou one that dost not fear? Thou sayst thou doth not. It might be thou sayest true. But it's not ordinary for those that do not fear God to say that [they] do, without it be in convictions. Now I say that there is a necessity of this renewing of repentance. As thou renewest thou will make one shift over another not to take comfort as it might be. Thou will say thou liest in some sin and art not in favor with

---

2. See March 2, 1640.

God and must be humbled before thou canst be healed. Now canst thou not find repentance in truth? Canst thou not? Yet thou must go unto Christ for repentance, and the blood of Christ will soften the hardest heart in the world. Now thou liest in this condition. Thou canst not repent. Yet thou will tire out.

Let it now comfort God's people:

1. Upon what terms is the soul welcome unto Jesus Christ? By coming to him. "Come to me, all that are weary," &c.[3] Art thou such? Then go to Christ, &c. He will ease thou [sic-*thee*]. So dost thou want anything? Go to Christ; then thou shalt be welcome. Jesus Christ took thee upon spiritual terms to pass by all thy sins. He took thee for better, for worse. He did forgive all the sins that ever thou wilt commit.

Now, use for exhortation to all to go to Jesus Christ for pardon of sin. The truth is, you must do it sooner or later. Your miserable, wretched estate will force you unto it. Plead and tire out yourselves never so long, yet in the issue you must be forced with a violence to go unto Jesus Christ. Go to Christ, the sooner the better. "Welcome, thou, at my father's house!" There is bread—Christ. Consider this and go to Christ.

All your carnal reasons, from whence do they proceed but from Satan's tempting, from one that never wishes you your good? Now press yourself on to seek after this healing in Jesus Christ, in pardoning your sins to your soul.

I have showed you how Jesus Christ heals the soul by pardoning sin. I cannot now proceed to show how he heals the soul by sanctifying the soul—sanctifying power or sanctifying grace.

DECEMBER 13, 1640

MALACHI 4:2

But to you that fear my name the Sun of righteousness shall rise with healing in his wings and ye shall go out and grow up as calves of the stall.

It hath been shown that in the text there is a promise of Christ to those [*who*] fear him:

1. a promise of healing;
2. that we shall grow in spiritual things as calves: the doctrine that in Christ there's healing enough to them that fear God.

1. There is healing enough in pardoning;

---

3. Matthew 11:28

2. There is enough in Christ to heal us in point of sanctification.

Concerning the first I spoke last Lord's Day. Now to show how there is healing enough in Christ for sanctification. Christ is able enough to sanctify—Psalms, Hebrews 10:10 and 14; Philippians 4:13—[*I*] will "do all things" through the help of Christ means that he will help to do this thing. Then there is help enough in Christ to do anything that God commands; thus much also is implied. Galatians 2:20—"I live, yet not I." I live by faith through the power of God.

Sanctification consists of two parts:

1. of mortification, dying unto sin;
2. of quickening grace, enabling unto holiness.

Now in Christ, first, there is enough in point of mortification to enable us to die to sin. Romans 6:3, 6—the "body of sin" is crucified with him, so Paul has said. Galatians 2:20—"I am crucified with Christ;" the meaning is, "I am crucified in my spiritual condition. My lust and temptation are as truly dead in me as ever Christ was crucified." Now there is power enough in Christ to crucify sin.

Second, there is enough in Christ to quicken grace. 1 John 1:4—"In him was life," and life was the beginning of the world; and so 1 John 5:12—"he that has the son and [sic-*has*] life;" Colossians 3:3, 4—"Your life is hid with God in Christ," and when he shall appear then shall ye also appear with him in glory. Christ is our life. Acts 3:15—he is called the "prince of life," and so he is said to be a quickening spirit. Yea, the whole work of sanctification is ascribed unto Christ. 1 Corinthians 15:45—"The first Adam was made a living soul; the last Adam was made a quickening spirit." John 5:21—the Father quickens "whom he will;" so doth the Son. Also, Ephesians 5:26.

First reason, to show that there is power enough in Christ to heal his people in point of sanctified walking. [*The*] reason is taken from the all-sufficiency that is in Christ as the mediator of the covenant. God is all-sufficient; then [*God has*] power enough to do all things well. Then is there power enough in God? Then there is power enough in Christ to do all things.

To prove [*there is*] power enough in God and Christ: Colossians 2:9—there is all "fullness" in Christ; yea, Colossians 2:3, 4—"in whom are hid all treasures of wisdom" and holiness and treasures of power; also treasures of all things. 2 Peter 1:3—according to "his divine power has given all things pertaining to life and holiness."

Now if there be divine power in God, then in Christ. If God have power, Christ has also; this is clear. John.[4] Though there might be difference

---

4. John 17:2

between the working of God and Christ, yet not between the power of God and Christ. Has God power? Then Christ. It's the soul God creates. Yea, and Christ creates: "Let us make man."[5] And oftimes it's said our makers, even God and Christ.[6] "God judges," sometimes it's said. And other times it's said, "God judges none, but has committed all to the Son." "I will pray to the Father and he shall send the comforter."[7] Other times it's said, "Christ will send the comforter"—that what the Father doth, the Son doth, and what the Son, the Holy Ghost. The Son doth what the Father doth, so that if there [is] grace enough in God's holiness, enough in God's divine power, enough in God, then in Christ also.

Second reason is taken from his kingly office. As he is a king there must of necessity be enough in him. There is an extraordinary divine power in him. 1 Corinthians 15:24, 25. Now he is a king and has dead men to deal with; dead souls and Satan to fight. As now he is a king, then he must be able to do all things well—his subjects able to mortify sin, to quicken grace, to tread down Satan even as God does. It's spoken of Christ, Psalm 45:3—"gird thy sword most mightily; thy throne, O God, endures forever. Thy arrows are keen and sharp," &c. So also Psalm 2:9—"Thou shall break them with a rod of iron; thou shall dash them in pieces with a potter's vessel." Is the wrath of a king like the roaring of a lion? Such is the wrath of Christ. He is able to subdue all his enemies; so Psalm 110, it being spoken of the victorious power of Christ, that he will make all stoop before him. [?] Psalm 89:19—thou hast "laid help upon one that is mighty; I have exalted one" above the people. David the type; Christ the antitype.[8] David mighty upon this earthly kingdom, but Christ mighty in the spiritual kingdom.

There is help enough in him, one that is mighty; so that there is power enough in Christ above death and sin and—and lust and all. Ephesians 1:19; so also 1 Corinthians 15:24—"Then cometh the end when he shall have put down all power," &c. For he must needs reign till he has put down his enemy under his foot, "that at the name of Jesus every knee might bow."[9] To bow at his name is to reverence him in authority, to be subject unto him. Christ hath such a kingly power as he makes all yield unto him.

Third reason: there is power enough in Christ to heal in [?], else these evils and absurdities will follow, for else all promises are in vain. Then the

---

5. Genesis 1:26

6. This usage is not found in either the Geneva or the King James Bible.

7. John 14:16

8. In classic Biblical interpretation, Old Testament models or "types" prefigure New Testament fulfillments, or "antitypes."

9. Philippians 2:10

new covenant is in vain, and a lying covenant. "Then I will put my laws in you and cause you to walk in his statute."[10] If there be not power enough in Christ in point of sanctified walking, then you might say that Christ promises more than he will perform. You must acknowledge all your faith is in vain. Nay, we might throw away all texts and say there is nothing in Christ.

And whereas the text says Christ works as the Father, you might say this is a lie. "Such texts are false. We grant God has power, but Christ has none." And so you condemn this text: "he that sanctifies and he that [*is*] sanctified are all one."[11] Hebrews 12:2—"Looking up to Jesus Christ, the author of our faith." He doth not say the object of our faith, but the beginning of our faith and the perfecter of it. Now this is in vain: "there is not healing enough in Christ." It's marvelous. Were there not healing enough in Christ, then how came God's people to be so holy? Abraham, Isaac, David, &c—whence have they their healing? Did Christ make them so holy, or was it nature made them so holy? If there be not healing enough in Christ, then how shall any get to heaven? How shall any, and how have any? No one can enter the door but by him. God is a God of all justice, but only through Christ. Will God the Father be reconciled with anyone without Christ? Will God work without Christ? Are men brought to glory without Christ? Is it not Christ [*who*] brings them to glory? Is [sic-*Are*] not all things of him and by him?[12] There is no way to heaven but by him.

You might say, "What need you to prove so much, that there is healing in Christ? There is scarce any man but think so. I never thought otherwise &c." It might be thou wilt say—and if thou wert to reason with any man thou wilt say—there is enough in Christ. Yet in thy judgment, thou thinkest not so. Now my strong proving that in Christ there is healing enough might convince thy judgment and may help thee as [*to*] thoughts that there is not help in Christ, if they should ever arise. The soul is afflicted: "I grant that in Christ there is power enough in point of healing us by sanctified walking, but that which I do doubt is:

1. the willingness of Christ to communicate;
2. how will the soul draw virtue from Christ?

Though Christ be full of power and is able enough to heal the soul, yet this is that which I stick at."

1. The soul sticks at Christ's willingness [?]. Christ is able yet not willing to communicate, aye?

---

10. See Ezekiel 36:27
11. Hebrews 2:11
12. Hebrews 2:10

1. Why then did Christ make such promises as Jeremiah 31:33—"After those days." Ezekiel 36:24[13]—"A new heart will I give." Some [?] these are precious promises. "If I had a new heart!" Christ shall give a new [heart]. "I shall want renewing." "I will put my spirit."

2. If Christ were not willing, why doth he bid us to ask and we shall have? "Knock, and it shall be opened. Ask."[14] But what shall we ask? We know not what to ask. Christ doth not set down what you should ask because he will not limit you. Ask what you have need of, for Christ himself reasons in [Matthew 7] v. 9, "what one of you, if his child ask [for] bread will he give him a scorpion? Much more will not your heavenly father give unto you?" And in Luke it's directly unto your hearts. "Seek." Luke—"I will give you the graces of the Holy Ghost."[15]

Now you that are children, you might reason, how willing is my father to give unto me? Christ is much more willing. So parents, you can tell how willing you are.

3. Jesus Christ has received the spirit for that purpose that he might communicate unto all the Elect. He has "led captivity captive and given gifts unto men."[16] Like as the sea which receives in all brooks and streams and spreads this abroad, so doth Christ receive gifts to communicate them to the Elect abroad in the world.

Then the more Christ gives, the more is he honored. Is he willing enough? The more of his spirit he gives the more you are able to improve it, and so honor [him]. ~~Now the uses.~~

Use: You will say we cannot tell how to draw virtue from Christ. "The well is deep and I have nothing to draw,"[17] and it's difficult. Yet take these directions:

1. If thou wilt draw power from Christ thou mayest see that thou hast need of the help of Christ. The whole have no need of the physician, but the sick.[18] A man might ~~wonder seeing~~ go to Christ and he will heal him. He will ease you of your sin and temptation when he seeth good.

2. You must resign up your hearts and your selves unto Christ. You must wholly be at his disposing. You must take him upon his own terms

---

13. Ezekiel 36:26
14. Matthew 7:7, Luke 11:9
15. Luke 11:13
16. Ephesians 4:8
17. See John 4:11
18. Matthew 9:12, Luke 5:13

and not stand higgling[19] with him; but you must give up yourselves wholly to Christ.

3. Prayer must draw—that is, in Christ. If any man will have wisdom, let him ask it of Christ, for he giveth wisdom and grudgeth no one.

I fear there are two faults in your prayer. You pray too indifferently. You pray so as if you cared to be answered, and yet cared not to be answered. I call such praying a sin: profane praying, taking God's name in vain. As you will find sins [*enough*] to pray [*only*] a little while, that is all you pray to God.

But not in the name of Christ. You do not bring Christ upon you. God's providence is not such [*as*] to bestow rich graces on men without they will fervently ask them. You must set faith on works. Faith believes God to be a rewarder of them that seek him. Faith must do it. By faith you must close with the promises. You must use faith to draw more rising power and quickening power from Christ. How should a man use his faith? ~~I say now turn to the~~ [?] to help your faith to believe Christ has healing enough.

Consider the experiences that the children of God have concerning the power of God in the soul. Have you never had no experience of any that Jesus Christ has communicated himself to him [sic-*them*] whether they will or not? Canticles 5—when the spouse would not open but lay in security, Christ put his finger in at the hole of the door.[20]

Says a poor soul, "I am so full of temptation that was never [*a*] poor soul the like over-burthened." Christ says his grace is sufficient for you.

1. Consider the time when Christ will help you. Stay his time. Wait upon him. There is power enough in him, and willingness enough in him, and he will do it in his time. Stay his time.

2. The measure and degree. How much Christ will heal you and how far you must leave to him. He will do it in his time and in his measure.

DECEMBER 20, 1640

Malachi 4:2

But unto you that fear my name the Sun of righteousness, etc.

Doctrine: there is healing in Christ to all those that fear God.

I have showed that there is healing enough in point of justification and sanctification. I have proved it by texts and text arguments. I have showed

19. haggling
20. Song of Songs 5:4

that he is willing enough in Christ to heal you. And I have given you directions how you might draw power out of Christ. And I think that the point may be more fully proved, and to answer some objections:

1. Objection. Seeing there is healing enough in Christ, what then is the reason that in God's people there is such complaining? For says a child of God, "I pray and pray in the name of Christ and do what I can to draw power from Christ, and yet I cannot get ~~power~~ Christ to heal me." Another: "I find but little to quicken up my dead heart and to stir me up. I cannot find myself but little better than a natural man, for I have but little of the spirit of Christ."

Before I answer the first point, I must know whether you have grounds thus to complain, that you have but little of the spirit and that you have but little or none of the power of Christ conveyed unto you in point of sanctification; you complain thus. I answer that you of yourself are like water. [*You*] have no strength in you. You are nothing but temptation, like the scales over [sic-*out of*] balance. One scale is down, so you are down. Would not the temptation that is in you keep you down, if it were let alone? Now it must be Christ strengthening you. You have power from Christ, and that abundance of his spirit communicated unto [*you*]. "We are kept by the power of God through faith unto salvation."[21] 1 Peter 1:5—now if God "keeps" you, you will not be care-full. "I am able to do all things through" [. . .]

Now have not you a share in the helping of Christ? "My grace is sufficient for thee."—2 Corinthians 12:9. Now have not you a share in this sufficiency of Christ? Do you not find that this sufficiency of grace is communicated to you? Galatians 2:20—"I live, yet not I." I live by faith. Now cannot you say, as Paul says, that in some measure you find Christ to be [. . .] Ephesians 3:16—"That he would grant you according to the riches of his glory to be strengthened by his spirit, with might in the inward man." Now if there were not abundance of, &c, you could never do as you do. Philippians 1:19—"For I know this shall turn for your good through my prayer and the supply of the spirit of Christ." Now you have abundance of the supplies. 1 Peter 4:11—"If any minister, let him do it as the ability God gives." Now have not you a share in this ability that God gives? Matthew 13:12—"to him that has shall be given." Now have you never found God making this promise good unto your soul? Do you not find God giving you more abundantly of his spirit from day to day? I do not believe but these days [?] have been when you would have been glad to have had the spirit so much as you have.

That which might make God's people the more complain is:

---

21. 1 Peter 1:5

1. that they cannot have that [*which*] they ask in their time;

2. that they cannot have it in their kind.

Nothing would content Abraham but a child. So nothing will content you but to have that very thing you ask.

3. You will have it in your measure. This is but a little, say you. If a man has 19 good turns he will not be satisfied without the 20. So you complain as sin, and this is that [*which*] I would have you to distinguish, between your complaining as sin and your [suffering?].

2. A second thing to be answered is, what might be the reason that God's people should so complain that they have so little from Christ as they say they have? Answer: the reasons might be partly from Christ and partly from ourselves:

1. from Christ, that he doth not give us in that measure he [sic-*we*] would have. Ephesians 4:7—"I will put my spirit in you." [?] He doth not tell you how much of his spirit, but according to the proportion of grace given you.

2. Christ doth oft deny to give us in that kind we ask. Paul sought the messenger of Satan to be taken away.[22] Now though he had not that, yet he had that which was as good. Paul had that which supported him. The soul says, "If I had that which should support and bear me up against temptation—but I have not." Luke 22:32—What doth Christ promise? That thy faith shall not fail thee, so that though Christ will not say that thou shalt not fall, yet Christ will take thee up again while you are fallen, so that though you are overborne with temptations, yet thy faith shall not fail thee.

3. Christ denies us to have our request at our time. Abraham should have a child, but not yet. So we shall have power over this temptation, yet not yet. We shall have many a knock first.

Now, in what manner Christ doth communicate? Not always at the same time, not always in the same kind, not always in the same measure.

Question: but why doth Christ thus hold the soul off? Indeed, Christ is wise and [*has*] wise ends known to himself. As a physician knows best how to cure the patient, so Christ as a wise God knows best when and how to heal us. Yet Christ might hold us off for these two or three reasons:

1. Christ may hold the soul off because we are not able to bear the communications of his spirit. John 16:12. The power of Christ when it raiseth up hearts makes us turn the grace of God into wantonness. We have such froward spirits, such deceitful spirits, such ticklish spirits, that whatever God doth we will make some bad use or other. We are not ~~the power of Christ~~ able to bear them.

---

22. 2 Corinthians 12:7–8

2. Christ may hold us off to keep us more hungry for Christ and for the spirit, that our stomachs might be more sharper. If we should wax fat would we not begin to kick? Luke 1:53—"he hath filled the hungry with good things." Christ will fill us when we are hungry, and he will not let us be always full, because that prodigal-like we might not spend all.

3. Christ doth hold us off to exercise our faith, exercise our condition; 1 Peter 1:7. Changes of condition put a man under the exercises of changes of grace.

4. God doth oft deny us, in that he might feed us so much the better with infirmities of our own weakness. God doth show us experience of our weakness, in that Christ is not always with us. If Christ did always supply us with his spirit we should be apt to say, "With our strength have we gotten power over temptation," and "I can pray effectually." You would ever think thus. But now Jesus Christ, that wise physician, withdraws his spirit that you might see your own weakness.

4) I have showed you the reason why God's people did complain that Christ withdrew his spirit lay partly in Christ and partly in ourselves: partly in Christ ~~our selves~~—why he holds the soul off, for what reasons I have showed.

Secondly, reasons in ourselves are these, for we do not use the means that God has appointed for our spiritual good:

1. Want of prayer. Either men do not pray or else not pray as they ought to pray. "In nothing be careful but in all things let your request be made unto God."[23] "In all things," outward and spiritual. In all things where you have need of a Christ, need of a savior, make your request known. Then if you are bid to make your requests, surely when they are known they shall be granted. James 1:5—"If you lack wisdom, ask it from God," for he "giveth liberally." Then ask heart, ask grace, ask understanding, and God will give it you; God will give you any other spiritual grace as well as wisdom.

Says the soul, "I have asked and I am never the nearer for asking." I bid thou [sic-*thee*] beware now of belying the spirit of God and of saying that thou hast no abundance of God's spirit when thou hast. Now do not say God will not grant; he has used to give liberally. Take heed of being too ready to say thou canst not obtain thy request, yet admit thou hast prayed and cannot obtain that which you pray for. I doubt the fault is in thy prayer. Thou dost not pray continually, or not fervently. Colossians—"Continue in prayer."[24] How long? As long as thou hast need of it. Ephesians 6:18—but pray "with all prayer and supplication." Do it with all perseverance. God would not have you to be weary of praying, and if you be not weary of pray-

---

23. Philippians 4:6
24. Colossians 4:2

ing God will not be weary of giving. But if you begin to slack in praying, God will begin to slack in giving.

Another fault in your praying might be that praying in the name of Christ, you must ask graces in the name of Christ. You must go unto a mediator. It's a wretched profaneness, a taking of God's name in vain, when we come unto God and not in the name of Christ. 'Tis a breaking the second commandment. "Hitherto have you asked ever in my name."[25]

Another fault in you is want of using means on your part. You must add one grace to another. You must strengthen your graces. You pray to Christ to strengthen your graces, and Christ bids you strengthen your graces. You must do it. You must pray. You must! It must be; you must do it. Revelation 2:5—Christ bids you to "repent" and to do your "first works." Revelation 3:2—Christ bids you "strengthen" yourselves, and you would have him to make you to stand fast. Christ bids you be strong in might and put on the armor of God. Now look to yourself. The fault lies most in you. Christ will enable you to stand if you labor for it.

3. Want of laying hold on Christ. The more the soul is estranged from Christ the less is it able to deal with temptation. The heart is never in worse temper than when it lays least hold on Christ. Take upon you the "shield of faith"—Ephesians 6:16. Faith in Christ bears off all the fiery darts of Satan so that your main hurt lies in want of application of Christ. Confess, "I am much to blame that I do not apply Christ. How should I apply Christ?" says the soul.

First, if you would apply Christ and act your heart aright on Christ, then:

1. Labor to see a promise. A promise must be your ground work. If you have your promises to seek,[26] you will never be able to apply Christ.

2. If you know yourself to have right to promises, then make that promise your own, and tell your hearts you have as good right to it as to any meat or drink that you eat.

3. Ask in prayer, according to the will of God, not to depend upon your lust. You will say, "Doth any man ask to depend upon his lust?" Yea, a man might ask to depend upon his lusts, to be proud of them.

4. You must show yourself thankful to God for that power he giveth you over your temptations. Now pray God for these things he bestows upon you, and then he will bestow more. You are apt to go in your [own] strength. Take heed of this: you think your prayer should do it, and not look beyond to a savior.

---

25. John 16:24
26. if you are still looking for promises

DECEMBER 27, 1640

MALACHI 4:2

But unto you, etc.

Doctrine: there is healing enough in Christ to all that fear God, healing enough in point of justification and sanctification.

Last Lord's Day I made a query that if there be healing enough in Christ, what is the reason God's people do so complain for want of the spirit? I showed the reasons were partly in Christ and partly in ourselves. Now to proceed.

Use for comfort and consolation to God's people, even to all that do labor to make Christ their sanctification—to you that complain for want of power that your temptations are too hard for you—you that complain for want of spiritualities, &c, [as] comfort to you. Though there is nothing in yourselves, yet there is enough in Christ. And it's of precious comfort and consolation to all those that do seek to live by faith in the son of God. You would fain live more by faith. You would that Christ would help you more to profit by ordinances. There is healing enough in Christ; and this might be of precious use to your faith, that though you have little or nothing, yet you know where to have enough, even in Christ. Is [it] that now doth Satan tempt you? Refer him to Christ and tell him Christ will deal well enough with him. Are temptations too hard for you? Call for Christ and he can deal with them—as children, when they fall out, the weaker will say, "Though I cannot deal with you, yet I will tell my father and he will." So you might say, "Though I cannot deal with temptation and deal with my heart, yet Christ Jesus can." Many times the devil gives us many a shrod[27] knock and we go weeping and sighing and complaining of our sins. Then comes Christ, and he doth not only pardon your sins but he helps you to be more watchful in future time. Is not this comfort?

'Tis a ground also of further comfort to keep us from apostasy. Aye, he will see what mettle you are made of. You need not fear small apostasy, such as Solomon's was. 1 Peter—we are kept "by the power of God through faith to salvation."[28] If God should leave us to ourselves we should fall; but we are kept not only for a day but for years. John 10:28, 29. There is a double union:

1. by faith—by the power of faith;
2. by the power of the spirit;

27. shrewd
28. 1 Peter 1:5

so that though faith might fail, yet the spirit will never fail. The spirit will never fail.

"Ah," says the heart, "this is all good. If I could but be persuaded of it." If thou canst but assure thyself that thou hast interest [*in*] Christ, then this heap[29] shall be yours and communicated unto you by virtue of that union that is but [sic-*between*] Christ and believers; John 17:22, 23. This union is beyond reason. Reason cannot apprehend it, but faith can, and the soul cannot tell which way it should come to pass, yet it finds [. . .] 1 Corinthians 6:17. I might say as the Apostle, "all is yours and yea [sic-*you*] are Christ's," so Christ is yours.[30] Canticles 2:16. All that healing that is in Christ is yours. The text doth describe this by sundry exhortations: "I am the vine and yea [sic-*you*] the branches."[31] The vine sends his sap into all the branches so: so Romans 11:17—you "partake" of the sap that is in the root. Romans 6:5. You need not fear the dying of the branches while the sap is in the root. There is enough in Christ to communicate to all the Apostles and patriarchs. And this is set out by the similitude of a husband—Isaiah 54:5, Hosea 2:19. 20.

3. Further to assure the soul of that healing that is in Christ, [*this*] is because there is as it were a union between Christ and the church as between the head and members. Colossians 1:18—"He is the head of the body." Now Christ is the head of the church, aye, and of every member of the church. 1 Corinthians 12—"For as the body is one and has many members, so also is Christ," that is, the Church. "Now one member says to another, 'I have no need of thee.' The hand cannot say to the head, 'I have no need of thee.'"[32] But by influence of the head does the body grow. So do the members, for whatever is received into the body the members do partake of. ~~and influence of other member~~

What is in Christ but in a sort it's said to be in believers. Is Christ dead? So are we. Is Christ risen? So we. Is Christ a King? So we. Doth Christ reign? So we. Romans 6:3 and 4. He speaks of [. . .] They are said, &c. v. 5—they are said [. . .] v. 6, v. 8. Do you think that Christ will have his body like Nebuchadnezer's? [*An*] image so unlike! v. 11. Romans 5:17. Is Christ a king? We are kings, too. Exodus 19:16. Peter has it, "a kingly priesthood."[33] Revelation 1:6—he has made us a kingly priesthood. We are said to reign as Christ reigns. And doth Christ overcome? Then we overcome. Where Christ is there is liberty from sin. Has Christ a crown to set upon his head?

29. collection
30. 1 Corinthians 3:22–23
31. John 15:5
32. 1 Corinthians 12:12–21
33. 1 Peter 2:9

So have believers crowns—crowns of pure gold. Revelation—"They threw down their crowns before thee."[34] Yea, in a sort we have crowns here; Zechariah 6:10, 11, 12, 13, 14. Thus much taken out of the text.

Jesus Christ has promised to me, if I will but fear his name, to be a healing unto me. Hence this is a ground of much comfort in Christ. There is enough to quicken up thy dead. The condemnable, wretched, damnable speeches of some that say Christ cannot heal! What will you make of Christ? What is he? Not a savior! You make him but an idle man. Did thou never say, "In Christ there is healing enough, and this is of great comfort?" I would fain have God's people to know where their comfort is and where a precious pearl is, even in Christ. Labor to draw full consolation from Christ.

Question: Whither are we to go if we want anything in point of sanctification? Answer: To Christ, for he hath the words of eternal life. And whither should, would [we] go else but to him? Can we mend ourselves anywhere else? If we should go to ourselves, what can we have? We shall soon draw the well dry if we go to ourselves. What then? Will you go to ordinances? There you will deceive yourselves; ordinances will not do it without Christ. We oftimes think that the word should beat lust and beat us so down and we should never meddle no more. Now go not to ordinances, but to Christ.

Use for information of the misery of natural men that do not question whether they have interest in Christ. You civilizers [sic-*cavillers*?] that have no power of godliness, you ungodly, you retainer of bosom sins, you that halt between God and the world, and would be half for God and the other half for the world—to you I speak. You that are thus full of sin, methinks it might make your very hearts to ache, that there should be so much in Christ, and thou hast none. The husband that has healing enough in Christ—and the wife none. The wife enough—and the husband none. The father enough—the children none. The servant enough—the governor none.

Some are taken and some refused.[35] Those that sit in the very next seat to thee might have no share nor part in Christ. You profane ones, one would wonder how you could go home and sleep so securely, and yet you have no share in Christ! Aye, but you say thou hast. Alas, I wish all that hear me this day were God's people. You now that say you have share in Christ: what ground have you to say so? How willst thou clear up thy evidence that thou hast share in Christ? There is power enough in Christ to be communicated to thee. Well now dost thou see it? So dost thou now say that thou wast a

---

34. Revelation 4:10

35. Matthew 24:40

cage of unclean birds[36] and that thou had a sweet morsel,[37] but now Christ doth wholly reign in thee? Ah, that this were true—that thou couldst say thus indeed! Has Jesus Christ been as fuller's soap in thy heart and as refiner's [. . .]?[38] Certainly where grace is there has been the power of Christ. Now evidence this unto God's people, if it be so.

Ah, poor creatures, that you should have no power nor share in Christ! You set about reformation, but you cannot reform thoroughly because you have not share in Christ. You are told of your sins and are wishing to reform, and you cannot. Why? Because you have no share in Christ. God's people, when they are convinced of a sin, do reform it. But why cannot you? They have Christ to help them; you are but a withered tree, [you] bring out no fruit, you that bind your heart by vows and covenants.

Yet you will never make thorough reformation. What is the reason men fall back so oft? They put a hand to the plow but hang back, so oft do fall off, though some continue longer. What is the reason now of this? Because Christ never took charge of you. Christ never looked after you. If they had been of the number of us—but they were not. "They went from us."[39] Some unclean spirit might send the devil packing for a while, but he will not keep out; he goeth a-walking and he will return again. Now what is the reason? Because they have not Jesus Christ. Though they get power over the pollution of nature, yet are entangled [with sin]. And why? Because Christ did not watch over [them?].

What is the reason?

You cannot say as God's people, "We are one with Christ." Now you cannot say such. Christ weeds the lust out of the children of God. But he does not out of the wicked man. Christ is oft calling to the one and to the other. A child of God many times might say, "I fear I shall be damned, and yet have not power to reform and to amend." Though the[40] they have feared hell many a time before they come there, yet they might drop into hell without remedy—and all because they have not share in Christ's healing. God's people, when God doth open their eyes, ah, how do they loath themselves! How can it be otherwise now, but [?] that there must be a world of filthiness in natural man. Ah, the foolishness that is in natural man! If they would buy the pearl, they might. If they would come to Christ, they should be welcome. And Christ bids you come, and buy milk without money.

36. Revelation 18:2
37. Proverbs 23:8
38. Malachi 3:2
39. 1 John 2:19
40. unnecessary extra word

I showed some reason why [the] godly could not draw power from Christ as they should was because they did not go to Christ. They wanted strength. Now, then, will Christ empty himself into you, rotten sinks? Let this be terror to all profane hearts! I tell thee, one day one drop of the pure blood of Christ will be of great worth to thee, more than all the world can afford.

Use: seeing there is so much healing in Christ, it teaches the godly to ask and to be persuaded of it. Do not think that Christ will deceive you. There is a reality in this. There is healing in Christ. Be now convinced of it.

2. Let it teach you to be thankful for your blessed condition that Jesus Christ has set you in. Who has made you to differ? Jesus Christ. Suppose two men should be stung with the same serpent. And how comes it to pass that one is healed and not the other? Says one, "I looked up to the brazen serpent," and the other looked but upon his wound. Now Jesus Christ makes them to differ. Jesus Christ enriches; "according to the riches" of his dear son.[41] Oh, now be thankful and behold the providence of the godly. Deuteronomy 33, last verse—"Happy art thou; who is like unto thee, O Israel?"[42] Now you might say that, "Let all the men in the world bend their heart to do hurt to God's people, they cannot, because they have healing in Christ."

Now acknowledge this privilege: was it not a curious robe to be clothed in, scarlet? Ah, you are clothed with better than scarlet, and with that which is better than a chain of gold, even with the righteousness of Christ; and this raiment have all the saints. Now ask the riches of God's free grace.

Use: is there such healing in Christ? Then the godly are to get as great a portion in this healing as they can labor for it. And lastly, then, never complain, (viz.) never so to complain as if Christ did not heal you of your temptation and of your dead heart and the like. If ever you should henceforth complain, sai your hearts deceive you and are full of sin. Never complain, seeing there is such healing in Christ. Either you know not where healing is to be had, or else [you] will not go for healing where it's to be had. Now labor to acknowledge yourselves bound in thankfulness to Christ Jesus, his healing—above measure.

---

41. Ephesians 1:7 or Philippians 4:19?
42. Deuteronomy 33:29

JANUARY 3, 1641

Malachi 4:2

And ye shall go forth and grow up as calves of the stalls.

In these words is set down a second ground of consolation: the benefit that shall come by healing. "They shall grow up as calves of the stall," that is, they shall grow up abundantly in spiritual [. . .] All of you have seen experience of the growth of calves. Now so shall Christians grow up. Hence note:

Doctrine: by virtue of that healing that is in Jesus Christ, God has promised that his people shall grow up as "calves of the stall"—or, has promised that they shall grow up abundantly in spiritual things. This, clearly proved, will be much comfort to the godly.

For proof: Psalm 92:12, 13, 14—"The righteous shall flourish," &c. The palm tree is always green; when 'tis old it's green. And the cedars of Lebanon, you know how they grow up. A little twig suddenly will be a tall tree. It will be admirable to see it. Now so shall the godly grow. A young Christian at his first conversion has but weak graces. But how wonderfully he is grown by his dying day, &c.

Isaiah 44:3, 4—Mark: the well "will pour water" upon the thirsty ground, that the herbs and flowers may grow. God will pour water. How doth he mean thus, that he will pour his spirit upon the godly? Aye, not only a drop of his spirit, but he will pour it. Aye, and what follows? "They shall grow up as among the grass" and shall flourish as the young willows. Some of you that have experience, how admirable they do grow. Now thus the godly shall grow. And the Psalm 1:3 may well be understood of the godly. And the godly are said to be a watered garden; Isaiah 58.

First reason why God's people, &c, is because they pray, and pray not only for growth in themselves but also for others. Now how do you infer strength from this? Thus the child of God, whatever [*he*] prays for, he has a promise of the spirit to have whatever he asks. Pray in faith. Hence a child of God cannot pray in faith without he have a promise that what he prays for he shall have. If we do but pray for growth in grace we might take it for a delivered truth that he [sic-*we*] shall have growth in grace.

Second reason: because God's people are bid to strive for growth in grace. Now then what duty is it [?] grace [?] to strive, without they shall have that which [*they*] strive for. This doth necessarily follow, that they shall have a promise of growth. If they strive they shall have what they strive for.

Third reason: God has commanded growth in grace. You will now say that there is little strength [*in that*]. Yea, I say there is most strength, for God never commands his people do anything but he enables them to do what he commands. Isaiah 26:12—thou wilt work "all our work in us." Whatever God commands, he first promises to do it for us. Thus I say that if God commands you to do a thing he first says you shall do it. There is not anything God requires of his people but he promises they shall do it as [they] grow in grace; this is the commandment. Well the promise goeth before: "You shall grow up as calves." God commands you. Ezekiel 18:31—he bids them cast away all their transgression and get them new hearts. Ezekiel 36:25, 26—he tells them he will take away all their "filthiness" and give them hearts. Deuteronomy 10:16—"circumcise the foreskin of thy heart." God bids them do it; and [in] Deuteronomy 31:6, he tells them they shall do it. Ecclesiastes 12:13—God commands them to fear him and "keep his commandments." Now Jeremiah 32—God tells them that he will make them to hear him. Ezekiel 36—he tells us that he will make us to know God and that we "shall know" God.[43] The Lord bids us pray to him; Zechariah 5—"Pray."[44]

Now whatever God bids you do, he first promises you shall do it. Doth he bid you grow in grace? Then he has promised your hearts [will] grow in grace. Doth God bid you gather yourselves into church condition? Then you shall. Doth God bid you flee lust? Then you shall.

Fourth reason: whyfor [we] "shall grow up as calves," is because of the means God uses for that purpose. He doth promise us that he [sic-we] shall grow in grace, yet he commands us to do it, that we might labor to grow in grace.

You must look upon all these arguments that God does intend you shall grow. God doth [not] only say you shall grow, but doth also make good. He promises what he doth but [sic-by] means and by ordinances. God gives [. . .] against these and these things that you might grow thereby.

Besides ordinances there is a second kind of growth, even exercises[45] under afflictions. "Feed thy people with thy rod,"[46] whether he means by affliction or what means such else. Yet Jesus Christ is compared to a shepherd which, with his rod, doth direct and feed his sheep. So Christ with a rod must feed his people: "and by thy rod am I comforted."[47] What doth the Lord intend by afflictions but to take away the sin of his people? God says, "Fury[48] thee not in me, but I do it for to purge you of your sin." When he will

43. Ezekiel 36:38
44. Zechariah 8:21?
45. fulfillment of duties
46. Micah 7:14
47. Psalm 23:4
48. drive oneself to fury

not make a man hearken and attend, then God useth another means, even affliction, to purge. He hath two ways to purge his people from sin:

1. When he makes them more to exercise their hearts and to reform—hear [sic-*bear*?] the rod and who has appointed it.

2. Another way how God does purge is but [sic-*by*] preventing sin by affliction, laying him upon his bed of sickness and so [?] now doth witness that sin. Christ has promised that you shall have healing. Why doth he deal thus else?

Besides, also the two titles that are given to Christ are an argument that we shall grow:

1. Christ is called a shepherd;

2. The vine which he purges that it might bring out more fruit; John 15:1, 2, 5. Job 17:9—"The righteous also shall hold on his way, and he that has clean hands shall be stronger and stronger." No wonder of that if Jesus Christ doth so dress us. [A] vine dresser does cut off superfluous branches and does pull up weeds that do hinder plants and does water them what need be. They do not only keep what they have but do also do what they can to make them, [*the*] plants, grow. So doth Christ what he can to make you grow. Has God ever [?] need of my help? [?]

Use for information to all of us, concerning, first, two things:

1. That the foundation of all our growth in spiritual [*things*] doth lie in Jesus Christ and in the promises made unto us in and through Christ, and not in the use of means, no more than salvation does lie in the word. I do not say but that in and through these means, Christ doth help us to grow in grace; but thus we are not to dote too much upon the means and not look beyond to a Christ. Look to Christ. For we by our doing and by our means do not cause God to give us growth in grace; but only he, by reason he has promised us, doth enable us in the use of right means to grow in grace.

Bear this in mind: your growth in grace lies in Christ and in the promises. You must of necessity grow in grace. I do not now speak of a dry, dry tree, (viz.) natural man, but of the godly. You shall grow in grace: Christ has promised. Though a child of God cannot find the growth in his soul, yet he doth grow; for the growth of a Christian doth lie in Christ and in promises. If you question whether Christ will make good promises then you might question whether you grow in grace. But if you take it for granted Christ doth make good promises, you grow in grace though you do not see it.

Second use: it informs us concerning natural man and civilizers [sic-*cavillers*?] and [*those*] which will not let Christ reign in them, why they do not grow in grace. What is the reason they do not grow in grace? Because Christ has made no promises at all to them. Christ has made promises unto his people, but let any natural man in the world say "Christ has made promises to me"—if he will—the children of God might say, "Christ has promised me that well." And what will the ungodly plead? No other than thus: "every branch in me that bears not fruit shall be cut down and cast into the fire."[49] Aye, but now says the ungodly, "I do grow in grace, &c. Now I have little ground to think myself to be an ungodly." Also, now to answer some scruple says the ungodly, "I grow in grace." How do you grow? "I have the gift of prayer. I delight in prayer and in good duties. I dare now to pray before[50] any."

Do you grow in grace no other than thus? This is not growing in grace.

Then says the ungodly, "Aye, but I am mortified to my lust." This were something indeed, were it true. You will say you love the ordinances. That might be because they are sweet to your taste. You get literal knowledge by [them]. Now do not deceive yourselves, you that love ordinances and God's people for carnal respect of your own. You ungodly are to be cut down and cast into the fire. You have no one to tend you. That vine which has no man to pluck up weeds and to cut off superfluous branches cannot bear such fruit as that which has [a vinedresser]. Now Christ is a vine dresser to the godly, but not to the ungodly. You cannot expect that [the] ungodly should grow in grace.

When the thirsty ground has no one to water, it cannot be fruitful; the ungodly have no one to water them. An ungodly stands at a stay where you find him. Now [if?] you shall find him [in] sin you sense this is a sad mark of an ungodly, where they [sic-there] be growth still the same.

Third use for exhortation: whether the godly grow in grace or not? Christ has promised they shall grow in grace. Now [Ex?] then, do you? Says the child of God, "It's a shrod sign of an ungodly when he stands at a stay. I do stand at [a] stay. I am as bad as an ungodly."

That proceeds through these mistakes:

1. Mistaking the measure and the degree of his growth. Christ promises he shall grow but not in what measure and degree he shall grow. Now Christians do grow though they cannot see, and this makes them condemn themselves that they cannot see they grow. If a man stand by a tree a whole summer he cannot see it grow. Shall he say it doth not grow? It must of necessity grow if it be a living tree, though it grows insensibly, though he doth not see [it] grows. Now this is it [mors?] all: that you will either have a large measure or else you will have none at all. Conclude that (Christ has promised you shall grow, therefore) you shall grow though you do not see it.

---

49. John 15:2,6
50. in the presence of

If you have not a full [*cup*], have you none? If the cup be but ~~brim full~~ half full, is there none [in it?]?

2. A second ground of mistake is this: that which is a true sign of grace you pervert and take it another way as the growth of grace and that the discovery of temptation and sense of belief [sic-*unbelief*], [*is*] power to [*do*] any good. You make this as argument of want of grace.

[*To*] prove this position by text, I believe it would nose[51] any man to do it. The more you see of your own vildness, the more you abhor yourselves in dust and ashes. Have not I showed you that the more grace, the more sense of temptation? The more you cry out of your vildness and want of grace, the more you are in communion with Christ and the spirit.

Do you not think you had as much temptation before, though you were not sensible of it? Had you not many sins in your hearts, though you know not of it? Yea, then more temptation and less sense of it. Examine your selves upon right grounds, whether you do grow in grace, and then accordingly it's for your comfort.

Use for comfort and consolation to God's people. It's a precious promise full of consolation. There is a deal of marrow in it. Though you have not such a measure as you would, yet such a measure as you shall be one day presented, pure, without "spot or wrinkle"—Ephesians 5:27. It's the will of God that his people should have some [comfort?] in them. Though you have not such a measure as you would, yet that as is sufficient for you and as is most for the honor of Christ. Would you ask or strive more?

You still complain of your temptations: "They are too hard for me," and "When will these temptations be mortified? When should I be rid of them? Ah, these my temptations," &c. Methinks it shall stint your complaining, that though you have your temptations still, yet you have something gotten power[52] over them, such as they shall not hinder your salvation. You seek [*that*] you might grow more than you do, as an heir does seek to grow as much in one day as in two, and he would seem [*to*] be a big man, and that he might have his inheritance in his own hands. Now you have grace [*in*] abundance; and where is your thanksgiving? Here is a ground of comfort as [*in*] all perpetual backslidings and apostasies:—————

"I had but a little grace in my first conversion, and now I have this [?] increase." As Jacob said, "With my staff I went," &c.[53] Now with a pure measure of grace you began at first; and by the blessing of Christ you are [more Christian?]. I had little faith, and now through the help of God I can more

---

51. reproach, confront, upbraid
52. gotten some power
53. Genesis 32:10

submit [?]. You think you honor Christ by ungodly manner, lying, but not so robbing both yourself and Christ at one clap lest trouble [. . .] proceed not from him that has called you to grace, thus to condemn yourselves.

Now [. . .] you shall grow in grace. Christ has prayed for me that my faith fail not.

Use for exhortation to [you?] concerning one [?] now to labor to grow in grace. The Lord has promised it through Christ. Be trading in the use of means, that you might grow in grace, and bewail it that you spend so many opportunities and grow no more. Has not Christ promised you shall grow? And would it not be more for your spiritual good and Christ's honor if you did endeavor more for growth? Labor for more growth. Let it be seen in the plantation and in the families, husband and wife [as] well, and be growing in the knowledge ~~and savior~~ of our Lord and Savior Jesus Christ. You have need of growth in grace.

vs serves to reprove all those yt doe not
beleeve ye word, they doe not acknowledge
a tenth of ye word, or if they doe will
not apply it to theire owne soules; to me
here to be required yt loose many a Sermon
lose a greate deale of labor & ye minister
loseth his paines: notwithstanding all yet
remaine inprofitable yu neyther get grace
nor increase grace & all bec of yr unbeleefe: mat 9th. fh. of Capnaum &c
did noe mighty workes there bec of theire
unbeleefe: yf give ye word a hearing
but for obeying it, beleeving it, & walking answerable to it, yf litle regard ye
how many yeares may a man live under
ye word & be never ye better if he beleeve
not ye word & revere yt: fora trifle away
yr tyme, will god beare it at yr hands
thinke yu: if yu be unprofitable hearers
as yu must needs be if yu be unbeleving
hearers, then yu are neere unto curseing
whose end is to be burned, burne in
fire of hell, & therefore it is, Cast ye unprofitable servant into outter darkenesse

John Pynchon's notes—May 13, 1649

3

April 1, 1649—December 2, 1649

Gratz Collection—Pennsylvania Historical Society, Philadelphia, Pennsylvania

APRIL 1, 1649[1]

ROMANS 7:9

But when the commandment came, sin revived, and I died.

I have opened the words already. By "Commandment" is meant any Commandment that comes to the conscience.

Doctrine: as men's hearts are rightly affected with the Commandments, so they become sensible of sin. The doctrine hath been opened and some uses made. In the use of consolation was this doubt propounded: says a soul, "I fear my heart is not rightly affected with the Commandments, and so I am not become sensible of my sin. I fear my heart is not affected with and truly sorry for my sin."

For full and further answer hereunto:

First, I would ask thee, "Hath God let thee see all thy sins committed in the time of thy ignorance or in thy former life, all thy remarkable sins? Hast thou seen thyself a breaker of all the Commandments?" Canst thou give an answer to this?

---

1. "The 1st of the 2d Mo (Commonly called Aprill), 1649."

Second, if thou canst not give a clear answer to that, yet dost thou labor in the use of means that God would let thee see all thy former sins? Dost thou pray to God to discover thy sins to thee that so thou mayest mourn for them? Dost thou daily meditate how thou hast walked, how thou hast carried thyself in this company and the other company, how thou has lived? Dost thou thus use means to come to the sight of all thy sins? What dost thou say? Canst thou give a clear answer to questions, and say that thou dost find it [thus?]?

Third, is thy heart affected with what thou seest? Thou wilt say, "Here is my fear: I fear that [. . .]"

These four things will clear it up, whether thy heart be rightly affected with those sins that thou seest:

1. If thou dost peruse them upon thy conscience, dost thou aggravate them more and more?

2. How far dost thou peruse sin upon thy conscience? What effects doth it produce? Doth it make thy heart as heavy as lead, as I may say? Doth it make thee to sigh up to heaven? Hath it broken thy sleep many times? Any time? Nay, further, hath it produced this effect, to make thee think thyself the greatest sinner in the world? These things will clearly evidence the heart to be affected with sin.

3. In what respects are [sic-*is*] the heart thus affected with sin? There are two: the former is the wrath of God, fear of hell and condemnation; secondly, God's dishonor; because God is dishonored by it, the holy commandment broken through breaking the law. Dishonorest thou God? That sticks with him, and this affects the heart. Hath thy heart thus been affected with sin, first in the former sense and afterwards in the latter sense?

4. Is thy heart so affected that it doth make thee weary of thy natural condition, weary of all sin as it is cross and contrary to holiness?

If thou find it thus with thee, then I tell thee thy heart is rightly affected with sin. The commandment is come to thy heart. By "rightly affected" I mean in truth, and so as the Gospel will accept; not that it is so far affected as the nature of thy sin requires, and what thy sin calls for—that I meddle not with, not with the measure of sorrow—but whatever sin thou art affected with according to the four particulars mentioned, thou art rightly affected, and so as God will accept. In strictness no man can sorrow sufficiently for his sin. But the Gospel will accept where such and such terms are performed.

Here I would advise: while the soul is troubling itself thus, "My heart is not so much affected as it should be," there is danger of running into this error—of being disorderly affected with sin, as:

1. When it strives to attain unto that which it cannot attain unto, and so God doth not expect [. . .] When Satan would set thee upon this gog[2] thou art not sufficiently affected and so screw thee up higher and higher till your spirit tires. It's not for good to your soul or that he would bring you to repent, but he would have you draw the arrow up [*to*] the head that so you may break the bow.

1. Sorrow is too much, and disorderly, when it doth hinder you from any other duties as prayer, reading, the works of thy calling;

2. When it takes away your hopes. If you strive so much for sorrow as it hinders your hopes, or actings upon [them?], it's disorderly. Hereby you weaken your hands, that you cannot go about the Lord's work. Yea, you make the work more tedious to you a great deal, and you become subjects for Satan to work up [sic-*upon*]. [*You*] give him advantage.

Afternoon]

Use last: it is for exhortation, to labor to get your heart affected with the Commandments, that the Commandments may come unto your souls. Such as have not repented, you have need that the Commandments should come to your souls. And the godly that have repented in the general yet fail so often in their daily walking that they also have need of the Commandments. Therefore all, one and other: labor to get your heart affected with the Commandments, that is, the word of God. Get your heart affected with the word.

How shall we get our hearts affected with the Commandments?

1. Learn the Commandments. Here I mean the Commandments given on Mount Sinai which we call the Ten Commandments. It is very necessary that you should be well acquainted with them, and know the meaning and extent of them. Every Commandment hath many branches, forbids many sins, and comprehends many duties. Now it's very necessary to be acquainted herewith, and therefore read the scriptures, be frequent and constant in them. We cannot come to see sin but by the law. How shall a man's heart smite him for the lusts of the heart if he does not know that they are forbidden? And therefore it's greatly to be bewailed that the younger sort are not better acquainted with the Commandments. This is the foundation of all: be well-acquainted with the Commandments. How can a man be a judge if he be not acquainted with the law? So how can our conscience judge us and condemn us if we are not acquainted with the Commandments that should tell us such and such things are sin?

---

2. set on gog = stir up, excite

2. When you have thus acquainted yourself with the Commandments, compare your actions and the word together.³ It may be conscience may hint to you that such and such actions are evil. Well then, go to the word, compare your actions and the word together, and see how far the law doth allow or disallow your particular actions. It may be your governors tell you, "You carry yourself stubbornly and disobediently." Well go to the word and see when [an] inferior may be said to be disobedient—that says, "Children, obey your parents in all things," "Servants [. . .]"⁴ Now compare your actions and the word together. This is the way to bring the Commandments home unto your hearts.

3. When you have thus weighed your actions and the word together, then see how far such an action according to scripture is to be aggravated—so often traded in lying, so often broken and sad, so that the oftenness of it may arise to many faults. "How often would I have gathered thee!"⁵ Aye, and "How often hast thou sinned against me!" The oftenness of it: this is a great thing. Aye, and the oftener sin is committed it argues the greater wickedness of the heart. For a man may, by the violence of temptation, be sometimes drawn into a sin; and to commit it often evidences a willingness and inclination of the heart.

Second, aggravate your sin by this: the persons with whom and against whom such evil hath been done. "With whom:" it may be with those that it hath done a great deal of hurt. Thy bad example hath done them much hurt. Or it may be thou hast grieved thy parents and governors, broken their hearts, &c. And it may be thou hast been vild against the godly, and such as thou shouldst have respected.

Third, aggravate thy sin by this: the evil frame of thy spirit, delighting in sin, running after sin as the horse rusheth into the battle, committing wickedness with greediness, as the Apostle says.⁶

Fourth, consider against what light, against what checks of conscience, what motions of the spirit, what means God and friends have used. "Against what light:" if thou hast done it against much light of conscience, this is great aggravation. "Friends hath [sic-*have*] told me, and parents, and yet I would not regard." This is committing wickedness with a high hand.

These directions—how to get your hearts affected with the Commandments. Now labor to get your hearts affected.

---

3. "togither;" so spelled consistently in the manuscript.

4. Colossians 3:20, 22—"Servants, obey in all things your masters according to the flesh."

5. Luke 13:34

6. Romans 1:29

1. If your hearts were but affected, the Commandments might be of great use to you. For scarce any week passeth over your head, but you are called to this—to let the Commandments come unto you.

2. Further, consider this is one end of all your hearing: to bring you to duty and to bring you to Christ. Why else do you attend at the posts of wisdom? Is not one end that you may be brought to the knowledge of your duty, and to repent where you come short? Then there is a necessity that you should get your hearts affected with the Commandments.

3. According as your hearts are affected with the Commandments, so do you get good or not good by the word, so have you benefit or not benefit by the ordinances. If men grow loose of the Commandments they will by degrees become scandalous. Therefore get your hearts affected with the Commandments. Life and death depends upon this: upon the Commandments coming or not coming to your comfort.

APRIL 8, 1649

Romans 7:9

Sin revived, and I died.

Sin revived. It lay as dead before, like some creatures in the winter season, frogs and snakes. They lie close, as if they were dead. You see none of them. But in the spring season they revive when the weather is warm.

So sin lay lurking in Paul all the while he was a Pharisee. But when he went to Damascus and God struck him, it revived. Not that he was a greater sinner now, but the condition [*revived*] and he was awakened to be sensible of his sin.

Doctrine: when God doth make man thoroughly sensible of his sin, he doth apprehend himself in a miserable condition. You may see this in Paul as here, so in the verse following, and verse 13. Likewise the Prodigal, Luke 15:17.

What is meant by this miserable estate and condition, the saying, "I died"? That is, he had the sentence of death in his own conscience, death eternal. The statute law concerning sin is, the day thou sinnest "thou shalt die the death."[7] Now sin reviving, the soul being sensible that it hath sinned, takes this sentence to itself, that it must die the death, die eternally.

---

7. Genesis 2:17. Moxon's patron William Pynchon also cited this wording from the Geneva Bible in his problematic book, *The Meritorious Price of Our Redemption*, (1650), 4, 108.

What is it makes the sinner to apprehend itself [sic-*himself*] to be in this miserable condition? The guilt of its [sic-*his*] own conscience, in the sense of the law broken. 2 Corinthians 3:6, 7. "Behold, a man that hath told me all that ever I have done."[8] I will set all thy sins in order before thee. When conscience doth this, the soul apprehends its condition [*as*] miserable. 1 Corinthians 14:24, 25—"The secrets of his heart" are laid open to his own conscience. Though he was never sensible of them before, never took notice of them, yet now he shall. Therefore Ezekiel 36:31—"They shall loathe themselves for the evil of their doings." They come to apprehend themselves in a miserable condition by this. They look upon God against whom they have sinned, and this is terrible.

When the soul hath to deal with God, then comes in:

1. God's dishonor. And therefore says the Prodigal, "Father, I have sinned against heaven and before [*you*.]" David: "Against thee, thee only have I sinned."[9] Through breaking the commandment dishonorest thou God. God is dishonored and this [is?] terrible, that it is a God, the great God, Lord over all, that is dishonored.

And therefore, secondly, comes in the displeasure of God; and God professes himself to be a revenger of the [?]. He is a God of [purer?] eyes than to behold any [iniquity?]. And Psalm 6:38.[10] He is a God of consuming fire to sinners, [*a*] God to be displeased to have to do with an [?] [god?]. If our own hearts condemn us, God is greater. The wrath of the Devil like a river of brimstone is kindled.

The third thing that makes the soul to apprehend its miserable condition to be the greater is the fear and natural unwillingness that it hath to perish. The soul is unwilling to be cast into hell, and yet fears it shall. This helps forward the apprehension of it [as?] not as bad as thou and as miserable as thou. In that thou art sensible of thy misery, it's a blessed condition that you are in—if God will but help you to carry it on.

---

8. John 4:29
9. Psalm 51:4
10. Possibly Psalm 106:30

APRIL 15, 1649

ROMANS 7:9

Sin revived, and I died.

I am now to proceed in the use of consolation. It is for comfort to all that are sensible of their sin.

    1. It's the ordinary way whereby God brings souls home to himself.

    2. It's the common condition of all the godly, and that which there is hope that you may get out of. Others have, and so mayest thou.

    3. Ground of consolation to those that are sensible of their sin, is this: the Gospel doth propound a great deal of grace and mercy to such. Psalm 126—"They that sow in tears shall reap in joy," &c.[11] You that go mourning and weeping in the sight and sense of your sin, your many sighs and groans, God takes notice of all. He puts all your tears in his bottle,[12] numbers all your groaning. Christ came "to seek and save that which is lost."[13] And that promise, "Come unto me, all ye that are weary and heavy laden, and ye shall have rest to your souls,"[14] is a precious ground of comfort.

    Fly to Jesus Christ when the law pursues thee, and grace and mercy shall be tendered. If a man were lapt[15] under so much guilt and there were no way out, it were [?] indeed. But the Gospel will help you out. There is balm enough in Gilead, if you will but make use of it.

    4. If you be so sensible of sin that you sense nothing but guilt, &c, yet this may stay your spirit. It's a frame of spirit that God would have all the sons of men be brought unto, and it's the damnation of many that they are not sensible of and affected with their sin. And it would have been a mercy to thee if God had sooner brought thee into this frame. It is of the devil that you should lay the thoughts of your condition and of your sin aside. It's a great dishonor to God that men should [be] so full of sin as they are, and yet so little affected with it. And it is an honor to God that men are sensible of their sin. Therefore be comforted in it. The issue of all will be happy. There must be sin-guiltiness and sorrow for it before Christ can be formed in you.

    Last, is for exhortation for the duties that do arise from this doctrine.

---

11. Psalm 126:5
12. Psalm 56:8
13. Luke 19:10
14. Matthew 11:28
15. wrapped

If sin makes man miserable, then take heed of sinning. It's a part of wisdom to foresee what may follow and accordingly to order actions. If you do sin and will take liberty to sin, be sure you will hear of it; it may be when you little think of it, either here or hereafter. And therefore Solomon says, Ecclesiastes 11:9, know that "for all" God will call you to judgment. I call on you to take heed of sinning. And if you will not regard me, to be sure God will judge you. Therefore take heed of sin. When men run on in wickedness, Satan persuades them there is no danger will follow. But he deceives you, who would destroy you thereby. Paul was once of this mind, and did not think to hear of his sin; but at last sin revived and then he died. God will one day indict thee of all thy sins and set them all in order before thee—either here to bring thee to repentance, or hereafter for thy eternal damnation. God hath set a conscience in man which will judge him as a judge, and also it will be as a witness to bear witness against you. Therefore take heed of sin.

Where God's law is broken the justice of God will require you to answer for the breaking of his laws; and then there will lay [a] load on you. And therefore take heed. Do not take liberty to sin. Do as you will answer God another day.

Let the godly also take warning here. Give not too much liberty to your own lusts and passions, to backsliding and decaying fits. God will reckon with [you] for them. Therefore do you also take heed of sin.

A second duty is, that men would labor to lay sin to heart. Labor to be affected with, sensible of, your sins.

Afternoon]

They that never yet had a sight of sin, it's necessary for them sooner or later to get a sight of sin.

It's necessary also for the godly that they should get a sight of their sin more and more, for:

1. The more that you see your sin and misery by it, the more your hearts cannot but be taken up with thankfulness to God. Yea, you will count it a mercy that you live, and that God hath done so much for you as he hath. If sin be thoroughly charged upon your soul, and [your will?] the misery that your sin hath brought you unto, you will have no cause to be discontented at God's dealings with you.

2. You will also admire the long-suffering of God. It will help you to walk humbly with God. All these things considered, labor to get your hearts affected with sin.

How shall we do that?

1. Labor ~~in the general~~ to see what wrath is due for sin in the general. Consider the sin of Adam. A man would think it were no great matter for him to eat of the fruit of a tree. And yet it was of sad consequence, that which harms millions. Look also upon the sin of the Angels that kept not their standing. Whatever their sin was, possibly the pride of their hearts not being willing to minister to man, and yet see what it hath brought them to. Had they kept their standing they had been the most excellent of all creatures; but now, by their sin, they are become the worst of all creatures, even devils, and without all hopes of recovery, but must be reserved in chains. The justice of God upon sins brought them to such a condition.

Then reflect upon thyself, what thou deservest. Yea, take this instance also, Sodom and Gomorrah. For burning in lust [*men*] must burn in fire, and not only, but must suffer the vengeance of eternal fire. Yea, if it were possible for thee to hear the yellings and howlings of the damned, it would let thee see what a miserable condition sin brings the sinner into.

2. The justice of God must have an infinite satisfaction for any sin, all sin, the least sin that may be: because they are committed against an infinite God—not the satisfaction of a man, but the blood, the sufferings, of the Son of God. And therefore the wicked that cannot make this satisfaction must suffer to eternity—an infinite time.

Ah, think what will the justice of God require of thee that hath committed so many sins?

3. Consider how it is, sometimes, both with the godly and the wicked. The godly, consider their tears that they shed for their sins, their sighs and sorrow. It is because their hearts are affected with their sins. And is there not as good reason that thou shouldst weep for thy sin? David tells us that rivers of waters run down his eyes because men keep not the law.[16] If he wept so for other men's sins, then much more for his own—so that, see how sin troubles the hearts of the godly.

Look upon the wicked. Cain complains the punishment of his sins was greater than he could bear; so Judas.

Look up to Christ to break thy heart and to set thy sins home upon thy heart. Pray unto God and earnestly entreat him to enlighten the eyes of thy soul. Who is he that can charge sin upon thy soul but God by his spirit? Therefore look up unto him and give him no rest till it be done.

Labor in the use of means to get thy heart rightly apprehensive of sin. A man is never fit for God nor fit for mercy till his heart be rightly affected with sin. Therefore get thy heart apprehensive of sin, that so thou mayest be fit for Christ. Sin must revive before a man can carry on the work of

---

16. Psalm 119:136

repentance. How can you ever come out of your natural condition till your hearts be affected with your sin? And the godly, if your hearts were more affected with your sin, it were better for you. Therefore get your hearts affected. How [sic-*What*] do you do to make confession of sin to avoid the occasion of sin? Labor against it.

APRIL 22, 1649

Hebrews 4:1

Let us therefore fear, lest a promise being left us of entering into his rest, any of you should seem to come short of it.

These words do contain in them an excitation to a duty which is for everyone: to fear, lest they should [?] come short of heaven.

In the words are these three axioms or definitions:

1. That there is a promise left us of entering into this rest;

2. Though there be a promise left us, yet men are in danger to come short of it;

3. Seeing there is such danger of coming short of it, we must fear lest any of us should come short of [*it*].

From the first, note this:

Doctrine: There are promises and encouragements to all those that will enter into the true spiritual rest.

There is a three-fold rest mention in this chapter. The first is in verse 4, which meant of God's rest from the works of creation. The second rest mentioned is in v. 8, the rest in the land of Canaan. The third rest is that here in my text and verse 1, which is the true spiritual rest in the kingdom of Christ. It's begun here in the kingdom of grace and perfected in the kingdom of glory.

Secondly, let us inquire what promise is made of entering into this rest?

Paul tells us there is a promise. It is not to be found in plain terms and express words, but it may be inferred: "I swear in my wrath they shall not enter into my rest."[17] This combination implies by way of contraries that if they had walked so and so they might enter it. Threatening where the duty is neglected implies a promise, if the duty be performed.

---

17. Hebrews 3:11, citing Psalm 95:11.

First use informs us that the state of the godly both here, after they come to be godly, but especially hereafter. Their state is a state of rest. They rest from their labors, from all their sorrows and miseries. All tears are wiped away from their eyes, and therefore heaven is called a place of joy. And when a man is brought from the state of nature to the state of grace he is beginning this rest; though the greatest rest is hereafter. When you are in heaven, then there shall be nothing to annoy you.

Second use informs us that all those discouragements and all those fears that men meet with [on] their ways to heaven are but temptations. They come not from God, for God's word [is a] word of encouragement, a word of promise. God's voice is, "Today if you will hear his voice."[18] The devil's voice is, "Nay, it's too late."

Third [use] informs us that if men get not grace and go not to heaven, it's not for want of proffers and encouragements, but from something else.

Last use exhorts every one, that you would labor to see the encouragements and promises that God doth hold forth unto you. If you could but see promises and encouragements that God doth afford you, they would much draw you on in the Lord's work. Therefore labor to see the proffers and promises and encouragements that God doth afford you whereby to carry on your spirits and draw you on in the Lord's work. Make use of them, that you may be encouraged to enter into this spiritual rest.

Afternoon]

From the second axiom:
Doctrine: though God be willing to bestow grace here, and glory hereafter, yet there is great danger that men may miss it, and come short of it.

For explication: wherein lies the danger? There is danger that men will not regard this rest, nor seek after it. There is danger when men have begun to seek after this rest, lest they should be turned away before they be aware.

Several things turned away the people of Israel:

1. Their unbelief. If men be not drawn out of a state of unbelief, it's impossible for them ever to enter into this rest provided.

2. The text doth mention hardness of heart. Hardness of heart doth disable men from using those means that God doth direct unto, that they may be found of God.

3. There is danger that the heart should be too much knit unto its old ways and old courses. Till the whole be made new, it will not desire newness of life.

---

18. Deuteronomy 28:1

Fourthly, danger lies in this, that men will not seek this rest for right conditions and aims—not in God's way, but their own way.

Fifthly, all these laid together will make the danger great here of apostasy and backsliding. When men seek and find so many difficulties, [there is] great danger but [that] they will give over before they have obtained it.

This may further be confirmed that there is a great deal of danger, even from these considerations:

1. Satan hath so many wiles and subtle devices that he keeps men off.
2. It's a way that men are unaccustomed [?]

1. Use serves to inform us that there are multitudes that in their apprehension may be fair for heaven. It's one of the difficult things in our ministry to persuade men what a condition they are in. You may be in danger to come short of all the good that you hope for. And if you come short, let me tell you what a condition you are in. How was it with the five foolish virgins? Are you willing to backslide? Would you have God to brand you for backsliders? Are you willing to be deprived of all your hopes? Can you be content to go without this rest? I tell you, the danger is great, and many of you may come short. Well, look to it. If you come short, your blood be upon your own head.

The last thing in the text is, seeing there is so much danger of coming short of this rest, it's everyone's duty to fear lest he should seem to come short. This fear should be rather a fear of carefulness, to make men careful, than a fear of diffidence and distrust.

Lest any should *seem* to come short: God would not have a man to seem in the least degree either to himself or others to come short of [*this rest*]. There should not be an appearance of this evil, not so much as gives any suspicion or jealousy of it.

Use: serves to reprove those that not only come short of this rest but appear so to others. It's a very sad condition that a man should walk so as a man may write upon his back, "Thou fearful backslider." There is a rest that God doth intend for his people, and it's open for every man that will but make use of it.

MAY 6, 1649

Hebrews 4:2

For unto us was the Gospel preached [afresh?] as unto them.[19]
But the word preached did not profit them, not being mixed with faith in them that heard it.

The scope of the Apostle you have heard was to exhort them, viz. the Hebrews, to take heed lest they fall short of heaven. Now to set it on he adds that they, viz. the Jews, formerly had the Gospel, so that though we have the Gospel as well as they (in the wilderness), yet they coming short, so may we. And he [*gives*] the reason of it: the word did not profit them because of unbelief. How did it not profit them? In that [?] it brought them not to this rest.

From the former part of the verse, note:

Doctrine: the Jews that lived after Christ and the Jews that lived before Christ, particularly those that were in the wilderness, had the Gospel preached [*unto*] them.

Answer: The Gospel was preached all alike to them in some respects, and so it was "as well." But in other respects it was preached better to one than to the other.

It was preached all alike in this respect, that it was the same Gospel, the same covenant of grace—the same in substance. But after Christ's time it may be said to be better preached because it was more fully and more clearly. Before Christ the Gospel was preached, but somewhat darkly and in general terms. Afterwards it was more particularly opened. For the New Testament is but an exposition of Moses and the Prophets.

These things will evidence that the Gospel was preached to the one as well as to the other:

All had the like promises, they before Christ as well as we since Christ. There is no new addition, but only an explication of former promises. They had the seals of the Covenant, yea, and extraordinary seals. They had ~~tpes~~ types of Christ. They had faith; the Jews of old, many of them had faith. Now this is an undeniable evidence, for a man cannot have faith without the Gospel. But many of the people of old had faith. Abel had faith; Noah, Abraham, &c.

Use 1. We are not to think that the Jews lived in so much darkness as many do take them, and in so much blindness. It's true they had the Gospel

---

19. Note in manuscript: "whereas the text saith, 'as well as unto them.'"

but darkly preached, lapt up in types. Yet they had those that expounded these.

2. Wherever God hath a people, he hath the Gospel preached unto them. He will not withhold the Gospel from his people.

But the word did not profit them because it was not mixt with faith in them that heard it.

Hence are two doctrines:

1. Many hear the word that do not mix it with faith. It was so in Isaiah's time—Isaiah 6, and likewise Isaiah 53:1. So in Matthew 13:14—Christ finds the faith in his time. And John 12:37, 38; Acts 28:26.

Afternoon]

When are men said rightly to believe the word when it is preached so as [*it*] may profit them?

Rightly to believe the word implies two things:

1. To believe it for ourselves; to [apply it?] believe the truth of the word. Therefore men cannot properly be said to believe the word when they are full of ifs and ands and stickings, as Nicodemus, John 9, and as Christ's hearers, Luke, that say of Christ's doctrine, "God forbid." [20] It's plain that they cannot mix the word with faith, for they do not so much as assent unto the truth of the word—though there should be this, that a man must go further, if he will mix the word with faith, namely, to apply it to his own case and condition, as the Ninevites did. And so the [?] disciples did apply the word unto themselves that Christ preaches, and therefore they say, "Is it I? Is it I?" Faith sayeth, "This word that is preached, it's spoken to me; God would have me to take it home."

First use informs us, though God on his part affords men the means, yet they on their part are apt not to improve the means aright. You see here the Jews: by unbelief they received not the word of promise. And many a man, he sleeps away the word, and it's the sin of many of you. And many a one, though they have the word, yet as second Commandment requires that we honor God with his own worship, so the third Commandment requires that we attend upon such worship and such ordinances with suitable qualifications.

Second use reproves such that do not believe the word, as do not mix it with faith. They that do not believe the word are here to be reproved, which is the sin of all that are in their natural condition.

---

20. Luke 10:16

What is the reason that men do not mix the word with faith?

Sometimes Satan will not let them. Jeremiah 42:2, 3. Another reason is the heart of man is full of strange conceits of their own. 2 Corinthians 10:4, 5. Till a man's heart be outed of these, he is not suited to hear a sermon. Sometimes men's having a base and low esteem of the word.

3. Third thing that keeps men from believing is some cross and contrary opinion that a man is in love with. So far as the word doth cross and contradict their opinion, they cannot believe.

4. Though a man should sometimes believe the word, in a sort believe it, and so far believe it as to apply it in part, yet this may keep him off from full [?] believing it: some dislike that he hath to the doctrine that is delivered. Or [they] see ends of their own that make them apply it more than love to it and mixing it with faith. Consider now whether any of these things do keep you off from believing the word or anything else. Why do you not believe the word? How can you have any benefit from it without believing it?

The next use for trial and examination, whether you do mix the word with faith. How shall I know it?

1. By the fruits. If the word be mixed with faith, it will certainly bring forth fruit. 1 Thessalonians 2:13—it works "effectually" in them that believe. Inquire now, therefore, what fruit doth the word bring forth? Any or none? Sometimes the word works convictions; sometimes it works humiliations, as Elijah's word did to Ahab. Sometimes it works consolation and comforts the hearts of the godly. Sometimes, again, it stirs up to duty and makes men more serious in their duty to God or man. Now if the word be believed, it works some of these things, some fruit or other. If thou dost assent unto the truth of the word and apply it unto thyself, to thy own soul—if thus, it will be an evidence that you received the word by faith.

Last use: exhorts everyone unto their duty: that they would labor to receive the word by faith. If you do not receive the word by faith, of all persons you will have the worst of it.

How [sic-*What*] shall we do to receive the word by faith?

1. Set yourself as in God's presence when you are hearers of it. Look upon it as an ordinance of God.

2. If ever any temptations arise in your mind that make you to question the word or the like, get a solution of such doubts and suppress such doubts as soon as possible may be. Yea, if ever a temptation come into your mind that cause a slighty[21] esteem of the word or of the person that dispenses it, labor to weed out evil thoughts and get a high esteem of the word and the dispensers of it.

---

21. neglectful, careless

3. Labor what you can to be fruitful under the word. For certainly, if God be displeased with you for unfruitfulness he might justly give you up to unbelief. Make consc [sic-*consequence?*] of it to mix the word with faith.

How can it be profitable ~~else~~ to thee else? It's a matter of great concernment. If thou dost not mix the word with faith, what a condition art thou in! Labor accordingly, therefore. Henceforth, you had need to receive the word with faith. The Jews did not mix it with faith and therefore they came short of the rest—and so may you, if you do not believe the word and receive it in faith.

MAY 13, 1649

HEBREWS 4:2

But the word preached did not profit them, not being mixed with faith in them that heard it.

The Apostle now shows the reason why the word did not profit them. It was because of unbelief, because it was not mixed with faith in them that heard it.

Doctrine: when the word is not mixed with faith it profits not the hearers. Hebrews 9:19, and Hebrews 4:6—the Jews entered not into the rest "because of unbelief." Why? Because they were unbelieving hearers. The fruitfulness or unfruitfulness of men under the word is often laid down under these terms, believing or not believing; Luke 8:12; John 12:37, 38. And where the word doth good it's expressed under these terms, "they believed." John 14:1. He that believes the word profits by the word. And Acts 28:24—is [sic-*in*] as much as some got good by Paul's preaching, and some got no good at all.

The reason: because if men do not believe the word, they do not see those glorious things that God doth make known in the word. 2 Corinthians 4:3, 4.

2. Reason: While men do not believe the word, the word is not applied to a man's own soul to particular condition. Faith applies the word to self: "He speaks to me, means me." Says unbelief, "Nay, he made a good sermon for such a man; he reproved such a man's sin very well." An unbelieving hearer lays not up the word [*in*] his own heart and soul. If David had not applied home Nathan's word—"I am the man; God speaks to me"—Nathan's words would never have done him so much good.

3. Where the word is not mixed with faith there is no receiving of the word, for the scriptures makes receiving of the word to be by faith. Acts 8:12, 14. Acts 17:11, 12. Ezekiel 33:31, 32.

4. If the word be not believed it's not obeyed. [*It*] calls on you to leave your sins and you shall gain good to your souls. If you do not believe it you will never obey it. If men do not hear the word in faith and apply it to their own souls they will never walk according to it. Romans 10:11.

First use serves to reprove all those that do not believe the word, they that do not acknowledge the truth of the word, or if they do, will not apply it to their own souls. Come here to be reproved. You lose many a sermon, lose a great deal of labor and the minister loses his pains; notwithstanding all, you remain unprofitable. You neither get grace nor increase grace, and all because of your unbelief. Matthew—it's said of Capernaum, Christ did no mighty works there because of their unbelief.[22] You give the word a hearing. But for obeying it, believing it, and walking answerable to it, you little regard it. How many years may a man live under the word and be never the better, if he believe not the word! And will you still trifle away your time? Will God bear it at your hands, think you? If you be unprofitable hearers, as you must needs be if you be unbelieving hearers, then you are near unto cursing, whose end is to be burned, burnt in fire of hell, and therefore it is [*said*], "Cast the unprofitable servant into outer darkness."[23]

Second use is for comfort and consolation to God's people that do mix the word with faith. If any get good by the word, it will be believing hearers that get good by it. 1 Thessalonians 2:13—the word works "effectually" in them that believe. If men will attend the qualifications that God requires in his own ordinances, God's blessing shall attend them. Faith is a qualification required in hearing.

Therefore be encouraged and be comforted. Labor to apply every word of God to your own soul. Believe the Lord; so shall you [*be*] "established."[24] Believe his prophets; so shall ye believe the ministry of the word. Therefore you will get most good by it in the latter end, and your way is according to God. Therefore be comforted in it.

Third use exhorts everyone to labor to receive the word by faith. It's God's word; and will you put no weight on the word of God? If God tells you, if God instructs you, labor to get good by it. And that you cannot do without believing. Labor therefore to hear the word in faith, to receive it in faith, to mix it with faith. So shall it be a blessing upon your souls, which

---

22. Matthew 13:58. The place in question was Nazareth.
23. Matthew 25:30
24. Romans 1:11

otherwise would be unfruitful to you. Look to it, therefore, that you hear in faith and believe the word. Your damnation or your salvation depends upon this: your believing the word or not believing it. Let no man therefore slight or reject the word.

Afternoon]

Now we come to inquire: how doth it appear that they did not profit? It appears that they did not profit because it did not bring them into the rest.

Doctrine: the Word doth not profit if it does not bring men into the rest.

Explication:

1. What ~~doth he~~ is meant by "rest"? Answer: The rest is the kingdom of heaven, that is, in the kingdom of grace here and in the kingdom of glory hereafter. Now if the word does not bring the hearers into this rest, it profits them not.

2. How doth it appear that the word profits not if it bring not the hearers to the rest?

First reason: because that which obtains not the end is unprofitable. Now the end of all preaching is to bring men into this rest.

Second reason: because all other things that come short of this rest are little or nothing worth in comparison of this rest. Whatever a man may read unto it will do him no good if it reach not to be in a state of grace here, that so he may be in a state of glory hereafter.

Third reason: because this sin of unprofitableness with all sins accompanying will deprive him of this rest—of life, of happiness, of eternal rest.

Use 1. This serves for reproof of two sorts:

1. Such as content themselves with common work under the word, though it does not bring them to a state of grace. It's the mischief of Satan and the deceit of men's hearts that if they have had any work of the word [. . .] Tell me, what is it that a man should rest in if he be not in a state of grace? He that was vild before, if he have left his profaneness, he thinks it a great matter. Ah, what pity it is that a man should be thus deceived and thus cozened! O therefore take heed! Let not any one or other content themselves without grace. Though you may be a little reformed, yet if you have not grace you are miserable.

Second use is for comfort and consolation to all the godly that have obtained a state of rest. You may be comforted in it, for it's better than all other things; and all other things are nothing worth in comparison of this. Though you have excellent knowledge, good gifts, and spirits, could give all your goods to the poor, yet not having a gracious principle, all will be worth nothing. O therefore let the godly rejoice in their grace, rejoice in the good things that God hath done for you—that the grace of God hath appeared unto your salvation!

And the rather may you rejoice in this mercy:

1. Because you find by daily experience that many come short of it; most do, and yet thou art holpen[25] on.

2. Thou hast the more cause to bless God and acknowledge his mercy considering how unable thou art of thyself to get into this state. How came thou unto it? It was the Father hath drawn thee.

3. This may add to thy mercy to make thee rejoice in it: considering what a rest this is. It's a rest of grace here and a rest of glory hereafter. It's one of the greatest gifts that the great God gives to any of the sons of men. Well therefore let the godly comfort themselves.

Use last: exhorts to those duties that do arise from hence:

1. Take heed of being an unbelieving hearer. If you be an unbelieving hearer you are an unprofitable hearer, and then you must answer for all the sermons and all the means of grace that you have had. If you come to the ordinances, and you do not believe the word, then you shall not profit [*from them*]. Take heed therefore of living in unbelief. Unbelief is the worst condition that a man can be left in. Romans 11:32.

2. Take heed of being an unprofitable hearer. If a man lives under means and helps and [*is*] not careful to grow up under means and helps, take heed of being as the barren fig tree. Assure yourself that God will expect fruit. And if God can find no fruits, woe unto thee! If God would have gathered you as a hen gathers her chickens and you would not,[26] take heed lest God in justice in a short time hide the things that belong to your peace from your eyes.

3. Take heed that thou dost not content thyself with anything beside this rest. Content not thyself with convictions, reformations, some change, &c. These are but common works and not such as the spirit of God will own another day. Therefore take heed of resting in these. My heart aches to think that any of you should content yourselves without this rest—a state of grace here that may bring you to a state of glory hereafter. You will but deceive yourselves.

4. Labor to hear the word so as it may bring you to heaven. Fear and tremble lest you fall short of it. And labor so to profit by the word as you may come to heaven hereafter. What if you see heaven—have a peephole into heaven—yet fear lest you should fall short? Labor therefore that you

25. helped
26. Matthew 23:37, Luke 13:34

make sure of grace here, and take heed that you be not deceived. Content not yourself with anything else.

A man should hear as though his main work were to get to heaven by hearing, to escape hell by hearing, and to do the work of God. You should hear for your life, hear as if heaven lay at stake. Be so serious in hearing the word and treasuring it up, that you may be sure of heaven. For if you miss of heaven, unavoidably you will drop into hell before you be aware.

MAY 27, 1649

Hebrews 6:11

And we desire that every one of you do shew the same diligence to the full assurance of hope unto the end.

In the former verse, the Apostle renders a reason why he was persuaded better things of them: because it [sic-*God*] is "not unrighteous to forget your labor of love to the saints."[27] Now he desires them to continue still in the same work with diligence.

Doctrine: exhortation to our duty is very suitable for the godly. It's not enough barely to tell them their duty, but exhortation to their duty is very necessary and requisite. 2 Corinthians 9:5. The need of it appears in these respects: it's necessary for the godly because, though they have grace and good affect in them, yet they have need of stirring them up. 2 Peter 1:12, 13. As the godly have need of it, so exhortation is part of an ordinance, and so comes in the blessing of an ordinance.

1. Because the subject matter that is preached or dispensed is for this end and purpose, namely, for exhortation. 2 Timothy 3:13.[28] And the word being ordained and appointed for this end and purpose, accordingly it is to be attended.

2. The ministry itself, part of his [sic-*its*] work is to be exhortation. Titus 1:9; Titus 2:15; and therefore Romans 12:8. The gift of some ministers is reduced to this head, that he [sic-*they*] attend on exhortation.

First use: teaches us what is the minister's work and duty. It lies in exhortation; as much as if the spirit of God should say in making use and application of what truths they deliver [sic-*it delivers*], the very life of all preaching lies in application. Acts 11:23; Acts 15:32; 1 Peter 5:12.

27. Hebrews 6:10
28. 2 Timothy 4:2; 1 Timothy 4:13?

2. For the people, there is a double duty belonging unto them:

1. According to Hebrews 13:22—"I beseech you thereon, suffer the word of exhortation." When you have exhortations, take them, apply them, be stirred up thereby, and be sure that you get good by such exhortation as you have. To what purpose is it for God to call on you for duty if you will not regard?

2. Duty for the people is to call on one another. Hebrews 2:13[29]—"Exhort one another daily while it is called today." Many men are greatly to blame here. And it argues a barren, cold-hearted Christian. If your hearts were heated and warmed by the love of God and duty you would be calling on one another and stirring up one another to duty. And it would be more for God's honor and your own conscience, if when you meet together, you would spend your time this way. Hebrews 10:25. Well be persuaded to exhort one another and to call on one another to duty that so your time may be spent more profitably.

Shew the same diligence to the end.

When God's people are in a fair way of performing their duty, they should be very diligent to continue therein. Hold on in a good way. If you be in a good way, continue therein to the end. 2 Corinthians 15:58. Hebrews 4:14—"Hold fast" to the end. If we have begun well, and be in a good way, hold to it. 1 Thessalonians 5:21—"Try all things, hold fast that which is good." Acts 13:43. Colossians 4:2. Romans 12:12. 1 Timothy 4:16.

First reason: because God that doth require duty doth also require the continuance in duty. There is no term set for men to give over duty. "Pray." Aye—but when? Always! A man is never exempted from duty till his life ends.

Second reason: because the reward of well-doing depends much upon our continuing in well-doing to the end. "He that continues to the end shall be saved"—Matthew 10:22. Matthew 24:13. Revelation 2:26. And therefore it is, "Be not weary in well doing, for in due season you shall reap if you faint not."[30]

Third reason: if men do not use a great deal of diligence they will hardly keep on in performing of duty as they should do.

Fourth reason: men that are in a fair way of doing must continue, because the honor of God depends upon it. God is honored or dishonored according as you do duty or neglect.

---

29. Hebrews 3:13
30. Galatians 6:9

Afternoon]

Second use serves to reprove such as do not continue in good duty:

1. All backsliders. As John the Baptist's hearers consider of it,[31] you that do backslide, look to it upon your peril. Proverbs 14:14—"The backslider in heart shall be [...]"

Is it not a sad sign of these two things:

1. that hitherto God doth not mean good unto your soul; that he gives you over to backsliding?

2. that for the present you do not desire [...] ?

2. This serves to reprove the godly, that though they do not backslide as the former, yet are exceedingly short of [...] You do not grow better, but rather worse and worse. Ah, the coldness of heart, the decay in grace! What says thy own heart? This, with grief you may think of it.

One use is for exhortation to stir up all one another. When you are in a good way, keep on it. And for that end, take these directions:

1. Get your heart stored with strong resolutions for what you undertake.

2. Get strong arguments. Do upon good judgments what you do.

3. If you would continue in well doing, then take heed of going on in your own strength. Resolve by the help of Christ, and beg power and strength from him.

If you would be encouraged in the Lord's work, then store your hearts with promises.

Unto full assurance of hope.

Doctrine: they that have assurance of their salvation should be diligent in the use of means, that they may get more full assurance of their salvation. It's godly, their duty, though they have assurance to get more and better assurance daily.

1. Reason: because though godly men have assurance, yet it's but imperfect here;

2. The godly have need to make their assurance more full because that assurance that they have, it's subject to change:

1. Through decays in duty and overflowing of corruption into scandalous sins;

2. through Satan's temptations;

3. forgetfulness of former experience.

First use: it is thus, that they that have assurance should labor to get better assurance. Then here is cause, and it serves sharply to blame many of you that have lost your assurance. You dishonor God exceedingly by your unbelief and your heart is gone in the Lord's works.

Second use: exhort everyone to labor to get full assurance, recover your evidences, and if you have assurance, hold what you have and get what you can more.

For this end:

1. some things are to be done;
2. some things are carefully to be avoided.

The things to be done are these:

1. Treasure up experiences. When God communicates himself to thee, treasure it up.
2. Be careful of holy walking. Keep close to God in duty.
3. Hold fast your love to the godly.
4. If at any time you have any doubts concerning your evidences, labor to get your doubts resolved in due time.

The things to be avoided are:

1. Gross sins, scandalous sins that may exceedingly darken things in your own soul.
2. Take heed of tampering so much with Satan.

Make use of these directions, for I tell you, brethren, it's a matter of great concernment to get sure evidences and to retain them.

JUNE 3, 1649

Hebrews 6:12

That ye be not slothful but followers of them who through faith and patience inherit the promises.

In the former verse the Apostle desires them to continue in their good work, &c.

Now he exhorts them further:

1. Negatively, be not slothful;
2. Positively, be "followers of them which through," &c.

From the first, note:

Doctrine: there is a sinful slothfulness in matters of God which should carefully be avoided.

First reason: because men in matters of God, for their soul and salvation thereof, have a great deal of work to do—so much as cannot be done with slothfulness. But men have need to "up and be doing."[32]

Second reason: because the adversaries of man's salvation and work of God, they will not be slothful but will be vigilant to take all opportunities. Therefore we must bestir ourselves [*to do*] what we can. The work of God will not be carried on if men be slothful.

Third reason: though sluggishness will not carry on the Lord's work and men's salvation, yet diligence will. By diligence we may come to inherit the promises. In matters of the world in getting or keeping, we cannot expect them without diligence, but the "diligent hand," Proverbs 10:4, "maketh rich" even in worldly matters. And so it is in spiritual things. He is a poor soul that is slothful; but he [*that*] is diligent is rich in spiritual things. And we find that where God makes promises of any spiritual good it's to diligence; Isaiah, and therefore Deuteronomy 28:1—"If thou shalt hearken diligently to the Lord," to thy good to observe and do, &c, then all these blessings, &c. Deuteronomy 11:13—"If you hearken diligently," and verse 22, "If you keep diligently." The promises are made upon condition of diligence. Hebrews 11—"He that comes to God must believe that he is a rewarder of them that seek him."[33]

Use for trial and examination, whether you are not slothful men in matters of God that concern your own salvation. You may be stirring men and women in the world, and yet lazy and slothful in God's work. Therefore try by these things:

1. A slothful person is apt to make excuses when work is to be done. Proverbs 26:13—"a lion is in the way." So Proverbs 22. Answerably in spiritual matters a slothful person makes excuses, will pretend this and that. "Why do you not pray?" "I have not a convenient place, children cry, &c." "Why do you not go to meeting on the Lord's day?" "I want a hat, want shoes," or "The weather is cold, snowy, or rainy. I cannot conveniently go." "Why do you not read, meditate?" It's the slothfulness of your spirit. Sloth will make many excuses, and poor, slender excuses, as Matthew 25:26.

2. A slothful person doth not improve time and opportunities as he might, and as a diligent person will. Look upon Solomon's good housewife, Proverbs 31. How comes all that work to be done? She takes her opportunities and improves them, which a careless housewife would neglect.

Tell me, how do you improve your time? Is not spiritual sloth too much in you? How do you take opportunities for prayer, reading, meditation? Do

---

32. 1 Chronicles 22:16 (Geneva Bible)

33. Hebrews 11:6

you improve your time—all opportunities for God? If you did bestir yourself to improve your gifts and the opportunities that are afforded you [. . .]

3. A slothful person will not work for ordinary hire, neither for ordinary wages, nor out of ordinary fear. Many times you find it, slothful persons will not work for that by the day that others [*will*]; neither will ordinary fear spur them unless it be a prickly, sharp one indeed. So in spiritual things, ordinary rewards will not carry on a slothful person. Neither will ordinary fear make him do the Lord's work. But when God puts him upon the wrack, frights him with wrath, hell fire flashing about his ear [. . .]

4. A slothful person usually chooses the easiest work, and to work with such persons and in such places as are easiest. Answerably in such spiritual things the sluggishness of our spirits makes us stick at a great deal of work that God would have us do. A slothful man casts off the Lord's work many times because of the difficulty of it. You will choose the easiest work. To come to meetings, to pray in your family—these are not so difficult. But to pray in secret, to search your own soul, humble your heart, meditate, spend time betwixt God and your own soul, wrestle with corruption and get power [. . .] Easy common works a slothful spirit may do, but [*not*] hard and toilsome work. If you let this lie it's a sign of a slothful spirit.

Well search yourself and try whether you are guilty of spiritual sloth; and so far as you are guilty, be ashamed.

2. Use for reproof of this sinful sloth: all of you so far as you are guilty take the reproof home. A slothful person loses what the diligent gets. Sluggishness of heart will not let you continue in the use of means; but God's work must be carried on in the use of means. Proverbs 6—Solomon speaks how unavoidably poverty will follow a sluggard;[34] and so Proverbs 20:4—"The sluggard will not plow," and therefore he shall beg in harvest and have nothing." Answerably you slothful spirits that neglect prayer, neglect ordinances—time may come that you may wish with all your heart you had used the means.

You may beg hereafter, and God deny to hear according to the sloth of your spirits. So will the curse of God be upon you.

Afternoon]

Three uses for exhortation:
1. That you would believe it as a truth that you are slothful. Believe it that there is such a distemper cleaves to thee in particular.
2. Labor to find it out wherein thy lazy heart doth lie. Whence doth it arise that you are no more drawn [. . .] ?

---

34. Proverbs 6:9–11

3. Where you have formerly been slothful you are called on to up and be doing and bestir yourself. Your laziness, your sluggishness, your lazy heart deprive you of many blessing. A lazy heart never brings good to a man in point of spiritual things.

But followers of them who through faith and patience inherit the promises.

Doctrine: by faith and patience the godly in former time inherited the promises. And we in these times must follow them in the like faith and patience—patience in respect of those hardships and difficulties that do accompany religion. Hebrews 11—the whole chapter is a proof of this doctrine. Hebrews 12:1, 2.

One reason: because religion is accompanied with many difficulties and hardships.

1. Hardships and difficulties from God.

When God doth delay and seem to deny, neither God [. . .] nor consigned that. O the sad complaints that the godly make under such delays! This is a heavy thing, for all their hope lies upon God. To have God displeased, this breaks the heart of God's people.

2. Sometimes hardships arise from something else, as from Satan's temptation.

3. This makes the work tedious and difficult—the hard work at home.

4. The hardness of the work sometimes lies on this: many exercises that they have from others.

Now God's people have need of faith and patience to meet with these difficulties and to carry them through all these hardships. 2 Thessalonians 1:4. Romans 8:25. Revelation 3:10. Revelation 2:3. Romans 2:7.

First use informs us what is the reason why many that are in a fair way of obtaining the promises do yet miss of them. Answer: It's a sullen, sinful fit of unbelief and impatiency. Your faith and impatience [sic-*patience*] doth not hold out, and therefore you do not inherit the promises.

Second use exhorts to a double duty:

1. Labor to get faith and patience;

2. When you have got it, set it on work. Faith sees that help will come and patience enables thee to wait till it does come.

JUNE 10, 1649

HEBREWS 6:13,14

For when God made promise to Abraham, because he could swear by no greater, he sware by himself, saying, Surely blessing I will bless thee, &c.

In the 12th verse the Apostle exhorted them to follow them who by faith and patience inherited the promise to be [?]. And here he picks out one select example to confirm the rest, as a man who through faith and patience inherited the promise. The person brought is Abraham. The promise is Genesis 22:16, 17.

Because he could swear by no greater.

Doctrine: hence, there is none greater than God. We do not mean it of bodily substance, but greatness in power and holiness, greatness in being.
1. God is said to be greater than all gods. If any be the greatest, it's gods. But God is above all gods—Exodus 18:11. He is greater than man—Job 33:12. He is greater than Christ—John 18:14. Now Christ is greater than any; greater than the angels—Hebrews 1:4, 5.
Reasons:
1. Reason: he that made all things is greater than all things that are made. God that made the world and all things in the world is greater than the world or anything in the world. He that gives being to all is greater than [*they*] that receive being from him.
2. Reason: he that hath his being from himself and receives not his being from another is greater than all those that have not their being from themselves.
3. Reason: he that is the ultimate end of all, and for whom all things are. The house is for the man and not man for the house; therefore the man is more excellent than the house. God is the ultimate end of all. Romans 11:36.
4. Reason: he that does do such things as none else do, or can do, he is above all and greater than all else. Now God does that which none else does, and he can do that which none else can do. That which is impossible with man is possible with God.
First use informs us that the godly should pick out some choice and select examples of the godly that have gone before them, to make use of; and among all examples no better than Abraham, because Abraham is the father of the faithful. This arises naturally from the text, though not so plainly

from this doctrine. I made [sic-*may*] have made it a doctrine of itself, but was willing to lay it up in a use of information.

Second use informs us that poor, doubting Christians may here receive information of judgment concerning doubtings, whether God will do so and so for them. It's too great a thing for them to expect: mercy for me, so undeserving to God, on my sin. It's too great a thing for me. Why? Man, the doctrine tells you that God is greater than all, and it becomes the great God to do great things. Here the poor creature may have a ground to expect great things from God.

3. Use for reproof to all those that live in their sins and live wickedly in base, lewd, sinful courses. Who have you to deal with, God or man? Psalm—"Consider this, ye that forget God, lest I tear you in pieces and there be none" to rescue.[35] Who is it that ye despise? Whose law is it that ye transgress? Against whom is it that ye kick and spurn? It's against God that is greater than all. O tremble at the greatness and majesty of God! He can destroy both body and soul in hell.

Afternoon]

Use for comfort and consolation of all the godly that have share and part in this God—the great God that is greater than all. Men of the world glory in it that they have great friends, &c. But to have the great God to be your friend, it's a happiness indeed. The mercy of God, the power of God, the wisdom of God—all shall be set on work for thee! Oh, it's a great happiness; and let it serve for comfort unto the godly.

Use for exhortation to the duties that do arise from this doctrine:

1. Is God greatest? Then fear God above all things. The Lord hath dominion above all in the world else, and therefore if any be to be feared, then God much more. Fear God above all things. Do not fear the creature so much.

2. Transfer all the honor that ever you can unto God. If God be greater than all, then he is to be honored above all. Whether you eat or drink or whatever you do, let all be done unto "the glory of God."[36]

3. Have all your dependence upon God. Let your faith act on him. The spirit is borne up while they have something in view that they place their expectation on. Therefore labor to place your faith on God.

If God will carry on a thing, if he say "aye," all the world cannot say "no." On the other hand, if God say "nay" all the world cannot say "aye." So that if you have God's consent, it's more than all the world. Have your

---

35. Psalm 50:22

36. 1 Corinthians 10:31

dependence on him. Therefore God is to be feared, to be trusted in, and therefore we should have our dependence on God.

You many times fear, corruption is so strong and devil hath such power that he will blast all the work of God's grace in your soul. Why, what is the matter? Is not God greater than all? Then have your dependence; you are bound to it as you are his creatures. It's part of that religious work that you owe him. And if you will worship God as you should, you are bound unto it. Besides that, you have this reason for it: he is greater than all.

Blessing I will bless thee, &c.

Doctrine: God makes promises unto his people which he would have them to make use of.

1. How is a person to make use of promises?
2. Why would God have his people to make use of them?

1. How is a person to make use of promises? Some directions:

First, promises that are made generally to all or to any: particulars may be applied to anywhere such promises are suitable. Where the promises be made in general to believers, any may apply them that are in such a condition as that promise. Joshua 1:5, 6, which afterward Paul makes use of when he dissuades against covetousness and the sinful care of the world. Hebrews 13:5. So 1 Kings 8:37, 40, which, 2 Chronicles 20:8, 9, Jehoshaphat makes use of and applies it unto himself.

Second rule: though the promises be known and certain, yet the way how promises shall be performed and the time when they shall be performed, that is unknown to us, and is uncertain.

When that great famine was in Samaria the prophet told them that by tomorrow that time corn and meal should be so cheap. Because [*of*] the way and manner how it should come to pass, they would not believe it. You will exceedingly wrong yourself and enter into secret things that belong to God if you trouble yourself and busy yourself about the manner how promises shall be made good, or the time when, unless it be expressed.

Third, in the application of promises when we expect the performance of them, it must be in that way which God intends; in God's way, and as God intends.

1. God intends one promise after another in an orderly way, for God will do things in order. God is like unto a skillful workman that always works things by degrees and in order.

2. God intends to make good promises, in the use of those means which God hath directed. Something must be done on our part—Jeremiah 29:10, 12, 13.

Fourth, the promises that God hath made, they are the grounds of our prayer and of our faith. We have no warrant to pray for anything but for that which God hath promised in general or particular. All the promises are made in Christ and to Christ. They are made in Christ mystical, as the head of the church.

Three things might exceedingly help the faith of God's people in this respect:

First, Christ hath power to see all the promises performed;

1. Power in respect of the Godhead;

2. Christ hath power in respect of his office. And as he is an officer, he hath power by virtue of his office. It's Christ's office to see the promises performed, to see the covenant of grace performed; thus Christ hath power enough.

Second, Christ hath will enough. As he hath power, so he hath a mind and will to see the promises performed. He is willing.

Third, he is careful also. He is careful to see the covenant of grace performed justly, exactly according to the intent of God.

These three things may exceedingly satisfy the soul. Thus you see that God makes promises, and he would have you to make use of promises.

JUNE 24, 1649

Hebrews 6:15

And so after he had patiently endured he obtained the promises.

You have heard that the Apostle brings in Abraham's example as a particular instance of that which he had spoken in general terms. In this verse you have the fruit of Abraham's patient waiting. He obtained the promise.

This verse affords three doctrines:

First doctrine: God, in making promises ~~doth~~ unto his servants, doth oftentimes and usually try and exercise the patience of his servants before he make good such promises. He did so with Abraham. He promised to multiply him, and yet it was a long while ere he had such multiplication.

Two things are to be opened:

1. How God doth try the patience of his people;

2. Why doth God thus exercise the patience of his people?

First, how doth God exercise the patience of his people?

1. God doth many times exercise their patience by delays, as David's. God promised he should be king when he was a stripling. And yet God delays him a long time. And what vexing passages he met with during that time, which tried his patience, the story will tell you.

In ordinary experience we find it. Suppose a person be about to mortify a corruption. God hath promised to help him. Yet what a long time doth God delay the soul: so in [...]

2. Sometimes God doth exercise men's patience by seeming denial, as in David's case. He had a promise to be King, yet Saul vexes him. He is in danger of his life, and his son rises up against him, sometimes one, and sometimes another. These are seeming denials, and therefore David himself concludes, "I shall one day perish by the hand of Saul."[37]

The Lord promised the Israelites that they should be delivered from the Egyptians. All things go so cross and contrary for [a] while, that one [?]. God tries the patience of his people by not letting Satan loose to tempt them and to try them.

Second, why doth God thus exercise the patience of his people?

One reason, that they may the more prize the mercy and consequently be the more fitted for the mercy.

Second reason: where God gives grace he tries it. That is a general rule. Job was an excellent man, one that feared God and eschewed evil. Well therefore God will try him. God will sometime or other try the graces of his people. 1 Peter 1:7—"That the trial," &c.

First use lets us see what we are to expect and on what terms we are to make use of promises. If you would apply promises then you must have patience. Expect that your patience will be tried. God will put his people upon delays and much try their patience. And the want of expecting this many times makes your patience mere impatience.

Second doctrine: though God in the performance of his promises does thus oftentimes exercise men's patience and try their patience, yet it's their duty patiently to endure until he perform his promise. Psalm 40:1. Psalm 123:2. Luke 2:25.

We do in this case as it's said of the husbandman, James 5:7. The husbandman, he sows, he plants, and when his corn is almost spoiled for want of rain, yet he waits still. He hopes, and when he doth not know what harvest he may have, yet he waits still. So should we. Or as the cripple that lay at the Pool of Bethesda.[38]

---

37. 1 Samuel 27:1
38. John 5:1–13

Afternoon]

One use serves to reprove all those who do not exercise patience in expectation of promises to be performed. We would have promises performed, but we would have them upon easy terms. And if they come out easily without much waiting, we are ready to reject them.

1. Let me tell you, it's your ignorance in applying promises that puts you upon these temptations.

2. It arises from your weakness of faith and weakness of hope, that your patience is so soon tired out, as it is. Romans 8:25.

You that are impatient, let me ask you this: if you be impatient with God and on so holy a matter, how do you do to hold out in other duties to God? Besides, again, who is it that you are impatient with? It's not man. It's not properly yourself. It's God. It's against God that you do wrangle, because he doth not perform what you expect.

Further, hath not God waited for thee? He hath had patience towards thee. Thou hast multiplied thy transgression towards him and yet he hath waited for thy return; and what, canst thou have no patience towards him, or so little patience, sith[39] he hath ~~so little patience~~ so much patience to thee? As it is your great sin, so there is a judgment accompanying it.

Second use: comfort to all the godly that do patiently wait upon God. You may be comforted in these respects:

1. You do [*your*] duty. God bids you wait and you do wait.

2. It's an evidence of the presence of God's spirit in your soul: God giving thee a heart above thy own and still following thee with the supplies of his spirit.

3. Though you yet have not the mercy and be delayed, yet in that God gives thee a heart to wait still in the use of means, it's an undeniable evidence that God means good, and that the mercy will come in the latter end. If you have not the thing promised, yet certainly you will have it.

Third use: exhorts all the godly that as you would set faith on work to lay hold on a promise, so you would set patience and hope on work. Psalm 37:7.

Helps against impatiency:

1. Always bear in mind that there is a great deal of difference to be made betwixt delays and denials, and that God ties not himself to times. Be not weary of well doing, for in due season you shall reap if you faint not.[40] You shall reap in due time. But when that due time is, you must leave to God.

---

39. since

40. Galatians 6:9

2. Do not trouble yourself about the manner of performing promises. Leave that to God.

3. If you would be patience [sic-*patient*] in spirit, take heed of giving way to any temptations that may weaken your faith and hope, and consequently your patience. Watch against those temptations and suggestions of Satan that strike against your faith, and labor to bring you into unbelief.

Motives to patient waiting for the performance of promises:

1. Consider that God hath waited for you, and had patience with you. He hath exercised a great deal of patience ~~with~~ towards you. Christ hath stood knocking for you till his locks have been met with the dew of the night.[41] God hath had patience with thee one year after another; and therefore thou mayest well have patience towards him. Again,

2. Bear this in mind, the great good that thou get if thy patience do but hold out: thou hast more experiences and more advantages, and lose nothing but rusty[42] graces. Romans 5:3; 4, 5. If God put your patience upon the trial and it holds out, you get a great deal by it. Not only the obtaining the promise, but your faith and hope grow the stronger, and the more patience you will have, which will be the greater blessing still. James 1:3, 4.

3. It is the good will and pleasure of God to try the patience of his servants. God will have it so; that should be enough to us. If God will try you, is it not your duty to say, "Lord, here I am; try me, and welcome"? Psalm 105:17, 18, 19—It is the good pleasure of God to try his servants till his "time" be come.

Third doctrine: if our patience do but hold out we shall certainly in the issue obtain that good which God hath promised.

First use serves to quiet the spirits of all that are in expectation of any blessing or mercy from God by virtue of a promise, whatever it be. Hold on, believing, continue still, and in the latter end you shall obtain.

1. The promise doth hold forth so much.

2. The precious experience, it may be of thy own soul—however, [*also*] of others.

3. God is faithful. The word of an honest man is of great trust, but the word of God more. Faithful is he which hath promised, who also will do it. Heaven and earth shall sooner pass away than "one jot or tittle" of his word fail.[43]

---

41. Song of Solomon 5:2
42. corrupted
43. Matthew 5:18

JULY 8, 1649

Hebrew 6:16

For men verily swear by the greater and an oath to them of confirmation is the end of all strife.

This verse contains in it the explication of the nature and use of an oath among men.[44] And the application of it he leaves to us, intending it should be applicable to this oath that he made to Abraham.

1. Concerning an oath as it respects men, I'll lay it down under this term: a human oath.

Three things in a human oath:

1. ~~for~~ by whom are men to swear;
2. for what are they to swear;
3. of what use is an human oath.

I do not speak of rash, vain swearing, but being called to it by authority.

First, by whom are men to swear? Answer: By a greater, namely a greater than himself, a greater than man is, and that for these reasons:

1. In an oath there is a calling that party to witness by whom we swear, that what we swear is true. Now to call a man to witness that knows not whether that [*which*] we [*sic-he*] swear be true or false, is an abuse.

2. In an oath there is an implication, a wishing a curse to ourselves if we swear falsely. Every man, when he takes an oath though justly called to it, doth call God to witness that what he speaks is true, and to plague and punish him if he speak false—not only in general, but if he speak false on any particular.

3. Swearing among men must be by a greater because swearing is a part of religious worship. Now to swear by any that is not greater than our selves is a profaning of swearing. It was a sinful custom that Joseph had gotten to say, "By the life of Pharaoh."[45]

Secondly, the use of an oath: it is for confirmation ~~It is for~~ of something that is to be confirmed. Suppose one says, "Such a beast is mine." "No," says another, "it's mine." How shall this be decided now? Now must an oath be for confirmation one way or other.

---

44. Several points in this sermon may be correlated with John Calvin, *A Commentarie on the VVhole Epistle to the Hebrevves*, (1605). See especially Calvin on 6:16, 18, and 19.

45. Genesis 42:15

Third thing in a human oath: it is for the ending of a controversy ~~when there is~~.

Thus far of a human oath, that is, an oath among men.

Now as the Apostle brings this, and as it is applicable to the oath that God made with Abraham, we are further to consider—

—Only, by the way, one thing I forgot from what I said before: we may infer that an oath among men is a lawful order. It's as lawful as to pray or hear the word. It's a part of religious worship and is commanded, Jeremiah 4:2—

—so that there being a command: "thou shalt swear," namely, in an orderly way. It is such a duty as to be attended. Yea, and of such necessity that many times controversies among men cannot be ended without it.

Yea, further, if we abolish an oath we must abolish the Ten Commandments, for the second Commandment takes in an oath. Yea, Psalm 63:11— an oath by synecdoche[46] is put for ~~all~~ the whole worship of God. Oaths are to be attended in an orderly way only. I won't have men contentious in these oaths.

Afternoon]

Now for what we are to consider in this oath as it is appliable to Abraham:

    1. It implies that there was a controversy between God and Abraham— and not only Abraham, but [?].

    2. That God's oath is for confirmation.

    3. That this oath should end and determine the controversy betwixt God and us.

    1. That there is a controversy between God and us appears several ways here in the text. God had said, "Blessing, I will bless thee."[47] We will not believe it. There is a controversy between God and an unbeliever, and Satan labors to maintain the controversy. If you would but take God's word the controversy would be at an end. But you will not; and therefore God must swear it.

    2. God's oath is for confirmation. Not for confirmation on God's part—his word should be enough—but your unbelieving [hearts] will not

---

46. A part for the whole: a figure of speech favored by William Pynchon.

47. Genesis 22:17

be satisfied with that, and therefore God takes an oath. God says, "Blessing, I will bless thee." We will not believe it, that God will be thy God, pardon thy sin. Here thou stickest. Tell me, hast thou not had need that God should confirm this unto thy soul?

These things will evidence so much. Says one, "I have heard many previous promises but I could not apply any of them to my soul." Says another, "I have sometimes thought that God was my God and that God would bless me, but now I know not what to think of myself." By this oath of God the controversy betwixt God and his people should cease. As an oath among men is for the ending of controversies, so the oath betwixt God and us is for the ending of controversy. We should now therefore never contend with God more, never doubt more. While we remain in unbelief the controversy remains. But when our unbelief is taken away, the controversy ceases.

From all this that hath been expressed, take notice of the mischief of unbelief. If there be anything that makes the controversy betwixt God and you, it's your unbelief. All the sins that a child of God might commit would not maintain the controversy, if it were not for impenitency and unbelief.

2. When God's word doth so far prevail in your conscience that you are persuaded of it, and can take his word, then the controversy betwixt God and you ceases. Therefore, while there is unbelief and doubting the controversy is not ended. Labor therefore against unbelief and doubting.

Why should you question God's word else, seeing he confirms it with an oath? Let not thy heart forever remain in that wretched sin of unbelief. If you lie in unbelief and will not put an end to the controversy, no wonder if God stands at a distance with you.

v. 17—*Wherein God, willing more abundantly to shew unto the heirs of promise the immutability of his counsel, confirmed it with an oath.*

The Apostle proceeds on to show the end and use of the oath he [= God] made to Abraham.

1. To show the immutability of his counsel to the heirs of promise.
2. To confirm it, for confirmation.

Doctrine: in all ages believers are as truly heirs of the promises that were made to Abraham as Isaac was, or, they have as truly right to the promises made to Abraham as Abraham himself had. All that should walk in the steps of faithful Abraham are heirs with [him], because they are sons, therefore heirs. They are heirs with Christ and therefore must needs be heirs with Abraham. Galatians 3:29—"If ye be Christ's ye are Abraham's seed and heirs according to the promise." Titus 3:7—"that being justified by his grace we should be made heirs according to the hope of eternal life." Romans 8:17.

First, what do you mean by this, "they are heirs?" Thus: you know among men the eldest son is the father's heir. And unless his undutifulness causes him to be disinherited, he shall certainly, if he live to it, not only have right and interest to his father's estate, but possess it. And so we are Abraham's heirs, and have truly right to all the promises made to him, to all the good things of the Gospel.

Secondly, how come we thus to be heirs?

1. It's God's counsel. He hath decreed it and ordained it. It's the immutability of his counsel. If there can be no other reason alleged but this, it's sufficient.

Reasons to evidence that we are heirs of the promise made to Abraham:

1. Experience shows that believers of what sort soever, be they weak, be they strong, yet if believers, they make use of the covenant of grace, the promises made to Abraham. And God doth not blame them but approve them for applying them to themselves.

2. Experience tells us that believers have need of all, and having need of all, God gives them right to whatever they have need of.

3. If believers have not right to promises, and be not heirs, then none in the world are heirs. For wicked men are not. They are esteemed but as dogs. "There's no place belongs to the wicked," saith God.[48]

One use: if that believers are heirs of the promises, then it serves to reprove those believers that do not apply the promises unto themselves. You will say, "Aye, if I knew certainly that I were a believer." In a word, if you be heirs of the promises, apply the promises unto your own souls. Take your portion. Say, "May I not eat my own bread, wear my own clothes—those that my Father hath provided for me?"

JULY 15, 1649

Hebrews 6:17

Wherein God, willing more abundantly to shew unto the heirs of promise the immutability of his counsel, confirmed it with an oath.

The end of God's making this oath is set down in this verse.

1. On God's part it is to show the immutability of his counsel to the heirs of promise.

2. On believers' part in v. 18, that we might have strong consolation.

---

48. Psalm 37:10

Doctrine: the counsel and purpose of God concerning the salvation of his people is immutable and unchangeable. It's true he propounds some conditions. But, Romans 11:29; Philippians 4:3; Revelation 3:5; Revelation 17:8.

Here are some things to be propounded:

1. The counsel and purpose of God in general, that shall stand for ever. There can be no changing or altering of God's decree. Psalm 33:11. Isaiah 46:10. Proverbs 19:21. If the decree and purpose of God could be changed, then it must be changed by God himself or some other. But God is not as man, that he should change his mind, nor as the Son of man, that he should repent. Neither is there any other that can alter it. Proverbs—there is "no wisdom or counsel" that can alter the purpose of God.[49] Isaiah 14:24, 27—"The Lord of host hath purposed it, and who can disannul it?"

2. Reason: believers, even so many as God hath ordained to life and salvation, so many are given to Christ. Now all that are given to Christ shall be saved.

One use informs us that the salvation of man doth not simply depend on man himself. Thus it depends on man that God will have him to use the means. But in respect of the decree of God, when God hath decreed a man shall be saved, nothing shall hinder it. All that God hath ordained to life and salvation, they shall be all saved—and not one more.

Will any say now, "It's in vain for me to seek to be godly? If God have a purpose to save me, I shall be saved; and if he will damn me, all that ever I can do will not hinder it."

Answer:

1. The purpose of God doth not lay a necessity upon thee to be wicked.

2. The counsel and purpose of God may be accomplished by sinful means, and so thou wilt smart in hell.

3. The purpose of God concerning man's salvation: it doth appear to some, but to some it's not made known in this world. And therefore we are to make our calling and election sure. This duty lies upon all. And it's very ungodly reasoning to say, "If I shall be saved I shall be saved and if I shall be damned, I cannot help it." This is ungodly and deceitful reasoning, for thou art to make thy calling and election sure. Though the purpose of God cannot be altered, yet man is bound to make his calling and election sure.

Second doctrine: God would have his people to know his counsel and the immutability of his counsel concerning their salvation. I mean, God would not only have you to know that God intends to save some believers in the lump, but that he intends to save thee in particular. God would

---

49. Proverbs 21:30.

have wicked men to know that he will save a company. But every godly soul should go further to know that God will save me in particular. And if you come not up to this you miss the intent of the spirit of God.

Objection: how shall I come to know that God purposes to save me in particular?

1. That it may be known doth appear by sundry scriptures. "Make your calling and election sure."[50] More particularly, it may be known by those things that God doth work in the hearts of his people. Acts 13:48—All that are "ordained to life" do some time or other believe. You cannot say the like of any wicked man.

2. In the 28 and 29 [verses of] Romans 9, God never predestinates any to life and salvation but he predestinates them to holiness, makes them conformable to the image of his Son (v. 30). If he [= a man] can but clear up his calling [. . .] Art thou effectually called? Then thou art elected—1 Peter 1:2.

Afternoon]

These things are too general—yet more particularly:

"Surely blessing I will bless thee"[51]—so that now, if thou canst find that God hath blessed thee with any spiritual things, that thou hast the qualification of any promise, thou mayest find the counsel of God for thy salvation in particular.

The heirs of promise may be considered in a twofold respect:

1. As coming home to Christ. Now you may know the purpose of God in this, "I shall have wine and milk without price."[52]

2. As already come home to Christ.

These things being promised, now by these four you may know the purpose of God for your salvation:

1. If you can but find that God and Christ and the honor of God and Christ is the main end and aim of your religion and your duties. When we labor that whether we live or die we may [be] accepted of him, this is more than can be in nature.

2. ~~Where the~~ If a person be an heir of the promise he will find a sorrowing and bewailing concerning the frame of his spirit and the thoughts of his heart. Heart sins, inward sins, close sins—do we bewail these? Sorrow them, and so as we can say as Job, "Behold, I am vile; I abhor myself in dust

---

50. 2 Peter 1:10
51. Hebrews 6:14, citing Genesis 22:17
52. Isaiah 55:1

and ashes."[53] If thou findest this thou mayest read the purpose of God for thy salvation.

3. When thou doth desire and endeavor that the image of Christ may be in thee and that thou mayest be ruled by the spirit of Christ, is it the serious thoughts of thy heart that thou wouldst have the image of Christ to shine bright in thee, that thou might walk holily as Christ did, &c?

4. Faith in Christ is another thing whereby any particular person may know whether God does intend to save him or not. "Believe in the Lord Jesus Christ and thou shalt be saved"[54]—faith in Christ for pardon of thy sin, faith in Christ to obtain any good blessing from God.

From these things laid down, if God will but help you to try, you may know the counsel of God concerning you, whether to save you or damn you.

Question two: Why would God have his people to know this? Answer: It's sufficient to tell you that he will have it so: partly that we might believe and partly that we might have strong grounds of consolation. God hath holy ends and aims why he would have us to know his counsel, and all for our good: if we be not in a state of salvation, that we might labor to get into a state of salvation; and being in such a state, might believe it, and believing it might have strong consolation by it.

One use informs us that no man is to be blamed if he does inquire into the counsel of God, so far as it concerns his eternal salvation. If God would have his people to know his counsel and purpose concerning their salvation, then it follows that God would have all men to know whether they shall be saved or damned, and to know it certainly. Ignorance concerning a man's estate is the mother of unbelief. You should as truly know the counsel of God concerning your own salvation as you should know whose sons and daughters you are and ~~whether~~ what your name is.

Art thou fit to die, thinkest thou, when thou dost not know whether thou shalt go to heaven or hell? Do not delay time; time is precious. Till thou knowest thy state and condition thou canst not so honor God as otherwise thou might. Take heed lest through the just judgment of God thou be given over, &c.

He confirmed it by an oath.

There was no need of this on God's part. His word is sufficient. And yet he swears to take away all doubts and distrusts out of our mind. Here let us take notice of our exceeding great weakness, that we will not take God's word.

53. Job 40:4; 42:6
54. Acts 16:31

JULY 22, 1649

Hebrews 6:18

That by two immutable things, in which it was impossible for God to lie, we might have a strong consolation, who have fled for refuge to lay hold upon the hope set before us.

In this verse is set down another end of the oath which God made to Abraham, namely, that he might have strong consolation.

2. You have the means how this is to be obtained: by two immutable things.

3. You have the persons to whom this consolation doth belong: to those who have fled for refuge to lay hold on the hope set before them.

That by two immutable things.

What are these "two immutable things"?
1. God's counsel and decrees touching man's salvation;
2. God's oath. Psalm 110.[55]

Doctrine: The true aim and intent of God in revealing his counsel, in revealing his promise and then confirming it by an oath, is that believers might have strong consolation; that they might have strong consolation in believing and applying what God declares.[56] For God by his promise, and confirming it with an oath, would have his people so to believe his word and apply it as never to doubt or distrust more. John 15:7. "These things have I spoken unto you that your joy might be full."[57] John 17:13. 1 John 1:4—as if he should say, "I write this epistle unto you that you might have strong grounds of consolation."

First reason: because God's command is that we should use the means to know his counsel. God aims at something—that he bids us use the means.

Second reason: the comfort and consolation which flows from promises, it's the children's bread. It's that which properly belongs to the godly. "There is no peace to the wicked, saith my God."[58] Isaiah 65:13, 14.

Third reason: God doth foresee that believers are then fittest for him and his service when they have strong grounds of consolation.

---

55. Psalm 110:4
56. "decleares"
57. John 15:11
58. Isaiah 57:21

One use informs us that the promises apprehended and applied by faith are able to give strong consolation.

1. Whether you respect the matter of the promises, the promises of the Gospel contain sweet comfort. Nothing can trouble thee; but there is something implied in the promises that will help. Or,

2. Whether we respect the person promising, it's God that cannot lie. Or, whether you respect Christ the overseer of the promises, Christ will see that they shall be performed.

Instance what you can that might hinder your comfort. Yet there is in the promises that which will afford strong consolation—against sin, against death, hell, let all combine. Yet there is enough in the promises apprehended by faith to afford strong consolation.

Ezekiel 36:25, 26—If you complain of your filthiness, that you are guilty of much sin, &c, "Then," says God, "I will sprinkle clean water upon you and you shall be clean."[59] If you say, "Though God should pardon my sin yet my heart is so bad and so vild that I shall procure his wrath," &c, then "A new heart will I give thee and a new spirit will I put within thee." If you will say you cannot do [*your*] duty, he tells you he will put his spirit in you. "Yet," says the soul, "I doubt much. I shall not be able to walk with God," &c, therefore "I will cause thee to walk in my statutes and my commandments, and thou shalt do them."[60]

A second use informs us that so far as men do apprehend and apply the promises less or more, so far they have consolation less or more. If men do fully apply the promises to their own souls they shall have strong consolation. If they do little apply the promises they will have less consolation. If no applying promises, no consolation by them. According as you apply promises, so will be your comfort and consolation.

"Now the God of hope fill you with joy and peace in believing."[61] Men have joy and peace by believing. 1 Peter 1:8—"Believing, ye rejoice with joy unspeakable and glorious." Philippians 1:25—"the joy of your faith." Our joy comes from our faith, and so much faith, so much joy.

Afternoon]

Next use: for reproof of all those that do not apply promises. I speak unto God's people that have right to promises. It's the practice of too many to put promises from them. It's Satan's work and a great wile of his to tell

---

59. Ezekiel 36:25
60. Ezekiel 36:27
61. Romans 15:13

God's people that they have no right to promises, and he uses arguments for this end and purpose.

You complain of your corruptions, &c.

1. Tell me, do hypocrites in an ordinary course complain of their corruptions and bewail them, when they are only heart sins, I mean inward and in the frame of spirits?

2. To see and bewail corruption is rather an evidence of grace than otherwise.

3. It's the general frame of God's people that they complain of corruption.

Again, you say you find not that you do mercy nor that you have such gracious qualifications. I answer, there are times when a man may find fruits and times when he cannot. We must look for fruit in its season. You deserve reproof.

1. You do not reach the aim and intent of God, which is that you should apply promises for your strong consolation. "Let not your hearts be troubled"—John 14:14. "Ye believe in God, believe also in me." God would not have the hearts of his people troubled, especially when there is means to the contrary; and therefore the duty is, believe, &c. "Rejoice evermore; yea, again I say, rejoice."[62] A child of God should be careful of this duty, whatever does befall him. Isaiah 52:9.

2. You do exceedingly reject dishonor God and the Gospel while you do thus reject promises that belong unto you. Is it not a dishonor to a Christian of a family when, though he keeps a good family, yet his servants [...]? You give way unto Satan whom you ought not to give place unto. For you are commanded to "resist the devil;"[63] and John 10:4, 5. I hope you hear his voice in the main; but in this particular you hear the devil's voice.

4. Hereby you expose yourself unto manifold temptations, as:

1. To give God the lie, and Christ the lie, and the spirit the lie. He that believes not hath made God a liar. "Did God say that I was his child? I now find it's a lie," says unbelief.

2. You dishearten and discourage yourself in the Lord's work by this frame of spirit. And a man hath little need to be discouraged in the Lord's work. And yet by such thoughts as these you do dishearten and discourage yourself in the Lord's work. Unbelief and distrust makes a man much to neglect duty.

3. You put yourself upon this temptation to live in unbelief, which is a great sin. The spirit shall convince the world of sin because they believe

---

62. Philippians 4:4
63. James 4:7

not. Unbelief is the great sin of the world. He hath shut up all in unbelief. "This is his commandment, that we believe in the son of God."[64] You break a commandment.

And besides, by your unbelief you deprive yourself of the shield of faith. If your faith be gone, the chiefest part of your spiritual armor is gone. And how can you do the Lord's work while you live in unbelief?

The means that God uses to bring thee to strong consolation is propounding of promises and confirming it with an oath. Your unbelief is a rejecting of God's means. And how you will answer God another day for it! Look you to it! Isaiah 61:3. It's Christ's work to comfort disconsolate souls. And doth not he labor to comfort you in all the sermons that you have heard on this text? "Therefore shall ye with joy draw water out of the well-springs of salvation."[65] Aye, but many of you draw water with little comfort. 1 Thessalonians 5:13[66]—"Comfort the feebleminded." How shall we comfort you when you refuse comfort? Isaiah 22:4. We go about to comfort you, and yet you put it off. "Labor not to comfort us." You will stick where you are.

Well I say the Lord reveals thy state and condition to thy soul in his season and humbles thee for thy refusing comfort through the wantonness of thy spirit.

Use last, for exhortation to a twofold duty:

1. Be persuaded that God's revealing promises to you is that you may apply them to your own soul. Be persuaded to be believers.

2. Labor thereby to get strong grounds of consolation. God would have thee have strong consolation. It's your portion. Take your own when God offers it. God would have you to have strong consolation.

JULY 29, 1649

HEBREWS 6:18

Who have fled for refuge to lay hold upon the hope set before us.

Here is a description of the persons to whom the strong consolation doth belong: to those "who have fled for refuge to lay hold on the hope," &c. It's a phrase borrowed from the Levitical law. Numbers 35:6. Deuteronomy 19:3–11. Joshua 20:2, 3, 4, 5, 6. There were to be cities of refuge for those

64. 1 John 3:23
65. See Isaiah 12:3
66. 1 Thessalonians 5:14

that fly from the avengers of blood. It was typical, and typed out their flying to Christ. Man in his natural condition, when God opens his eyes, he sees sin and death and hell and all pursuing him. Now he knows not what to do, but flies to Christ, lays hold on the offers of the Gospel. And that preserves him.

Doctrine: those that from sin, death, hell, and condemnation do fly to Christ ~~for~~ as a refuge, laying hold on the hope before them in the Gospel, they are the persons to whom God swears that he will bless them, and to whom he intends these strong consolations. It's a precious doctrine.

But the persons to whom it belongs are:

1. Such as fly from sin, hell, and condemnation as from the avenger of blood. Says the law, "Thou hast done thus and thus, committed such and such sins." And it pronounces the sentence: "Cursed is he that continues not in all things."[67] The persons are such as are sensible of their lying under this curse, and therefore fly.

2. The persons are such as have such an apprehension of Christ, as that they take him to be a sure refuge to them, and therefore have an honorable esteem of him. It cannot be expected that a man will fly to Christ unless he esteem him a refuge, and a refuge to him in particular to keep him from hell and devils and God's wrath and all.

3. There must be a going higher. The terms must be to forsake all friends and pleasures and to go to the city of refuge. Answerably he that comes to Christ must be willing to part with all and forsake all for Christ.

4. There must be an actual flying to the city of refuge, a coming up to the terms of Christ—actually lay hold on him. If a man does not actually fly to the city of refuge, he hath no benefit by it.

You will say, "Suppose I have done all this. Yet may I not be an hypocrite? May not an hypocrite do all this?" Answer: Some of these things mentioned an hypocrite may do. An hypocrite cannot do all of them.

1. An hypocrite may through the terrors of the law see himself cursed and undone.

2. An hypocrite may see no way to help him but Christ, and therefore esteem of Christ.

3. An hypocrite may seem to desire Christ, and therefore be content to fly to Christ.

But here he fails; he mistakes his own heart in it. Therefore,

4. An hypocrite cannot actually lay hold on Christ further than some fruits of temporary faith.

---

67. Galatians 3:10; Deuteronomy 27:26

"I am not yet satisfied," says the soul, "whether I am any more than an hypocrite." Therefore I will further describe this person by his fore fruits and after fruits:

1. He that flies to Christ as a refuge sees grounds of hope for what he needs and desires suitable to his condition, and upon terms he may have them: "Come," and "here is healing." He sees upon what conditions ~~hath the performance of~~ [?] the good things of the Gospel may be had.

2. He labors to bring his heart to the terms of Christ as in a sort compelled to it. "Can I endure the wrath of God, the flames of hell?" Therefore because he will not perish, he will come to the terms of Christ. Rather than perish he will give up himself wholly to Christ, to be ruled and guided by Christ.

3. When he hath thus labored with his own heart, he actually applies Christ, and lays hold upon him in some promise or proffer of the Gospel. He rests on him. Some know it; others cannot see it. And therefore such I will describe by after fruits:

1. Such a one desires the honor of Christ as the main bent of his spirit and breathes, "Oh, that I could do more for Christ!" And if it were left to his choice what request he would have granted, it should be to honor God more.

2. He groans in his spirit under the body and strength of his daily sins. It is not satisfying to him that Christ hath owned him, but [he] is troubled at overflowing of corruptions.

3. This follows a frequent trading with Christ concerning such sins as are daily discovered to him.

1. In way of pardon: desiring pardon thorough Christ, praying thorough [sic-*through*] Christ they may be pardoned, hoping and believing thorough [sic-*through*] Christ they may be pardoned;

2. In way of power: trading with Christ for power, praying for power, hoping for power, strength to mortify them [sic-*his sins*], he looks upon Christ as the fuller's soap and refiner's fire.[68]

First use informs us that the godly, in the work of conversion, are much drawn on by a principle of self. Necessity compels them. They lay hold on Christ because they are afraid of hell and damnation. I do not deny but there are other things do accompany, but this in a great measure the soul is most sensible of. Therefore fly to Christ, if it be but for your own safety.

Second use informs us that no sinner needs to perish in his sin for want of help or want of remedy; for there is means enough of salvation afforded—offers enough, proffers enough. God takes care that you may not

---

68 Malachi 3:2.

go to hell except the fault be in yourself. This will be the aggravation of your torments in hell.

Afternoon]

Use next: it's for comfort and consolation to all those who fly for a refuge to lay hold on the hope set before them. Hast thou examined thyself by the marks laid down, and will all reach to this, that thou hast actually laid hold on Christ? And canst thou manifest it by any of the fruits? Dost thou labor [to] the honor of God and Christ? Dost thou bewail thy daily sins? And lastly, dost thou trade with Christ, both for pardon of thy daily sins and power and ability to walk better?

If thou dost find these, let me tell thee, thou art one to whom this strong consolation is intended. If you have fled to Christ for a refuge and laid hold on the hope set before you, though your walkings have not been so exact, though they cast never so much dung in your faces, yet it's a ground of precious consolation to you.

Last use: exhorts all of you to labor to fly to Christ as a refuge. The want of flying to Christ and laying hold on the hope set before [them] is the destruction of many a soul. The devil would keep thee from it. But if thou wouldst make sure, work for thyself. Thou must fly to Christ for a refuge. Are you willing to perish in your sins? Are you willing to be deceived that you content yourself without Christ? He that flies to Christ, Christ will in no wise refuse him.

If you will fly to Christ, Christ will secure you. If you might be secured, and will not be secured, the fault will lie upon yourselves. Seeing there is such a remedy, why will you die in your sins? I call on you once again, to fly to Christ as a refuge, and lay hold on the hope.

v. 19. *Which hope we have as an anchor of the soul both sure and steadfast.*

The Apostle compares the state of the soul to seamen on a ship riding at anchor. A good anchor, seamen make great account of. Now the Apostle tells you this hope is an anchor, and describes the anchor to be "sure and steadfast, entered within the veil."[69]

Doctrine: though God's people have not full profession of those things offered in the Gospel, yet they have fast hold of them by faith and hope. God's people are like children under age. They have but a little of their

---

69. Hebrews 6:19

father's estate in comparison of what they shall have when they come to have their full inheritance.

2. Though they have but a little, yet the godly have fast hold of that which is behind. Hebrews 11. Romans 5:2—"and rejoice in hope of the glory of God."

First use shows us the reason why God's people sundry times are so borne up in their spirits concerning those things that they have waited for.

2. Hence it follows that though God's people, while they live in this life, are but in a poor condition. Yet in a sort they are in a rich condition in this life. You possess something, but it's but little in comparison of what you shall enjoy.

Objection: you tell us we have fast hold of it by faith and hope. But may not our fast hold be lost, and so the thing itself be lost? Answer: There is a great deal of difference betwixt letting our hold go in our apprehensions, and letting our hold go really and indeed. The actings of faith and hope may be gone, and yet there is faith and hope in the soul, for it cannot be lost.

2. If it were possible that faith and hope could be lost, yet the thing hoped for cannot be lost, because it is not in our keeping.

Second doctrine: the state and condition of God's people is such as they are subject to much tossing and tumbling. And yet notwithstanding all, the anchor of their hope holds.

AUGUST 5, 1649

Hebrews 6:19

Which hope we have as an anchor of the soul.

He describes this hope:
    1. By comparing it to an anchor;
    2. by the properties of it:
    1. It's sure;
    2. Steadfast;
    3. It entereth that within the veil, according to Exodus 26:32, 36.
    It is a type of heaven; Hebrews 10:19, 20.

The state and condition of God's people is resembled to a ship on the water, which is subject to tossings and tumblings and therefore hath need of an anchor.

Doctrine: the godly are subject to tossings and tumblings, to troubles and temptations, as a ship at sea is subject to tossings by waves and tempest. By troubles and temptations I mean both inward and outward trouble.

1. Outward, such as concerns a man's outward [*affairs*]—any that affects the outward man: our good name subject to many infamies, our estates to losses, &c, our bodies to sickness—and these are troubles.

2. Inward troubles, such as concern the inward man: soul troubles, troubles of conscience, troubles about a man's spiritual condition, temptation to sin, Satan following, God hiding his face, &c.

How come the godly to be subject to these troubles?

Partly thorough their own folly and weakness;

Partly thorough corruptions;

Partly thorough God's trying them, or chastening them;

Partly thorough the malice of the common enemy of mankind.

1. Through their own folly and weakness, as by negligence and not using the means to prevent these troubles.

2. Sometimes through the strength of corruption, corruption being strong.

3. Satan's temptations that make God's people so subject to troubles. His main work is to run to and fro and to compass the earth to do what mischief he can. Satan puts in both himself and what instruments he can. He is as "a roaring lion."[70]

4. It sometimes comes from God, partly trying his people and partly as a just judgment. Men through their careless walking cause God to give them over to be buffeted by temptations.

First use informs us that a man may be a godly man and yet be strangely exercised with tossings and tumblings, both outwards and inward. Great troubles, strange troubles, and temptations the godly may be exercised under, and yet remain a child of God.

Second use for comfort to God's people in the midst of all their troubles and temptations. Count it not strange in the midst of such temptations. Do you know all the experiences of other godly persons?

Which hope we have as an anchor of the soul, sure and steadfast.

Doctrine: hope is to the souls of the godly as an anchor is to the ship.

1. The anchor is necessary for the ship—so necessary that no wise seamen will ever go to sea without it. Answerably hope is as necessary for a Christian. For a man to enter upon profession without hope, he will lose all.

---

70. 1 Peter 5:8

2. The anchor is for a ship to hold by, and a ship hath nothing to hold itself by in a storm if its anchor be gone. Answerably take hope away from the soul and it hath nothing to hold by. For in many troubles, many trials, temptations, the child of God hath nothing but hope to hold—by no other help.

3. The anchor keeps the ship fast and unmovable in its place, without danger while it holds. So the godly, while their hope holds, all is well. There is no danger that while—a man is never in any danger while he doth depend on God; and while he doth wait on God the issue will prove gracious. "They shall have a blessing at the latter end." Psalm 22:4, 5.[71]

Inquire here:
1. What this hope is.
2. What kind of hope is here meant.
3. The properties of it.

What hope is: Hope is a virtue whereby we are inclined to the expectation of those things from God that he hath promised us.[72] The exercise of this hope lies much in expectation. Philippians 1:12; Psalm 40:1; Romans 8:25. Hope acts upon things in relation to future. And three things must concur for the object of hope:

1. That the thing we hope for be good, for else we rather fear it, than hope for it.
2. It must be difficult.
3. It must be a thing to come that we have not yet.

There is a double property of hope:

First, the text tells you it's sure and steadfast. It's firm, it will not deceive or fail a man, and therefore it is that "hope makes not ashamed." Romans 5:5. Isaiah 40:31.

Second property: it's entered into that "within the veil."[73] It's entered in heaven: our hope is in heaven. Romans 8:24. We are saved by hope. Psalm 2:12—"Blessed are all they that hope in him." It's so sure, as it brings a man to a state of blessedness. Psalm 84, ultimate verse—"Blessed is the man that trusteth in thee."[74]

---

71. Psalm 24:4,5

72. Ames, *The Marrow of Sacred Divinity* (first Latin edition, 1623; English translation, 1643), II, vi.1:"Hope is a vertue, whereby we are inclined to expect those things which God hath promised us. Rom. 8. 25. 2." See Eusden, *The Marrow of Theology*, 245.

73. Hebrews 6:19

74. Psalm 84:12

Afternoon]

First use: is it thus that hope is to the soul as the anchor to the ship? Then it shows us the reason why Satan does act so much against our faith and hope. When God seems to hide his face and withdraw himself from the soul, Satan works upon it. His main reason is he wants to take our hope from us. If Satan can take your hold from you, then you are left. You may sink or swim or what you will. What a spite and mischief would it be if an adversary should come and cut the cable and let the anchor go! The ship is lost in a storm. So Satan taking away your hope does you a great spite and mischief.

Second use: lets us see what kind of hope this is that is as an anchor to the soul, that is sure and will hold. Every kind of hope will not hold. But it's such hope as:

1. Is placed in God, bottomed in God.

2. Such a hope as carries a man on in the use of means to obtain that which God hath promised, in the use of those means that God hath appointed for that end and purpose.

3. This hope of the godly is subject to changes: sometimes stronger and sometimes weaker.

Next use: serves to reprove all wicked men that have no hope. Or if you have any it's not sound hope, but you place your hope on something else besides God. Such a kind [of] hope in plain speaking is no hope. No wonder therefore if wicked men be put upon such kind of tossings and disquietings as they are. When they have no anchor, no fast hold, then they must make what other shifts they can. Do you not think that Judas had hopes concerning his spiritual state? And yet his hopes, proving but the hopes of an hypocrite, what became of him?

Next use: for comfort and consolation to all the godly, all that have this anchor. The God of hope hath filled you with hopes and strong consolation. It's much that God hath done for you. Look into the experience that you have had. And have you not found the hopes that you have had by this scripture and the other scriptures much bearing up your spirits and comforting you in times of affliction? It's often. In Psalm 119—"I have waited for thy salvation."[75] Your hopes have upheld you and preserved you. Can you not say that from time to time God hath been your hope? When outward troubles have been on you, and inward troubles, God hath been your hope.

Use last, for exhortation to a double duty:

---

75. Psalm 119:174

1. Such of you as have no sound hopes, get hopes. Labor to repent of what you have done and come in unto Jesus Christ.

1. Such of you as never saw yourselves undone and lost and in a miserable condition, labor to see yourself in a miserable condition, without God, Christ, and the hope of salvation.

2. When you see yourself without hope, labor to attain it. Fly to the refuge. Get an anchor that will hold, hope that is sound. And lest you should mistake false hope for sound, my advice is that you go to those that are better able to discern than thyself. Desire their help, lest you build your hope upon uncertain sandy foundation, and fail you in a storm; or if your hopes be built upon good grounds, yet not knowing it. How doth Satan hinder the actings of your hope?

3. When you have gotten this hope, make use of it. Use and exercise your hope, else you will be as David was in Saul's armor.[76] For you to have hopes and yet not know how to make use of them, how unsuitable is this to religion. When a man hath done all that he can, striving and pleading against hope, yet you must be necessitated to put forth actings of hope, even for your own safety. What will become of poor creatures if they do not exercise faith and hope?

You have many encouragements to hope in God—encouragements from the experience of others. And you have encouragements from the scriptures—invitations and promises. Yea, the benefits of hope might exceedingly encourage you.

Put forth your hope, therefore. You have an anchor that, if you can but keep to it, you shall come to heaven in spite of all hell devils' army. Pray that the God of hope would fill you with hope. Make use of your hope.

You have heard a great deal out of this Hebrews 6, and when God may afford me the like opportunity to call on you again I know not. If you be not the better for all, he may justly deny you the like opportunity again.

---

76. 1 Samuel 17:38–39

AUGUST 12, 1649

Hebrews 6:20

Whither the forerunner is for us entered, even Jesus,
made an high priest for ever after the order of Melchisedeck.

Two main propositions are in this verse. First, from the former part of the verse:

Doctrine: Jesus Christ our forerunner is entered into heaven for his people. Here are sundry things to be opened:

1. When did Christ enter into heaven?
2. Why did Christ enter into heaven?
3. Why is Christ said to be our forerunner?

First, when did Christ enter into heaven? Answer: at his ascension.

Second, why did Christ ascend into heaven? Answer: There is a double [reason]:

1. In John 14—"I go to prepare a place for you."[77]
2. End of Christ ascending into heaven is to make intercession for his people; to do the office of a mediator.

Third thing to be opened is, why is Christ our forerunner? There are many to go to heaven, and Christ goes before to make the better preparation for them.

First use informs us that the hope of God's people should be in heaven, where Christ is. To place your hopes upon men, upon the creatures, &c, these may fail you, will fail you. But Christ will never fail. Place your hopes on Christ your forerunner, therefore.

Second, it informs us that Christ is the forerunner to all the godly. He is gone before you, and therefore you may conclude with yourself the time will come that you shall follow him.

Third, "he is entered for us." It informs us that the godly have the benefit of Christ's ascension. It's not so much for himself as for our good that he as mediator sits at the right hand of God.

Next use serves to reprove all those that are without God, without Christ, and consequently without anchor of hope for their salvation. Christ is entered into heaven for the godly. But what benefit have the wicked by it? Christ is not a forerunner for you. He is entered into heaven, but what hopes have you to go after? None at all, that are sound.

---

77. John 14:3

Use for comfort and consolation to all the godly: Christ is your forerunner. It assures all the godly that nothing shall hinder their salvation, but they shall as surely come to heaven in their time as Christ is gone thither before. John 12.[78] John 14:3. This may exceedingly rejoice the godly. Nothing can hinder your salvation.

Use last, exhorts to those duties that do arise from hence:

1. Labor to place your hopes in Christ. Get strong hopes in Christ. The more your hopes do act upon Christ, the more benefit and advantage it will be unto yourselves. I told you, "hope makes not ashamed."[79] Keep your hope firm on Christ. Therefore let your anchor be in heaven. Continue your hope. Let it hold out under all trials and afflictions. Though Satan may toss and tumble you, yet say, "My hope is in heaven, and I shall one day come there. He cannot hinder that."

2. Labor to fit yourself. Christ is gone before, you must follow after. Therefore prepare for it. Is disorderly walking the way to fit yourself for heaven? Oh, no! Labor to be without spot or wrinkle. Duty lies upon you to strive against all corruption.

3. Labor to apply it to your own soul, that Christ is gone before to heaven, for you. His being in heaven is an advantage for you.

Second doctrine is from the latter part of the verse: note that Christ is a Priest forever after Melchizedek's order.

Afternoon]

"Forever"—it is before the foundation of the world and to eternity. "After the Order of Melchizedek." Two things are here to be inquired into:

1. What is meant by Melchizedek?
2. What by the order of Melchizedek?

1. What is meant by Melchizedek? Melchizedek properly signifies "King of Peace" or righteousness. The story we must fetch from the 17 and 18 [*verses of*] Genesis 14. It's much controverted among divines who this Melchizedek should be, some interpreting it one way, some another. In Hebrews 7 he is said to be without father, without mother, &c.[80] Some hence think him to be some King of Canaan extraordinarily raised up. This to me is most unlikely. Some think him to be the Holy Ghost, without father, mother, &c, and like the Son of God. "Who can this be?" say they, "but the Holy Ghost?" Others say think him to be Christ himself. But then Christ should be a type of Christ, which is impossible. What shall we think, then?

78. John 12:26, etc.
79. Romans 5:5
80. Hebrews 7:3

That which I pitch upon, is that Melchizedek was Shem.[81] You will say Shem was dead before Abraham's days. I say it's but conjecture. Inquire into the genealogy and you will find that he was alive in Abraham's days till after Isaac was born. Now they that search the Jewish writers shall find they had a high account of Shem, and therefore it's not impossible but that this Melchizedek was Shem. By the name Shem he was known, but by the name Melchizedek he had neither father nor mother, &c.

2. What was the order of Melchizedek? Or wherein doth Melchizedek's order differ from the order of other priests?

Now then it's to be inquired into, wherein these two to differ. I shall not reckon all the differences, but only the most material.

1. Melchizedek was made a priest without any calling from man or without any ordination from man into that office. He was immediately called by God to that office. Aaron had a calling from man with certain ceremonies, pouring oil, &c.

2. The order of Aaron's priesthood [. . .]

3. This Melchizedek, we never read that his order was continued by succession.

To open a little more the priesthood of Christ. It's a large subject, but I intend to be brief and therefore shall only gather up the most considerable things.

Wherein lies the priesthood of Christ? It lies mainly in two things:

1. In his oblation;

2. In applying it by his intercession.

First, Christ must offer a sacrifice, and that is himself. Hebrews 9:26. Christ as priest laid down his life. No man took it from him. He was offered to bear the sins of many; and Ephesians 5:2—"Christ hath given himself for us a sacrifice to God of a sweet smelling savor." Christ was both the Altar priest and sacrifice. Revelation 8:3. Isaiah 53:4, 5.

Second thing wherein the priesthood of Christ lies is in the application of it by his intercession. He applies it to all those for whom it was intended, and therefore he is said to sit "at the right hand of God" to "make intercession for us."[82]

We are to conceive that the intercession of Christ is not as man's intercession is. He doth not kneel down before his father and say [. . .] &c, as man doth. But he makes intercession by presenting himself and his sacrifice

---

81. Following Hugh Broughton, *A treatise of Melchisedek: proving him to be Sem* (1591). "The summe being cast, Sem is founde to outlyue Abraham his nephew in the tenth degree thirtie and fiue yeeres." 20R

82. Romans 8:34

before God. And he unmoveably wills and desires that such and such things may be done for the elect.

What necessity was there that Christ should thus become a priest?

1. There was so much guilt and wrath contracted by man that there was no other way to reconcile God and man. Though we should commit no sin of our own, yet Adam's sin, the guilt and wrath that is contracted thereby, is such as cannot be taken away without this priest, the sacrifice of Christ himself. One man may intercede for another. But who is there to stand betwixt God and man, but only Christ Jesus, the high priest?

2. There is a necessity of this priesthood because of the impotency and inability of man to [*save*] himself. If any could help themselves, the damned in hell would. But they cannot; they are bound hand and foot.

What benefit hath the godly by the priesthood of Christ? The benefit lies in diverse things. It's an endless benefit, an unconceivable benefit.

First, we are thereby so reconciled to God as that we have fellowship with God and Christ, that they may be one with us. The wicked have no fellowship with God; the godly have.

Second, hereby we have the spirit of God. And all that the spirit doth for us, it's founded in this: John 14:16, 17. Romans 8:26.

Third benefit that we have hereby, is strength against our corruption by the sanctification of our natures.

Fourth benefit is the sanctification of our services so as to make our services acceptable. 1 Peter 2:5—we are said to "offer up spiritual services acceptable to God by Jesus Christ."

Fifth benefit is boldness and confidence to come before God in prayer. We may come boldly, seeing we have such a high priest as this to make intercession for us. Hebrews 4:14. Hebrews 10:12.

1. Is it thus, that Jesus Christ is a priest for ever after the Order of Melchizedek? Then it reproves the ungodly and wicked that are without Christ. Is Christ a priest? The more is your misery. The godly have benefit by his priestly office. But you will not lay hold upon it, and so you have no benefit by it, but will perish in your sins. Christ offered himself a sacrifice, but not for you; he prays not for any wicked. It's your misery that you are wicked and if you die in your wickedness you will perish eternally.

2. It serves for comfort and consolation to the godly. Christ is a priest for you; great is your happiness! Christ is a sacrifice for your sins and he hath satisfied the justice of God, reconciled God to thee. And if God be reconciled to thee, there is nothing but love, fatherly affections, towards you. All your services are accepted—services, prayers, persons, graces—all accepted thorough the mediation of Christ. You have a friend in the court—a Christ sitting at the right hand of God to make intercession for you.

3. Use exhorts you when you have committed any sin, fly to the priestly office of Christ. He is the Lamb of God that takes away the sins of the world. Let faith act upon Christ. Come with boldness to the throne of grace, &c. He makes your prayers and services accepted. Therefore make use of him. Believe in him and rely upon him.

SEPTEMBER 16, 1649[83]

JOB 31:1

I ~~have~~ made a covenant with mine eyes;
why then should I think upon a maid?

In this chapter Job makes a declaration of his life in sundry particulars, wherein you have several properties of a godly man.

The first thing he mentions is his carefulness to prevent unchastity. He "made a covenant" with his eyes, for which he renders three reasons:

1. Because the fear of God was before his eyes;
2. Because he feared God's judgment;
3. Because else there were not portion for himself.

"I made a covenant with mine eyes." That is, there hath been in me such a carefulness, and conscientious, strict endeavor, as if his eyes had been under a covenant.

"Why then should I think upon a maid?" It's an interrogation carrying with it the force of a negation, as much as if he should say, "I cannot ~~look~~ think upon a maid." Why is it not lawful to think on a maid? In some sense it is, and in some sense it is not. To think upon a maid to lust after her, lusting thoughts—it is that makes the matter sinful.

Doctrine: it's the duty of all men in general, and the care of good men in particular, to keep their eyes and thoughts as under a covenant.

Job's meanings: "I have pitched a reflection and am careful in the practice of it, not to pitch my eyes upon any sinful, unchaste object. Nay farther, not to let my thoughts run upon any unchastity; and for this end, as it were, [*I*] engaged myself in a covenant." Thus should all men do.

Solomon in Proverbs 4:23 gives direction concerning the heart.

First reason: because the eyes are as it were the doors or windows of the house to let in what ought not to be let in. So the heart of man is as it

---

83. "The 1st Sabbath after my return from the Bay"

were the house; the eyes, ears, and other senses are as the doors to let in. James 1:14,15.

There may be many instances of much corruption let into the heart by the eye that drew Eve into that great [*sin*]. She saw the fruit, that it was pleasant, and so took and ate. The sight of the eye brought her into the great soul-damning sin of the world. Genesis 34—Shechem saw Dinah, that she was beautiful, and took her and defiled her; and Genesis 38:15—Judah saw Tamar. The wickedness was let into the heart by that which the eye saw. So David, 1 Samuel 11, saw a woman washing herself.[84] He should have guarded himself and turned away his eyes; but the temptation stayed upon him. So Genesis—it's said of Joseph's mistress, "She cast her eyes upon Joseph and said, 'Lie with me.'"[85] So Achan, Joshua 7:21—"I saw the wedge of gold and the Babylonish garment, and I coveted it, and took it."

In point of idolatry, Ahaz going to Damascus, 2 Kings 16, sees an Altar, and the seeing it sets his heart on work that he will have such a one made.[86] Proverbs 23:11—"Look not upon the wine when it's red in the cup"—implying that the eyes seeing it will entice a man to drunkenness. This is the first reason why men must be careful to keep[87] their eyes.

Second reason: because good men are careful to avoid the occasions of sin as well as sin itself. And the same commandment that bids us avoid ~~of occasions~~ any sin bids us also to avoid the occasions of it. Proverbs 1:10 and then v. 15—"My son, walk not thou," &c. The Lord requires that not only sin be avoided, but the very occasions of it.

First use informs us what a difference there is betwixt good men and bad, a godly heart and a wicked. Good men are careful to avoid the occasions of sin, sinful thoughts. "Why should I think upon a maid?" But an unsound heart makes little conscience of thoughts.

Second use informs us that the patriarchs that [*did*] go before the law was given were as careful to avoid sin as the godly since the law was given. They were not loose and careless because there was no law written. Job before the law was a careful, conscientious man as any nowadays.

Use next, serves to reprove all those that are loose spirited, that take no care of their thoughts and looks, a carnal heart so he can keep himself without the compass of the magistrate. He looks no further—gives way to unchaste thoughts, and unchaste actions too. If it were only the sin of the younger! If it were only [?]. It's certain the heart is a very den of devils and

---

84. 2 Samuel 11:2-4
85. Genesis 29:7
86. 2 Kings 16:10
87. guard

cage of unclean birds[88] that is not careful of thoughts and looks. Giving way to the eyes to see inflames the heart, pleasant before the eyes of such things and the other; and the heart is inflamed with it, and caught unaware. It's certain a man must be more than a man ~~if he can~~ that can avoid committing of sin sometime or other, if he be not careful of his thoughts and looks.

And the truth is, if you will be loose, you do not know how far God may leave you. ~~while such~~ A man cannot always quench a fire when he please. The best is therefore to prevent or quench it in the beginning.

I add further, [the] very looks may be sinful in themselves, and thoughts, though they never come to action. Matthew 5:28—he that looks upon a maid "to lust after her hath committed adultery with her in his heart." So much the heart is unchaste, so much it trades in unchaste looks and unchaste thoughts. And the very looks where the eyes are not guarded, though there be no other sin follow, yet may be such and so displeasing to God as may bring fearful judgments.

Afternoon]

Use next, for exhortation to all men, young and old, one and other, to labor to prevent sin betimes.[89] Look to your thoughts. Look to your looks. Keep your eyes, your ears, the whole man, lest the members of the body become instruments of iniquity.

First direction: let everyone get strong arguments to persuade himself of the necessity.

First, that may be an argument which shows you the evil of such a course, if the spirit be possessed with this, that there is a great deal of evil in such courses. They are a sin against God, a shame to me [sic-*men*], a dishonor to men. Think, how could I look my friends in face if my thoughts should proceed to actions? Consider first if thou give way to wandering thoughts and looks, it's just with God, thou shouldst go further. And if the Lord do leave thee to thyself, who can tell where thou mayest stop? For a little sin begets an aptitude to more. Get such arguments as these to help thee. Proverbs 21. ult.[90]

Second direction: labor to maintain strong and sound principles within, in your spirits, against such loose and vain carriages: principles of modesty which makes persons to be ashamed and blush at anything that's shameworthy. When men and women have left the principles of modesty, they are laid open to temptation. Advances in gestures and carriages may

---

88. Revelation 18:2
89. beforehand
90. The last verse of the chapter, Proverbs 21:31—"safety is of the Lord."

weaken modesty—unsuiting speeches, &c. If the principles of modesty be gone, no wonder if you are not ashamed of that which is shameworthy. Maintain the fear of God in you, which is the best principle of all. This principle among the rest: the shame of men.

Look to yourself, especially when the time of trial and temptation comes. When a temptation to such and such a sin comes, then use the time of trial. That is the very instant time when you should make use of all. If you have sound principles at other times, and cannot make use of them at that very instant that the temptation doth beset you and besiege you, it will not be so excellent.

4. Pray over whatever resolutions, purposes, considerations, or meditations you have concerning this matter. "Except the Lord keep the city, the watchmen watch in vain." David says, "Turn away mine eyes from beholding vanity."[91] When men have strong resolutions of their own and they are but their own resolutions, they may sooner fall than they are aware of. Therefore look up to God.

Why then should I think upon a maid?

Doctrine: where there is a conscientiousness over the looks, that they be not sinful, there will be conscientiousness over the thoughts also. But I shall not insist on this.

v. 2. *For what portion of God is there from above,* &c.

Here Job tells you one reason why he pitched upon such a resolution, &c: "When I consider what portion of God is to them that be unchaste, if I should [*be*] wanton, what can I expect?"

Doctrine: It's a great help for preventing of sin to consider beforehand what portion or reward we are to expect from God for such sins.

Reason: because the heart, when it weighs things well and is in debate about sin, it usually fears both God and his judgment.

Use for comfort to the godly that find these considerations in their own hearts.

Use last: for exhortation to all the godly, that you will arouse yourselves with some considerations and meditations that may help you against sin.

---

91. Psalm 127:1; Psalm 119:37

SEPTEMBER 30, 1649

JOB 31:3

Is not destruction to the wicked?
and a strange punishment to the workers of iniquity?

You have heard what moved Job to give an account of his walking and to make profession of what duties he was careful of, namely, Eliphaz' unjust accusation against him. In the first place, he manifests his care to avoid unchastity, v. 1; and he renders his reason of it, v. 2—"What portion of God is there to such," (which you have heard of it). And now he goes further: "Is there not destruction to the wicked?," as if he should say, "If I take liberty to unchastity, God will ~~destroy me~~ punish me and bring destruction upon me."

Doctrine: destruction and strange punishment is the portion of wicked men and workers of iniquity.

What is meant by "destruction"? Answer: outward plagues and punishments here in this life. And in scripture phrase, eternal misery; that is called destruction also. 2 Thessalonians 1:9. That destruction is the portion of the wicked appears [*from*] Proverbs 21:15 and Job 21:30. Psalm 73:27. Psalm 92:7, 9. In Isaiah 1:28, it's threatened. The destruction of the sinners and transgressors shall be together and they that forsake the Lord shall be consumed; and Psalm 7:11, 13, 15. Thus you see destructions to the wicked.

Let us look into the next part of the doctrine, that strange punishments are to workers of iniquity, and you will find plentiful instance of it in scripture. Begin with Cain, Genesis 4:11, and you will find a strange punishment inflicted upon him. Genesis 7—the old world, all excepting Noah's family, had strange punishments inflicted on them, that all must be drowned. And Genesis 9:25—Ham was accursed, and is accursed to this day. Sodom and Gomorrah that followed strange flesh had a strange punishment inflicted on them, that they were burnt up with fire.

So likewise we shall find a strange punishment upon Haman and Sachem and Er and Onan; Genesis 38:7, 9. The text says of one he was wicked, therefore the Lord slew him; of the other, he displeased the Lord, and he slew him. Nadab and Abihu. Korah, Nathan [sic-*Dathan*], and Abiram—the earth swallow them up for stubbornness and rebellion. The forty-seven[92] children for mocking and deriding the prophet; a bear comes out of the wilderness and tears him [sic-*them*] in pieces. A strange punishment! Judas for betraying Christ, a strange punishment befell him: he hangs himself, and

---

92. 2 Kings 2:23–24 puts the number at forty-two.

Acts 1, he falls and bursts asunder in the midst and his bowels gushed out. Acts 13:23—Herod, a worker of iniquity, was eaten up of worms. These are but a handful of instances. Both the scripture and other histories are plentiful in giving instances of strange punishments to wicked men.

First use: lets us see the misery of wicked men and workers of iniquity. "Aye," you will say, "such are miserable. But I hope I am no wicked man." And so everyone hopes of himself, though he have no more saving grace in him than the soles of his shoes. It's the devil's work to persuade that you are better than you are, for while the strong man keeps the house all is in peace.

Some of you, whose wickedness is apparent to all—yet when I have come to speak with you, I have found you persuaded that Christ was yours—you do not see your wickedness, and eternal destruction hanging over your head. Are there not among you such as live in lying and are not[93] liars, workers of iniquity? Are there not among you disobedient to governors: proud persons, unchaste persons? If you should be asked particularly, "Do not you think you are workers of iniquity?," what could you answer? Well whether you fear strange punishments or not, God's justice hath intended it. And so sure as the Book of God speaks it, you shall find destruction come on you when time comes, unless God make you better men hereafter. Proverbs 11:21. Proverbs 16:5. Consider seriously of it.

Are you willing God should break in upon you with everlasting judgments? Or would you avoid destruction to your souls? Then:

1. Labor to come out of your condition, and labor to be godly. Lay aside your working of iniquity and strive to do that which is just and holy, and God will take away the punishments threatened against you and bestow on you blessing everlasting. Therefore labor to come out of thy natural condition. Hast thou not been vild long enough? Be not wicked overmuch. Let not the devil have all your time. Now at last before God, hath [he] not called on you, preserved you fair? Then give up yourself to the ways of Jesus Christ.

2. Labor to avoid sin. All of you godly, one other [sic-*another*], let me exhort you to take heed of sin. Sin is displeasing to God, and he will bring strange punishments for sin, even upon the godly. David was followed with strange punishments for his working iniquity. Hezekiah, &c.[94] Avoid sin as you would avoid God's judgment. If you be about to sin, think with yourself, it will bring destruction on you.

Afternoon]

---

93. unnecessary extra word?

94. 2 Kings 20:1–5

v. 4. *Doth he not see my ways and count all my steps*[95]

This is another reason why Job was so careful to prevent unchastity: because God sees and takes notice of all that he doth. "Doth he not see my ways and count all my steps,"[96] as if he should say. "I could do nothing in secret but God would see it, and when I considered it, the fear of his all-seeing eye did overawe me."

Hence observe two doctrines:

1. God doth see all men's ways and take notice of all their actions.

2. The consideration of Gods all-seeing eye will keep men from sinning.

For the first doctrine: God sees all men's ways and takes notice of all their actions. Proverbs 5:21. Proverbs 15:3. We shall find the scripture ascribes unto God all that men do. When there was wrangling in the congregation, it's said the Lord heard it, took special notice of it. And as the Lord takes notice of speeches, so also of thoughts. Deuteronomy 31:21. God knows the hearts of men. Proverbs 15:11—"Hell and destruction are before the Lord, how much more the hearts of the children of men?" 1 Samuel 16:7. The Lord knows and sees the actions of men before they are done. The Lord knows what men will do. Exodus 3:19; 1 Samuel 9:15.

First reason is taken from the power of God in creation. Thus, God creates man, and creates all things besides man. Now he that created all things knows what is in man that he hath thus made and created.

Second reason: God is to judge the world another day, and to judge the world in righteousness, to render unto every man according to his deeds. Now if he must render unto every man according unto his deeds, then he must know what is in man and what he doth, and so ~~accordingly~~ take notice of all that man does, that he may be able to pass righteous judgment. It's often spoken of God in scripture that he renders unto every man "according to his deeds," which is impossible unless God knows the deeds of all men.[97]

Third, to question whether God knows the hearts of men is to make God like a creature that knows things but according to the circumstances of time, place, and person—which were atheism.

Fourth, if God does not know the hearts of all the sons of men he is unfit to be worshipped. We may flatter, deceive, be hypocritical, and what we will, if God did not know it.

First use serves to inform us of our duty towards God even in this, that religious worship is due to him, if he knows our thoughts, our actions,

---

95. "steeps"
96. Job 31:4; "steeps"
97. Romans 2:6

our hearts. The heart is desperately wicked; who knows that? Aye, the Lord knows it. Therefore he is worthy of all religious worship.

Second use serves as a ground of comfort and consolation to all the godly. It's a great happiness to you that you have to deal with God that knows your heart. He that knows your heart, your temptations, your troubles, your corruptions, your requests, will help you, and do for you what is good. 2 Chronicles 16:9. Psalm 38:9—"Lord, all my desire was before thee and my groaning is not hid from thee." This is a comfort to the child of God. So Hezekiah: "Thou knowest that I have walked before thee with a good, perfect heart."[98] Is not this a great comfort to a godly soul, that God knows this? Says Abimelech, Genesis 20:4, 5—"Thou knowest that in the integrity of my heart I have done this." This was his comfort, that God knew it. Psalm 56:8—"Thou tellest my wanderings and putest my tears in thy bottle; are they not in thy book?"

Third use: it's for terror to the wicked. Doth God know all your wanderings and count all your steps? It's your misery. It were a great happiness to you if God took no notice of your walking. He looks to the ends of the earth and seeth all under the heavens; the more is the misery of wicked men. Psalm 90:8. Though you can hide your wickedness from man, yet you cannot from God. He knows it, and takes notice of it. There is no juggling with God. Proverbs 24:12—"Doth not he that pondereth the heart know it, and will not he render unto every man according to his work?" It argues a great degree of atheism in the sons of men that they do not consider [this].

Fourth use: for exhortation, to set God before your eyes always. Consider God. Behold all your ways, and stand in awe of his presence. 1 Samuel 2:3. Take heed what you do: God is a God of knowledge. God weighs your actions, your speeches, your frames of spirit. Set God always at your right hand.

OCTOBER 14, 1649

Psalm 86:11

I will walk in thy truth.

This Psalm was penned by David under some straits and difficulties, and therefore [he] begs God to make known his way unto him: "Teach me thy

---

98. 2 Kings 20:3

way." You heard of this last [Lord's] Day. Now says he, "I will walk in thy truth." That is his resolution.

"Truth" is taken four ways in scripture:

1. It's sometimes taken for that which we call truth in speeches and doctrine: "Speak every man the truth to his neighbor," &c.[99] Galatians 3:14.[100]

2. Truth is taken for sincerity and integrity in opposition to dissimulation and hypocrisy. Philippians 1:18.

3. Truth is taken as it stands in opposition to legal ceremonies and conceits of men's [ani?] in the worship of God.

4. Truth is taken sometimes for the way of well and right living according to God, and thus it's opposed to unrighteousness. Romans 2:8; 1 Peter 22.[101] And in this last sense I take the word "truth" here in the text: "I will walk in thy truth," that is, in thy way, according to thy rule.

Doctrine: it's the purpose of the godly, and it ought to be their serious endeavor, to walk in God's way so far as God makes it known unto them. For proof: Psalm 119:33, 34; Psalm 119:106. In the doctrine are two points:

1. That it's the purpose of the godly to walk in God's way so far as God makes it known unto them.

2. They do accordingly desire and endeavor to walk in that way which God reveals unto them.

For the first:

One reason, because the hearts of the godly are fitted to do God's will, when God makes it known unto them. If we look into the godly we shall find such a spirit in them as this [in] David. And Numbers 14:24—Caleb followed God fully. The same may be said of Joshua. Romans 6:17. 1 Thessalonians 5:23. Jeremiah 33:31—"I will put my law into their hearts and write my law in their inward parts." If God will do this, then the godly have a heart to obey his law. It was wont to be the prayer of Austin, "Lord, give me a heart to do what thou commandest and then command what thou wilt."[102]

The heart is carried on by a three-fold motive:

1. They see God commanding them, for when God makes known my duty, it implies a command, and a gracious heart takes it [as] his work [to?] do the commands of God.

---

99. Ephesians 4:25

100. Galatians 5:14

101. 1 Peter 1:22

102. Moxon conflates two quotations. The Augustine quotation is from Confessions, 10.29.40: "Give what you command, and command what you will." The additional words are from Puritan devotional writings.

2. They are encouraged by this: the commands that God hath annexed to walk in his word. There is no duty that God commands but he hath promised to help us to do it.

3. This motive helps [*to go*] forward. When God hath made known a duty, if the heart should not purpose and desire it, God will be displeased. He fears, "God will be highly offended." To want the smiles of God's love is punishment enough to a gracious heart.

For the second part of the doctrine, which is, it ought to therefore be the serious desire of the godly, and endeavor, to walk in that way that God reveals, to do what they purpose to do. This appears by two considerations:

1. Every purpose that is according to God doth necessarily call for and require performances. Psalm 119:106—"I have sworn, and I will perform that I will keep thy right judgments." Psalm 39:1, 2. Ruth 1:16, 17, 18—according as she had purposed, she performs. So Daniel 1:8, when he came to the Babylonian Court he resolved not to defile him [sic-*himself*] with uncleanness, and then he performed accordingly.

2. The end of God's making known his will to us is that we may do it, and therefore we should be very careful to perform what duties God reveals.

Afternoon]

First use informs us what a difference there is betwixt the spirits of the godly and the spirits of the wicked. The godly, when they know their duty, desire to perform it. The wicked do not, except in time of special conviction. And then a Pharaoh may resolve to do God's will. But naturally the frame of every wicked man is according to Job 21:14—"Depart from us. We desire not the knowledge of thy law;" and Romans.[103] Jeremiah 18:12—"We will walk after our own devices and we will every one do the imaginations of our own hearts." But the godly—now, they are steadfastly purposed in their hearts to do whatsoever God reveals unto them to be their duty.

2. Use for reproof of two sorts of people:

Firstly, the wicked that have no desires, no purposes, much less suitable endeavors to walk in God's way. Their purposes are to walk in their own way and in the imaginations of their own evil hearts. God makes known his will and discovers his way in the ministry of the word. But you let it have a highway through your head because you have no desire to walk in the way of God.

Let me reason with you, you that are of ungoverned tongues. Hath not God told you your duty? You that are proud, hath not God told you you

---

103. Romans 3:11—"There is none understandeth, there is none that seeketh after God."

ought to walk humbly? Hath not God told you it's your duty to repent? If you do not purpose to do what God makes known unto you, then tell me these things:

1. Why do you pray that God would make his will [*known*] unto you? Why do you desire to know it when you have no purpose of heart to perform it?

2. Why do you frequent ordinances when you lay stumbling blocks of iniquity before your hearts?

Secondly, it serves to reprove those that have some imperfect desires and feeble longings to know God's will, and yet are not so forward to perform it.

What is the reason of this?

1. There may possibly be some strength of lust or reigning corruption that disables from performance. Lusts in the heart drive a man from his purposes as a blast of wind drives the arrow from the mark. The stronger the distemper of a man's body, so the less able is he to perform what work he purposed and intended to do. The thing that hinders may be the weakness of grace and weakness of sanctified affection. "How weak is thine heart, O Jerusalem."[104]

2. There is such a material difference betwixt purposes and performing, that a man may be stirred up to purposes when he will not to performances. A powerful sermon is enough to beget purposes, a cross providence, or the like. But to perform is another [quest?] work. A man must wrestle with all his corruptions, break thorough all difficulties. And performances require a long continued time in practicing. It will not be done at once.

Fourth reason why men may be so forward in purposing and so slow in performing, may be because, when men have purposes they are on the heat of affection, begun with the heat of conviction. And as convictions do decay, so performances will be the slower and the less apt to hold. Thus you see the reasons why men are so backward in performing their purposes and so fall short of what they should do. Now let me press the reproof a little.

1. Purposes without performances loose a great deal of that reward you might have. For you to be in such a fair way and to come short and lose all, it's pitiful.

Again, if you have purposes, and yet feeble purposes that reach not to performances, they will be evidences to you another day that you knew your duty, and so you will be left without excuse. The Lord hath let so much light into yourself as to leave yourself without excuse. The doctrine needs no more witnesses; thy own conscience will be sufficient.

---

104. Ezekiel 16:30

Add further, what a spirit doth it discover, that thou shouldst have purposes without performances? It shows what a weak heart thou hast. What canst thou make of thy life? Weigh all these things, you that are so slow in performances.

Use next, for comfort and consolation to all the godly that find such a frame of spirit as this, to purpose and endeavor to walk in God's way and in some comfortable measure performing it. When God makes known his will to a heart that is in a right frame, that heart echoes, "I will do it, Lord," and accordingly endeavors. This is a gracious frame of spirit. If it reach to all known duties, it's a great trial of the heart. And if it reach to universality of obedience, a child of God will not make a slight matter of any known duty. If you find yourself in this frame you may be comforted.

Question: what if a man find in himself that he hath purposed sundry times to do the will of God in some things that hath been discovered to him to be God's will, and hath endeavored a little, and yet falls short of performing? What will you say of such a one?

1. I would ask, "What is it that thou hast purposed and endeavored and yet come short on performing? Is it in some fundamental, as in believing?" Repent. Or is it the suspension of some gracious act? For a man not to pray at all cannot stand with grace. But for a man to omit for some or for a whole is but the suspension of a gracious act, and may stand with grace.

2. I would ask, "With what willingness are these defects in performance? Within what frame of spirit dost thou mourn that thou canst not perform Gods will?" Grieve in thy spirit. Grieve under it. Then let me tell you, that a godly heart may find both ground of comfort and ground of humiliation.

1. Ground of comfort that God did give thee a heart to purpose and in some measures to endeavor—ground of comfort, that God did give thee a heart to close with his will; that thou hast such a frame of spirit; that God hath thy heart, though thou canst not reach to actual performance in all things. You testify what you would have done if God had given you abilities.

2. There is matter of humiliation—that you are so unstable in your spirit, that you are so unconstant, that you should leave undone that which is for God's honor. You may see the Lord had not need to trust you with much. Besides, I doubt you have cause to be humbled in this respect, that you do not so seriously endeavor.

Use last, for exhortation to everyone that they would purpose and promise and seriously perform to walk in God's way. Bring your hearts to it. When will you say, "I will walk in thy truth?" Resolve on it. Get strong resolutions. And then:

Secondly, see what a necessity there is in performing. Be serious in it. Do what you can do, waiting for power from above. If you have promised God to walk in his way, conscience will expect you should do it. Whatever duty God discovers unto you, bring your hearts to perform it.

OCTOBER 21, 1649

PSALM 86:11

Unite my heart to fear thy name.

Some read it thus: "Apply my heart to thy fear, and that with simplicity."[105] Some expound it thus: David being sensible of various temptations begs God, "Keep my heart close to thee that I may have thy fear always before me."

Doctrine: it is and ought to be the serious desire of the godly that their hearts might be united to God and the fear of his name.

The first reason consists of these particulars:

1. Godly men, yea all men, meet with many temptations. Everything, yea every condition, hath its temptations. Repentance hath temptations. Comfort and consolation hath temptations. What way some ever a man can be exercised, he will meet with temptations.

2. The heart of man is apt to comply with every temptation, temptations of any kind. If God should not keep your heart and mine, we are apt to consent unto [them]. How willing are your hearts to listen and hearken to any temptation? David complied with his temptation of prosperity: "I said in my heart, I shall never be moved."[106] David complied with his temptation of adversity, "I shall one day perish by the hand of Saul," and so with other temptations. Abraham's heart complied with the temptations of fear: "Say thou art my sister."[107]

3. The longer that the spirit sits from God, the more apt it is to comply with all these temptations. The more of God in the heart, the less will temptations work upon us. The soul's misery properly lies in its separation from God so that the more the heart is disunited from God and from his fear, the

---

105. Henry Ainsworth, *Annotations upon the Five Bookes of Moses, the Booke of the Psalmes, and the Song of Songs, or, Canticles*, (London: Iohn Bellamie, 1627), the section on "Psalmes," 130.

106. Psalm 10:6

107. 1 Samuel 27:1; Genesis 12:13

more apt it is to close with temptation. All these three things considered make up the reason why the godly should and ought to desire that their hearts may be united to God and the fear of his name.

Second reason: The godly do find that to have their hearts united to God and his fear is a great advantage unto them in three particulars:

1. They are in the most suitable frame for God's honor.

2. It makes much for our holy walkings to be closely united to God. If we can but draw near to God we shall walk the more holily. David found it so, and therefore could say, "It's good for me to draw near unto God."[108]

3. It makes much for our inward peace and comfort. The closer that any man's spirit is united to God and the fear of his name, the more advantage it will be to them [sic-*him*].

1. The first use informs us that it is usual with the godly, what they see they have need of, to commend unto God in prayer. When the godly want anything they go to God and make their wants known. Only the great misery is, we want praying hearts.

2. It informs us that prayer should be carried on according to the sense of men's wants. It's a fine frame of spirit when sense of wants teaches us to indict. So also when sense of sin teaches us to confess, it's a fine frame of spirit.

3. The desires of godly men oftentimes carry them after those things which they do not so fully attain unto. The desires of the godly are carried beyond that they can reach unto.

Next use serves to reprove two sorts:

First, wicked men whose hearts are not in any measure united to God or the fear of his name. Psalm 73:27—"They that are far from you shall perish." Wicked men are said to be far from God, and as the prodigal who went into a far country in his own actions, so in his spirit he was far from God. All men naturally, their spirits are at enmity and stand at a distance with God. There is little fear of God before their eyes. Take the reproof therefore.

Secondly, it serves to reprove that looseness of spirit that is in the godly, that your spirits sit so loose from God and his fear. And if you question whether your spirit sits thus loose from God, try:

1. Whether your spirits do not sit loose from God in ordinances, public or private. Do you never, when you come home, bewail the looseness of your spirits? And your absence from ordinances, especially on the Lectures, is it not much from looseness of spirit? And when you are at ordinances, how do you attend upon God? With what weakness, distractions, may be in your closet services? See whether you do not find looseness of spirit:

---

108. Psalm 73:28

slightiness,[109] slubbaring[110] over duty, neglecting it. How little reading or taking book in hand—but for fashion, not meditation. If your spirit sits loose from ordinances it argues you sit loose from God and the fear of his name.

2. Is there no looseness of spirit in your comfort, food, raiment, children? To close with the comforts rather than God in the comforts argues looseness of spirit.

3. Try whether your spirits do not sit loose in providences. The spirit that is tied to God and the fear of his name is the same in all providences.

Afternoon]

Several other things there are that may help to try our spirits in this point.

1. By inconstancy in duty and in purposes and resolutions. Whence doth all your inconstancy arise? What doth it argue but looseness of spirit, and that your spirits are not so united to God and the fear of his name as ought to be. Besides, again, let the godly look into the breaking forth of their sins and their corruption: some a worldly heart, some a passionate heart, some an unchaste mind, some one sin, some another, which the godly bewail at the throne of grace.

When you think upon these things and what [several?] temptations draw forth these corruptions, do they proceed from a loose spirit? So far as there is any guiltiness in you of looseness of spirit, you come under this reproach. And fasten on the reproof that you may take it to heart and be humble and consider the loathsomeness of such a frame of spirit.

2. How come you unto this frame of spirit? Your hearts have been more closely tied to God; then how came you to this looseness of spirit? By neglect of duty or breaking forth of corruption, not renewing repentance? That your hearts have been this out of frame is the more loathsome. Besides, again, looseness of spirit doth always evidence neglect of your watch;[111] and neglect of your watch brings looseness of spirit. Besides, again, looseness of spirit doth always argue decays in grace and in thy affections. Besides, looseness of spirit will plainly evidence that a man is in a greater measure laid open to sin, Satan, and temptation. Again, looseness of spirit doth plainly evidence slightiness of spirit in the spirit's work. A loose spirit is a cold spirit also—cold in the Lord's work. And where are those warm hearts, affections that you have had? And where there is looseness of spirit, a man carries on

---

109. neglectfulness
110. performing carelessly, going through quickly
111. watchfulness

the Lord's work by his own spirit. By these things you may see now what a bad frame of spirit it is. Truly it is a frame of spirit that is much to be bewailed.

Use next for comfort and consolation to all the godly.

1. The godly have great cause to be comforted, that do desire that their spirits should be united to God and the fear of his name.

1. It's a precious frame of spirit if you can attain unto it.

2. It's a comfort because it is a thing that may be attained unto. James 4:8—"Draw nigh to God and he will draw nigh to you." You may have your heart brought near to God if you will but draw nigh to him. And it's that frame of spirit that many of the godly have attained unto.

3. There is this ground of comfort: it argues much of God in that soul that doth desire to have his heart united to God and the fear of his name. A natural heart cares not to fear God.

2. It may serve to comfort those whose spirits are ~~they~~ already united to God and the fear of his name. It's a great blessing and that which you may take a great deal of comfort in.

Last use. Exhortations: 1. to get your heart united to God and his fear; 2. to keep your heart in that frame.

First, get your heart united to God and the fear of his name. What means should I use? For I find that my heart hath been tied closer to God than now it is.

Directions:

1. Find what it was that brought your heart out of frame. How camest thou to looseness of spirit? Find it out. If it be neglect of duty or breaking forth of corruption, whatever it be, bewail it and repent of it. Remember from whence thou art fallen, and repent.

2. When this is done, in the next place, renew thy watch. Neglect of watch hath brought you to this frame and temper; renewing thy watch must bring thee out of it. Thou must not now go from day to day without reading. Thou must not go from day to day without praying. And desire a blessing of God upon thee. Thou must not go from day to day without considering the sins of the day, without meditation, etc.

3. Prize and improve ordinances. Kitchen physic, the country people will say, is good physic. More skillful will say that there need [*be*] more wholesome diet to recover the body. The ordinances and afflictions of God are as kitchen physic. But the misery of the soul is that it becomes guilty with ordinances. Formality under ordinances will not recover the soul from its looseness of spirit. Isaiah 12:3—"With joy shall ye draw water out of the wells of salvation." Therefore I say, improve ordinances to God's honor and your own spiritual comfort.

Second duty that you are exhorted to is, if the spirit be united to God and the fear of his name, that you would labor to keep it in that frame. It's good to keep your heart in this frame, as David says when he and his people [*were*] offering willingly to "keep it forever in the purpose of the hearts of thy people."[112] So should a Christian ever labor to keep his heart in this frame.

You have need enough to keep your heart close to God; for if you do not your heart may lead you into soul-damning ways that you may have small comfort in. Our hearts are of such mettle that we cannot [*hold*] them to good behavior. Therefore we must go to God to entreat him to keep our hearts to good behavior and to keep them in his fear. And let us earnestly endeavor to keep them close to God, and so as may be most acceptable to God.

NOVEMBER 4, 1649

MATTHEW 15:22

And, behold, a woman of Canaan came out of the same coasts, and cried unto him, &c.

At this verse begins the story of the woman of Canaan, so famous in scripture.[113]

1. You have a description of the woman herself;
2. of her acts.

The woman is described
[1. by her sex;
[2. by her country.

2. Her acts are two:
[1. that she comes out of the same coast;
[2. she cried unto him.

3. A description of the manner of her crying. The manner of it is laid down in this request: "Have mercy upon me," and secondly, in this point: "My daughter is vexed with a devil."

---

112. 1 Chronicles 29:18

113. Moxon's introduction of Biblical material in this sermon follows a Ramistic form, and exhibits several close similarities to *Syrophaenissa or, The Cananitish Womans conflicts: In twelue seuerall Tractats discouered at Horndon on the hil, Essex*, 1598, attributed to Robert Wilmot (1601), 16, 20, 52.

The persons she calls upon are two:
[1. O Lord,
[2. thou Son of David.

Note from the woman: "and she was a Canaanitish woman," that is, in a sort a heathen; yet living among the Jews, was converted.

Doctrine: where God hath a people it often falls out that other strangers that live among them receive something of that religion, if not the power of it to their effectual conversion.

1. This may often fall out partly by the godly conversation of God's people who will dispute about religion.

2. This may fall out by reason of the people themselves. They will come to see and hear, though not out of any love [of] ordinances.

3. It falls out by this means, that people of differing nations and languages conversing together come in some measure to be acquainted with one another's language and so important matters of religion.

Use 1. Informs us that it is of great use [. . .]

"Have mercy upon me." Here is a double doctrine inferred.

First doctrine: children's sufferings are their parents' sorrows. "Have mercy upon me, for my daughter is grievously vexed."

3. Genesis 37:34 and 35—we shall find this: Jacob concerning his son Joseph. And likewise in David's case: 2 Samuel 12:16—his child begat in adultery, he weeps and mourns and will not be comforted. So in Absolom's case: 2 Samuel 18:33.

First reason is taken from the natural affections of parents to their children. Isaiah 49:15. 1 Kings 2:26.

Second reason: children are part of a family, and the affliction that God lays upon children is part of the family's suffering. 1 Kings 17:18. Lamentation 2:11, 12. They make it ground of lamentation that God should afflict them in afflicting the children. Ezekiel 24:21.

Third reason: because children are the delight of parents and the desire of parents.

Fourth, children are the greatest of God's outward blessings, a choice blessing, a chief blessing. Psalm 124:4, 5. Now when God doth begin to curse his blessings, to afflict us in our blessings, this becomes an affliction to parents.

1. Use reproves those parents that lightly regard the sorrows and sufferings of their children. Some regard not their children—spendthrifts that waste their estate and regard not to provide for their children. Do you regard your children when you care not how they go, and yet can help it? Do such regard their children as give them away? Those that care not for their children, it's pity they should have any.

2. For exhortation to a double duty:

1. Children, take heed of yourselves. If anything be amiss in you, it's your parents' sorrow. Therefore do you do your duty to your parents? Now you are grown up; if your aged parents need your help, requite them. If they be in any affliction, pity them. Help them. Make your parents' suffering your own, else it will be just with God, if ever you have children, to make them unnatural to you. And if you be helpful, and do lay to heart your parents' suffering, God may bless you in your children and make them as pity-full, as helpful, and as full of natural affection to you.

2. Let it exhort parents to their duty. Make the case of your children your own. If you can help your children, do. If you can prevent their sufferings, you should. Make their sufferings yours. You know how tender old Jacob was of Benjamin.[114] Do your duties; prevent what may be of your children's sufferings, and sorrow with them in their sufferings.

Afternoon?]

Have mercy upon me, my daughter is, &c.

She comes to Christ for mercy—uses the means.

Doctrine: it's parents' duty to seek help and remedy for their sick children. We shall find it the care of parents to seek help in such cases: Jeroboam for his sick child—1 Kings 14:2, 3, 4; the Shunamite woman—2 Kings 4:25; and Matthew 9:18—Jairus, a ruler among the Jews, comes to Christ in the behalf of his daughter; and Matthew 17:14, 15.

1. Reason: children are part of the care and charge in the family that God hath committed to parents. 1 Timothy 5:14. And indeed, if children should suffer through the neglect of parents, as it would be their sin, so God would requite their blood at their hands.

2. Reason: children are not able to help themselves—and yet holpen they must be. Common works of mercy require it of parents. If it be but a man's beast is sick, rather than he will lose his beast, he will use what means he can to cure it. And it's a work of mercy much more to a child.

First use serves to reprove parents that are negligent of their duties this way. Parents may be wanting in using the means out of various principles. Sometimes they delay, hoping it will be better. Sometimes they neglect it for fear of charges; there is a great deal of defect this way. We owe many duties to our children, and among others this is one: to seek remedy for their distempers, and that seasonably.

---

114. "Benjamean"

Second, it exhorts you to your duty. Nature teaches this duty, but grace should engrave it much more. Be helpful to your children, partly out of mercy to the child, and partly out of [. . .]. Attend your duty in this case. You have many examples in scripture.

Have mercy upon me, O Lord, thou Son of David.

She acknowledges Christ to be such a one as he is.

Doctrine: they that go to Christ for help had need know what and who Christ is:

1. Because if they be ignorant of Christ, they cannot so earnestly seek help of him nor so patiently wait for an answer from him. The woman of Canaan, it seems by her expressions, was thoroughly informed what a one Christ was.

2. When persons go to Christ for any help or remedy it's necessary they should ask in faith. And if they be not thoroughly instructed who Christ is, they cannot ask in faith. Therefore if men would proceed and take no denial it's necessary they should know who Christ is.

Use: serves to reprove those that do so little inform themselves concerning God and Christ and especially about the nature and offices of Christ.

Two things a man must have that would have a blessing:

1. A tongue to ask it;
2. Faith to receive it.

Prayer is the tongue to ask it, and faith is the hand to receive it. What a case had the woman of Canaan been in if she had said, "I hear Christ is the Lord and the son of David, but I cannot tell whether he be so or no." Labor to be rightly informed concerning Christ.

My daughter is grievously vexed with a devil.

Doctrine: it sometimes falls out that the children of godly parents are as grievously vexed as any others. Sometimes God doth not spare the children of godly parents. To have the hand of God upon children is a common calamity. The plague is one of God's great judgments, and yet it falls upon the righteous as well as the wicked.

Use: look up unto God as a great mercy to you, in that he restrains and rebukes Satan. God might let Satan loose and might vex you and your children. Bless God that doth keep you free.

Is grievously vexed with a devil.

Doctrine: if God give Satan liberty and let him loose upon any person, the devil will grievously vex that person. You have a story in Matthew and Mark that proves this: Matthew 17:15; Mark 9:17, 18. You may see the same likewise in Job. God let Satan loose on Job, and how grievously did he vex and torment him! If Satan be let loose, how grievously will he vex men. And the reason is this:

1. partly from his nature, which is to do mischief.
2. Devils are enemies—God's enemies, man's enemies.

Use: serves to reprove those that are willing to be bondslaves of Satan. All wicked men are bondslaves, to do his will at his pleasure. Hence it follows that the torments of the devil themselves hereafter shall be exceedingly great.

Lastly, let it exhort all men to labor to keep near and close unto God. Keep close to God, lest ye provoke God to let Satan loose on you to vex you with temptations and to vex you with torments. Oh therefore keep close to God and Jesus Christ! The looser you are, and the more vain and frothy, the more just with God to let Satan loose to vex and torment you.

NOVEMBER 25, 1649

Matthew 15:24

But he answered and said,
I am not sent but unto the lost sheep of the house of Israel.

These words are Christ's answer, not so much to the woman as to the Disciples. The woman had made a request, and Christ gave no answer. Now the Disciples come and mediate: "Send her away, for she troubleth us." Christ answers, "I am not sent but to the lost sheep of the house of Israel. This woman is a Canaanite, and I am not sent to help her. I am sent to the lost sheep of the house of Israel."

Two things are in these words:
1. Christ is sent to lost sheep;
2. Christ was sent to the lost sheep of the house of Israel.

First doctrine: Christ was sent to lost sheep. Here must several things be opened:
1. what is meant by sheep?
2. what is meant by lost sheep?

3. for what end was Christ sent, or, what is Christ to do to these lost sheep?

First, what is meant by ~~lost~~ sheep? It usually means the godly; yet, notwithstanding, any of the Jews and such as profess Christ may be among them. The godly are here meant by sheep, Christ's flock. "Fear not, little flock. Feed my sheep. Feed my lambs."[115] And the godly do resemble sheep in these respects:

1. Sheep are harmless creatures. So the godly, they are not willing to do anything that may offend God or man. Some carry matters according to their lust and corruption. Some, their wills lead them. But the godly desire to submit to God's will.

2. Sheep are profitable creatures. There is nothing of sheep but is useful and profitable: their flesh for meat, wool for cloth, skin for leather, their guts for lute strings. Their bones burnt to powder are good to dry up some sores that will not [heal] with other means. Their dung good for the ground. Their very horns some have used to make clout[116] leather for their shoes of them. So the godly are fruitful and profitable. They bring forth the peaceable fruits of righteousness. Colossians 1:10—they are fruitful in the fruits of the spirit. And Paul says of Onesimus, "now profitable to thee and me."[117]

3. Sheep are and ought to be under the hands of a shepherd. So all the godly are under the hands of a shepherd. Jesus Christ is their shepherd, the chief "Shepherd and Bishop of their souls."[118] Others are but under Christ, the ministers of the Gospel in Christ's stead, to whom he gives charge to feed his sheep. Christ hath not such care of the wicked as of the godly. The main end of all ordinances is in relation to the sheep, to the godly.

Second thing to be opened is, what is meant, "lost sheep"? Peter—"Ye were as sheep going astray."[119]

1. They may be said to be lost sheep going astray as they are in their natural condition. Luke 19:9, 10—Zacchaeus is a lost sheep, and Christ came to seek him and bring him home—and Zacchaeus in his natural condition yet.

2. Persons may be said to be lost that are lost in their own apprehension, such as judge themselves lost. Matthew 11:28—"Come unto me, ye that are weary and heavy laden," as much as ye that are lost on your selves, lost on [sic-*in*] your own apprehensions.

---

115. Luke 12:32; John 21:15–17
116. patch
117. Philemon 1:11
118. 1 Peter 2:25
119. 1 Peter 2:25

Third thing to be opened is, for what end did Christ come, or what is he to do to these lost sheep?

It's set down in three Scriptures: first, Luke 19:10—"The Son of man is sent to seek and save that which was lost." This is his work, according to the parable, Luke 15:4. To seek them, Christ must seek out his sheep and secondly, save them. Christ must save his sheep: therefore he is called a Savior.

The second scripture that shows why Christ was sent is Luke 4:18, 19.[120]

The third scripture is Acts 10:38—"whom God hath anointed with the Holy Ghost and power, who went about doing good and healing all that were possessed with the devil." God sent Christ for this end and purpose.

1. We are here to take notice of the exceeding great care the Father hath of his people, that he will send his Son from heaven to take care of them.

2. We are here informed of the end of God's sending his Son: it's for the sake of his sheep. The work of the ministry is for the lost sheep. It's for the elect's sake that God affords ordinances. There are a great many that hear the word and are in the number amongst the lost sheep; and yet notwithstanding, Christ was not purposely sent to them.

3. It informs us that that work that Christ was sent to do he will, and doth carefully attend.

4. Sometimes Christ's answers to your requests may seem to hold forth a denial. And yet in very deed, there is no such denial intended.

Afternoon]

I am not sent but to the lost sheep of Israel.

Why was Christ to meddle with none but Israelites? He did meddle with the woman of Samaria and others that were not Israelites.

1. Christ's meaning is that he was chiefly and in the first place sent to the Jews and house of Israel. "He came to his own, and they received him not"[121]—his own, his own nation, his own stock, the Jews. He came mainly to them, though others might receive good by him.

2. This woman might have said that she was of the house of Israel, for she was a proselyte among the Jews. Though she were not the stock of the Jews and of that nation by birth, yet being joined unto them she becomes one of them by profession. Now though Christ seemed to deny her by saying, "I am not sent but to the lost sheep of Israel," yet it's but a seeming denial, no real denial, for Christ never intended to deny her.

120. "The Spirit of the Lord is upon me"
121. John 1:11

Next use is for comfort and consolation to all lost sheep. I speak not to reprobates, but to lost sheep.

1. Christ is sent to lost sheep that are yet in their natural condition. Christ is sent to you. Though he be mainly sent to the lost sheep of the house of Israel, yet he is sent also to all lost sheep—and the rather [that] you have a ground of comfort; because Christ, though in his own person he was sent but to the lost sheep of Israel, yet by his ministers and servants he is come to seek all lost sheep. Christ will send one man and send another, that his lost sheep may be found. And they shall be found and saved. Where God hath persons to save, he will send men and means and instruments for such purpose.

1. It's a ground of confirmation and consolation to all that are lost in their own apprehensions. I would there were enough that did apprehend themselves lost. I know there hath been many of you that within a twelve month space were lost in your own apprehensions; and how it is with you now, I know not. But I fear God hath given you over to walk in your former ways and courses. There is a great deal of difference betwixt lost sheep and lost sons of perdition. Lost sheep shall be found and saved. Is there any lost sheep, therefore, among you, such as are lost in your own apprehensions? Here is a word of comfort to you. Though you may meet with backsliding fits and think Jesus Christ will never seek you more, yet let me tell you, Jesus Christ never rejects any but upon their not consenting to him. If ye consent to Christ's conditions, he tenders himself unto you. Art thou willing to consent? Then there is blessing enough in the Gospel, and mercy enough to thee. Christ came to seek thee. And if thou wilt come in and repent, thou wilt be saved.

Use for exhortation to everyone to labor to see when Christ is offered to you, is tendered to you. The ministry of the Gospel tenders Christ to you. And if Christ comes to you and tenders himself to you, and you will not receive him, you may justly perish in your sins. Oh how precious would Christ have been a while ago with many of you! What a spirit of prayer! Now what little regard of Christ! Doth not such a frame of spirit argue a curse of God on your spirit? Well Christ was sent to lost sheep, and Christ is tendered to lost sheep. If you will not accept him you may smart for it. Oh take heed, therefore, of putting him from you, lest he depart from you!

Doctrine: though Christ is sent to all lost sheep, yet he is mainly sent to the lost sheep of the house of Israel. ~~This will appear~~ I mean it of Christ being personally sent and coming in his own person, in his human nature. Thus Christ was mainly sent to the house of Israel. That appears by these considerations:

1. The promise was made to them. Romans 9:4. Acts 13:(26 or) 46 v. Matthew 10:5. John 1:11—"He came unto his own." He came first and chiefly to the Jews. The reason and ground is mainly because they were the only church in the world.

First use informs us the Jews are our elder brethren. They have had the proffers of Christ before we Gentiles.

Second, if Christ was sent to the Jews, then this clears the justice of God in leaving them to such a woeful condition at this day.

DECEMBER 2, 1649

Matthew 15:25

Then came she and worshipped him, saying, Lord, help me.

She still renews her former request and adds more to it.
First doctrine: religious worship was due to Christ when he was in his human nature upon the earth. We [have] many examples in scripture of many that worshipped him: Matthew 8:2; Matthew 9:18; Matthew 28:9; Luke 24:52. He was truly God though accompanied with the manhood, and therefore religious worship was due to him. But I intend not to insist on this.

Second, if God's people do not prevail they must continue and renew their request. (This I pass over.)

Third doctrine: (which I shall stand on) is, faith in the godly makes them continue, earnest in seeking, though they meet with some delays and seeming denials. Genesis 32—Jacob, wrestling with the angel, continues and would not give over till he obtains a blessing.

First reason: because faith rightly bottomed makes the godly to see that the promises are sure and certain, whatever they may meet with to the contrary. Acts 13:24[122]—they are called "the sure mercies of David." Psalm 19:7—"Thy testimonies are very sure." Romans 14:6[123]—the Apostle tells you that God doth what he doth out of grace, that "the promise might be sure." Faith apprehends the promises [are] sure, partly from the faithfulness of God; Titus 1:2—"God that cannot lie" hath promised. Hebrews 10:23—"Faithful is he that hath promised." 1 Thessalonians 5:25—"Faithful is he which hath called you, who also will do it."

---

122. Acts 13:34
123. Romans 4:16

Faith looks upon God as able to do that which he hath promised. God can do it. He can do according to the requests of his people. Says the Apostle, "To him that is able to do exceeding abundantly above all that we can ask or think."[124]

[*Second*] reason: faith carries the godly on to obey God, and to do duty as God bids. It's called "the obedience of faith;" Romans 1:5, Romans 16:26. Faith hath such an influence where it is strong that it carries the soul to obedience.

Now the reason lies thus. Duty requires God's people to continue seeking, though they meet with delays. And faith carrying them to do their duty. That duty requires the godly to continue [*in*] earnest appears by those instances of the importunate widow with the unjust judge, and the loaves that were earnestly borrowed—beginning [*at*] Luke 18:8. Romans 12—"Continue instant in prayer."[125] Colossians 4:2—continuing in prayer, as if he should say, "Continue and continue till you overcome," as Jacob continued wrestling till he had overcome. Continue in prayer. And watch thereunto; a man must add watching. And "be not weary in well doing."[126] This adds strength to the other commands. It's a duty, and where there is a duty faith carries the soul unto it.

Third reason: wherever faith is there are other graces accompanying, which help [. . .] duty, as hope and patience. Where there is faith there is hope, [. . .][127] and 1 Peter; where there is faith in God [*there is*] hope in God.[128] And I will show you also that where ~~hope is~~ faith is there is patience also. 1 Thessalonians 1:4 and 6. Hebrews 12—"who thorough faith and patience inherit the promises."[129] James 1:3—"the trial of your faith worketh patience." Revelation 2:19—"I know thy faith and thy patience." Yea, 1 Thessalonians 1:3—faith, hope, patience, all go together. So that now if men have but faith, they have hope and patience. And hope and patience will make a man continue earnest in duty. Psalm 4:1. Romans 8:25—"If we hope for what we see not then do we with patience wait for it." Where there is faith, hope, and patience a man's spirit will not sink, but he will be carried on through all difficulties.

One use informs us why many persons are so discouraged that they lay aside using the means and give over seeking—or at least are guilty of a great

---

124. Ephesians 3:20
125. Romans 12:12
126. 2 Thessalonians 3:13
127. Colossians 1:23?
128. 1 Corinthians 13:13, 1 Peter 1:21
129. Hebrews 6:12

deal of omission of duty. Now what is the reason of all this? The great reason is the weakness of your faith. Your faith failing [tear] unbelief is the ground of all. An evil heart of unbelief makes you to de [sic-*depart*?] [tear] from the living of God. You know the [spe?] 2 Kings 6 ult.—"This evil is of the Lord; wherefore should I wait for him any longer?"[130] Thus many begin to [. . .]

Afternoon]

A second use serves to reprove all those that do thus give over in the Lord's work. The woman, you see, gives not over, but renews her request, though she had denials. Therefore those that say, "The Lord hears me not, regards me not, and I had as good give over," and the like—to give over on such grounds as these are, your sin is great.

1. You are commanded to continue in prayer and to watch thereunto. "Be not weary in well doing. Stand fast in the faith. Quit you like men," &c. Now for you to lay duty aside, you plainly break all these commands.

2. Your laying aside duty, though it be but for a time, arises from temptation: temptation from Satan. And you ought resist Satan. 1 Peter—"whom resist steadfast in the faith."[131]

3. Give no place to the devil. Ephesians 6—"Stand against the wiles of the Devil;"[132] and v. 13—"take [*the*] whole armor of God that you may be able to stand;" and v. 16—quench "the fiery darts" of the devil.

3. Your sin is the greater in respect of the root from whence it proceeds. It proceeds from that evil root of unbelief. To let faith go and to sink in your spirits through unbelief, it's exceedingly dishonoring to God. 2 Corinthians 1:24—"By faith you stand." Then if you stand by faith, by unbelief you fall.

4. By laying duty aside you may here see the frame of your spirit. You will serve God while it is for your own advantage. But if it come to hard work, you will give over. You serve God, as I may say, for hire. Nay, inquire into your own heart, whether there be not a spirit of indifferency in you.

1. If you were as this woman [*you*] would take no denial, would not [tear] [way?] She had obtained her request
[tear] something, but when you will [apply?]
[tear] fall It argues indifferency

130. 2 Kings 6:33
131. 1 Peter 5:9
132. Ephesians 6:11

Appendix

Sermon at Windsor, Connecticut by the Rev. George Moxon[1]

10 BOOK 5 SERMON BY MR. MOXON AT WINDSOR— OCTOBER 21, 1638

1 Corinthians 11:28
"But let a man examine himself,
and so let him eat of that bread and drink of that cup."

Doctrine: that Christians by <u>due examination of themselves</u> should prepare themselves before they come to the Lord's table.

Reasons taken partly from God, partly from the duty, and partly from ourselves

One reason: God is present in the assembly.

Second reason: the ordinance is a spiritual ordinance; therefore bodily exercise profits not.

[Reason 2] <u>It is an ordinance</u> of spiritual communion wherein Christ and the soul must have spiritual union.

---

1. Douglas H. Shepard, "The Wolcott Shorthand Notebook Transcribed," Ph.D. diss., State University of Iowa, 1957.

Three, reasons from ourselves:

1. There is a great deal of unfitness in us for such service.

4. Ground of reasons in respect of examination itself doth much fit the soul.

One use of humiliation: to humble every one of us for our unpreparedness when we come before God in duties of this nature.

Glossary of Archaic Words and Usages

aggravate (verb) = exacerbate, exaggerate, make more serious

> "God does some way or other make us to aggravate our sin so far as we do condemn ourselves."—February 9, 1640

caviller (noun) = a captious or frivolous objector; a quibbling disputant.

> "You [cavillers] that have no power of godliness, you ungodly, you retainer of bosom sins, you that halt between God and the world"—December 27, 1640

challenge (verb) = lay claim to

> "you do not lay hold of these manifestations of the spirit and so challenge comfort."—March 2, 1640

contrivency (noun) = scheme, scheming

> "The heart of man is apt to be filled with abundance of care, nothing but contrivency."—January 26, 1640

contumation (noun) = insubordination, rebelliousness, disobedience

> "And they are puffed up . . . so far that they make themselves guilty of [contumation]. They do not see it is sin."—February 9, 1640

exercise (noun) = practice, fulfillment of duties

> "Besides ordinances there is a second kind of growth, even exercises under afflictions."—January 3, 1641

exercise (verb) = practice, perform, train

> "Under many trials God doth exercise his people."—February 16, 1640

fury (verb) = to drive to fury, to infuriate

> "God says fury thee not in me, but I do it for to purge you of your sin."—January 3, 1641

gog, as in *set on gog* (verbal phrase) = to stir up, excite, make eager

> "When Satan would set thee upon this gog thou art not sufficiently affected and so screw thee up higher and higher till your spirit tire."—April 1, 1649

heap (noun) = collection

> "If thou canst but assure thyself that thou hast interest [*in*] Christ then this heap shall be yours"—December 27, 1640

higgling (verb) = haggling, close bargaining

> "You must take him upon his own terms and not stand higgling with him"—December 13, 1640

insist (verb) = to stand or rest upon

> "... religious worship was due to him. But I intend not to insist on this."—December 2, 1649

instance (verb) = offer an example of

> "All the men in the world cannot instance one time that God did ever fail his people."—February 2, 1640

lapt (adj.) = wrapped

> "If a man were lapt under so much guilt and there were no way out, it were bad indeed."—April 15, 1649

lay down (verb) = prescribe, formulate

> "I lay it down, the godly; for so was David, and therefore it certainly holds true in others."—February 2, 1640

moidering (adj.) = bothering, bewildering

> "Now say our sinful, moidering hearts, 'We might pray—but what of that?'"—January 26, 1640

nonplus (noun) = inability to proceed

> "Yet still we are driven to a nonplus; and this teaches us to cast our care on God."—February 2, 1640

nose (verb) = to find out, to detect, to reproach, confront, upbraid, oppose

> "I believe it would nose any man to do it."—January 3, 1641

overly (adv.) = haughtily, superciliously, slightingly; also used by Moxon as an adj.

> "it might be you confess, but it is overly."—February 9, 1640

> "Do you not lie in overly confession many months before you confess aright?"—February 9, 1640

pitch upon (verb) = fix, settle

> "Now you must pitch upon this: what do you find of the spirit of God working in thee that an ungodly might not have?"—February 23, 1640

shrod (adj.) = shrewd

> "many a shrod knock"—December 27, 1640

> "It's a shrod sign of an ungodly when he stand at a stay."—January 3, 1641

sith (adv.) = since

> "canst thou have no patience towards him, or so little patience, sith he hath so much patience to thee?"—June 24, 1649

slighty (adj.) = superficial, negligent, careless, trivial

> "if ever a temptation come into your mind that cause a slighty esteem of the word . . . , labor to weed out evil thoughts and get a high esteem of the word"—May 6, 1649

slubbering (adj.) = hurriedly gone through; done or performed carelessly

> "See whether you do not find looseness of spirit: guiltiness, . . . slubbaring over duty, neglecting it."—October 21, 1649

sorrow (verb) = give pain to, make sorrowful

> "Heart sins, inward sins, close sins—do we bewail these? Sorrow them . . ."—July 15, 1649

GLOSSARY OF ARCHAIC WORDS AND USAGES

stick (verb) = linger, be unable to make progress

> "the sluggishness of our spirits makes us stick at a great deal of work that God would have us do."—June 3, 1649

sum up = summarize, as a judge in a trial

> "Now this is the reason that you have not drawn comfort, because you do not sum up the testimony of your conscience."—February 23, 1640

vild (adj.) = vile

> "we are vild, full of temptation, nothing but sin"—February 9, 1640

write upon (verb) = make a record of

> "you might write upon it that God will care for you"—February 2, 1640

Definitions from J. A. Simpson and E. S. C. Weiner, ed., *The Oxford English Dictionary*, second edition. Oxford: Clarendon Press, 1989.

List of Works Consulted

Ainsworth, Henry. *Annotations upon the Five Bookes of Moses, the Booke of the Psalmes, and the Song of Songs, or, Canticles.* London: Iohn Bellamie, 1627.
Ames, William. *The Marrow of Sacred Divinity.* London: Edward Griffin for Henry Overton, 1639.
Bailyn, Bernard. *The Barbarous Years.* New York: Random House, 2012.
Bremer, Francis J. *Congregational Communion: Clerical Friendship in the Anglo-American Puritan Community, 1610–1692.* Boston: Northeastern University Press, 1994
———. *Building a New Jerusalem: John Davenport, a Puritan in Three Worlds.* New Haven: Yale University Press, 2012
———. *First Founders.* Durham, NH: University of New Hampshire Press, 2012
Bridenbaugh, Carl, ed. *The Pynchon Papers.* Vols. 1, 2. Boston: Colonial Society of Massachusetts; distributed by the University Press of Virginia, 1982.
Bright, Timothie. *Characterie; An Arte of shorte, swifte, and secrete writing by Character.* London: 1588.
Broughton, Hugh. *A treatise of Melchisedek: proving him to be Sem.* London: for Gabriel Simson and William White, 1591.
Browne, Robert. *A Treatise of Reformation Without Tarrying for Anie.* Middleburgh: [Richard Schilders], 1582.
Bruchac, Margaret M. "Revisiting Pocumtuck History in Deerfield: George Sheldon's Vanishing Indian Act," *Historical Journal of Massachusetts* 39:1 & 2 (2011), 30–77.
Burt, Henry Martyn. *The First Century of Springfield.* Springfield, MA: 1898, vol. 1
Calamy, Edmund. *An Account of the Ministers, Lecturers, Masters, and Fellows of Colleges and Schoolmasters, who were Ejected or Silenced after the Restoration in 1660.* London: J. Lawrence, 1713.
Calvin, John. *A Commentarie on the VVhole Epistle to the Hebrevves.* London: by Felix Kingston, for Arthur Iohnson, 1605.
Capp, Bernard. *Cromwell's Navy: The Fleet and the English Revolution, 1648–1660.* Oxford: Clarendon Press, 1989.
Cogley, Richard W. *John Eliot's Mission to the Indians Before King Philip's War.* Cambridge, MA: Harvard University Press, 1999.

Demos, John Putnam. *Entertaining Satan*. New York: Oxford University Press, 1982.

Earle, Alice Morse. *The Sabbath in Puritan New England*. New York: Charles Scribner's Sons, 1891.

Eusden, John Dykstra. *The Marrow of Theology*. Boston: Pilgrim, 1968.

Forbes, Allyn B., ed. *Winthrop Papers*. Boston: Massachusetts Historical Society, 1947—.

Ford, Worthington Chauncey. "Letters of William Pynchon." In *Proceedings of the Massachusetts Historical Society* 48 (1915):35-54

Francis, Keith A. *The Oxford Handbook of the British Sermon 1689-1901*. Oxford: Oxford University Press, 2012.

Gordon, Alexander. "Moxon, George." *Dictionary of National Biography*, ed. Sidney Lee (London: Smith, Elder and Co., 1894). Vol. 39.

Gordis, Lisa M. *Opening Scripture: Bible Reading and Interpretive Authority in Puritan New England*. Chicago: University of Chicago Press, 2003.

Green, Mason A. *Springfield, 1636-1886: History of Town and City*. Springfield: C.A. Nichols and Co., 1888.

Hall, David D. *A Reforming People: Puritanism and the Transformation of Public Life in New England*. New York: Alfred A. Knopf, 2011.

———. *Witch-Hunting in Seventeenth Century New England*. Boston: Northeastern University Press, 1991.

Hardman Moore, Susan. *Pilgrims: New World Settlers and the Call of Home*. New Haven: Yale University Press, 2007.

Herget, Winfried. "Writing After the Ministers: The Significance of Sermon Notes." In Herget, ed., *Studies in New England Puritanism*. (Frankfurt am Main: Peter Lang, 1983), 118-120.

Innes, Stephen. *Labor in a New Land: Economy and Society in Seventeenth-Century Springfield*. Princeton: Princeton University Press, 1983.

Johnson, Edward. *A History of New-England: From the English planting in the Yeere 1628. untill the Yeere 1652*. London: Nath: Brooke, 1654. [i.e. 1653]

Karr, Ronald Dale. "'Why Should You Be So Furious?': The Violence of the Pequot War" In *The Journal of American History* 85(1998) 3:876-909

Matthew, H. C. G., and Brian Harrison, eds. *Oxford Dictionary of National Biography*. Oxford University Press, 2004.

Miller, Perry. *The New England Mind: The Seventeenth Century*. 1939. Reprint, Boston: Beacon, 1961.

Neuman, Meredith M. *Jeremiah's Scribes: Creating Sermon Literature in Puritan New England*. Philadelphia: University of Pennsylvania Press, 2013.

Norton, John. *A Discussion of that Great Point in Divinity, the Sufferings of Christ; and the Questions about his Righteousnes-Active/Passive: and the Imputation thereof*. London: A.M. for George Calvert, 1653.

Ong, Walter, S.J. *Ramus, Method, and the Decay of Dialogue*. Cambridge, MA: Harvard University Press, 1958.

Perkins, William. *The Arte of Prophecying, or, A Treatise Concerning the sacred and onely true manner and methode of Preaching*. London: 1607.

Powers, David M. *Damnable Heresy: William Pynchon, the Indians, and the First Book Banned (and Burned) in Boston*. Eugene, OR: Wipf & Stock, 2015.

———. "William Pynchon and the Meritorious Price: The Story of the First Book Banned in Boston and the Man Who Wrote It." In *Bulletin of the Congregational Library*, Boston, Spring 2009, 4-13.

Pynchon, John. "John Pynchon Moxon Sermon Notes (1640)," unpublished manuscript, Springfield History Library and Archives of the Lyman & Merrie Wood Museum of Springfield History, Springfield, Massachusetts.

———. "Notes of the Rev. Mr. Moxon's Sermons by the Hon. John Pynchon of Springfield (1649)," unpublished manuscript, Simon Gratz Collection, Historical Society of Pennsylvania, Philadelphia.

———. "Sermon Notes; possibly those of John Pinch (1625–??)," unpublished manuscript, in *Sermons Collection, 1640–1875*. Box 3, folder 26. Mss. boxes "s," American Antiquarian Society, Worcester, Massachusetts.

Pynchon, William. *The Covenant of Nature made with Adam Described, and Cleared from sundry great mistakes.* London: 1662.

———. *An Endevour After The reconcilement of that long debated and much lamented difference between the godly Presbyterians, and Independents.* London: by M.S. for John Bellamy, 1648.

———. *The Meritorious Price of our Redemption, Iustification, &c. Cleering it from some common Errors.* London: by J. M. for George Whittington and James Moxon, 1650.

———, and John Pynchon. "Account Book," manuscript volume, Forbes Library, Northampton, Massachusetts.

Roberts-Miller, Patricia. *Voices in the Wilderness: Public Discourse and the Paradox of Puritan Preaching.* Tuscaloosa, AL: University of Alabama Press, 1999.

Shelton, Thomas. *Short-Writing, the Most Exact Methode.* London?: 1626.

Shepard, Douglas H. "The Wolcott Shorthand Notebook Transcribed." Ph.D. diss., State University of Iowa, 1957.

Shurtleff, Nathaniel B. *Records of the Governor and Company of the Massachusetts Bay.* Boston: William White, 1854.

Smith, Joseph. *Colonial Justice in Western Massachusetts (1636–1702—The Pynchon Court Record.* Cambridge, MA: Harvard University Press, 1961.

Stout, Harry S. *The New England Soul.* New York: Oxford University Press, 1986.

Thomas, Peter A., "Bridging the Cultural Gap: Indian / White Relations." In *Early Settlement in the Connecticut Valley.* Deerfield: 1984, 5–21.

———. "Contrastive Subsistence Strategies and Land Use as Factors for Understanding Indian-White Relations in New England." In *Ethnohistory* 23:1 (1976):1–18.

Trumbull, J. Hammond, ed. *The Public Records of the Colony of Connecticut.* Hartford: Brown & Parsons, 1850, v. 1

Tyacke, Nicholas. *Anti-Calvinists: the Rise of English Arminianism, c. 1590–1640.* Oxford: Clarendon Press; New York: Oxford University Press, 1987.

Walker, Williston. *The Creeds and Platforms of Congregationalism.* 1893. Reprint, Boston: Pilgrim, 1960.

Williams, George H., ed. *Thomas Hooker—Writings in England and Holland, 1626–1633.* Cambridge, MA: Harvard University Press, 1975.

Willis, John. *The Art of Stenographie.* London: 1602.

Wilmot, Robert? *Syrophaenissa or, The Cananitish Womans conflicts: In twelue seuerall Tractats discouered, At Horndon on the hil, in the countie of Essex,* 1598. London: 1601.

Winship, Michael P. "Contesting Control of Orthodoxy among the Godly: William Pynchon Reexamined." In *William and Mary Quarterly*, 3rd series, 54:4 (1997):795–822.

———. *Godly Republicanism; Puritans, Pilgrims and a City on a Hill.* Cambridge, MA: Harvard University Press, 2012.

Wright, Harry Andrew. *Meeting Houses of the First Church of Christ, Springfield, Massachusetts.* Springfield: 1945.

Index of Sermon Topics and Names

Abel, 129
Abimelech, 180
Abraham, 55, 97, 101, 129, 143, 146, 150, 151, 152–53, 157, 171, 185
Achan, 175
Adam, 53, 54, 81, 88, 95, 125, 172
adversity, 48–49, 78
affliction, 45, 46, 47, 48–49, 52, 65–66, 110–11, 125, 168, 170, 188, 190–91
Ahab, 131
Ahaz, 174
angel, 92, 125, 143, 197
atheism, 51, 74, 180
Arminianism, 82
Austin (St. Augustine), 59, 181

backsliding, 61, 113, 124, 128, 138, 196
baptism, 83
belief—see faith
Benjamin, 191

Caananite woman, 189–90, 192, 193–95, 197
Cain, 125, 177
calling (as a Christian), 119, 154–55
cares—human, 45–47, 100, 145
children—youth, 48–49, 52–53, 55, 60, 72, 76–77, 80, 81, 83, 91, 98, 101, 104, 106, 109, 119–20, 140, 163–64, 174, 177, 187, 190–92

church governance, 80–84, 110
commandments, 103, 110, 117–21, 122, 130, 151, 158, 160, 174
comfort, 63–79, 87, 93–94, 104, 106, 109, 111, 113, 121, 123, 131, 133, 134–35, 144, 157–58, 160, 165, 167, 172, 180, 184, 185, 186, 187, 188, 196
complaining, 52, 59, 90–93, 100–102, 104, 108, 113, 142, 159
confession, 57–63, 69, 77, 87, 103, 126, 186
conscience, 46, 58, 64, 68, 69, 70–71, 75, 76, 84, 85, 86–87, 117, 118, 119–20, 121–22, 124, 137, 152, 165, 174, 183, 185
covenant, 48, 63, 72–73, 74, 75, 82, 83, 95, 97, 107, 129, 146, 153, 173
creatures and creation, 53, 55, 74, 121, 125, 126, 144, 145, 179, 194

David, 48, 54, 55–56, 57–58, 60–61, 62, 69, 73, 75, 77, 96, 97, 122, 125, 132, 147, 168, 174, 176, 178, 180, 181, 185, 186, 189, 190, 192, 197
death, 96, 105, 121, 161
diligence, 136–41
Dinah, 175
doctrine, 80–88

211

INDEX OF SERMON TOPICS AND NAMES

duty, 46, 50, 52, 60, 78, 85, 86, 87, 88, 121, 124, 126, 128, 131, 136–39, 142, 147, 148, 149, 151, 154, 158, 159, 160, 167–68, 170, 173, 179, 181–82, 183, 184, 185, 187–89, 191–92, 198–99

Eliphaz, 177
excommunication, 68
exhortation, 105, 136–37

faith, 46, 47, 49, 51, 54–57, 60, 63, 64, 72–73, 80, 81, 82, 86–87, 92, 93, 95, 97, 99, 100, 101, 102, 103, 104–5, 109, 113–14, 129–34, 142–43, 144–45, 146, 148–49, 156, 158, 159–60, 163–64, 167, 168, 173, 192, 197–99
faith-set faith at work, 46, 56, 99, 142, 148
famine, 49, 77–78, 145

God
    caring of, 49, 50, 52–57
    character of, 54–55
    dependence on, 51–52, 144–45, 166
    grace of, 71–72, 76–77, 79, 88, 94, 95–96, 99, 100, 101–2, 107, 108, 123, 127, 133, 134–35, 145, 147, 178, 184, 192, 197
    judgment of, 81, 96, 124, 148, 165, 173, 175, 178, 179, 192
    justice of, 61, 97, 124, 125, 135, 172, 178, 197
    love of, 55, 68, 137, 172, 182
    promises of, 46, 47–48, 56, 59–60, 61, 67, 69, 70, 71–72, 74, 75, 92, 94, 96–97, 98, 99, 100, 101, 103, 106, 109–14, 123, 126–27, 130, 140, 142–43, 145–49, 152–53, 155, 157–60, 162, 166, 168, 182, 184–85, 197–98
    providence of, 47, 48, 51, 54, 55, 56, 70, 73–75, 77, 99, 108, 183, 187
    word of, 48, 64, 70, 74, 76, 77, 106, 111, 119–21, 127, 129–36, 149, 151, 152, 156, 157, 178, 182, 195

good works, 55, 79, 86, 134
growth (in grace), 109–14

Ham, 177
happiness, 91–92, 134, 144, 172, 180
healing, health, 77, 91–95, 96, 98–100, 101, 104–8, 109, 111, 162, 195
heaven, 48, 54, 59, 85, 97, 118, 126–27, 128, 129, 134–36, 149, 156, 164, 166, 168, 169–70, 195
hell, 107, 118, 122, 133, 136, 141, 144, 154, 156, 161, 162–63, 168, 172, 179
Herod, 178
Hezekiah, 178, 180
Holy Ghost, 98, 170, 195
    as comforter, 64, 96
hope, 59, 71, 119, 123, 128, 142, 147, 148–49, 153, 157, 158, 160–61, 162–64, 165–70, 178, 198
hypocrites, 68, 159, 161–62, 167, 179, 181

inconstancy, 87–88, 184, 187
inheritance, inheritors, 113, 140, 142, 143, 152–53, 163–64, 198
instability, 83–85, 87, 88, 184
Isaac, 65–66, 97, 152, 171

Jacob, 73, 92, 113, 190, 197, 198
Jairus, 191
Jeroboam, 191
Jesus Christ, 93, 94–99, 104–8, 110, 111, 114, 178
    and God the Father, 95–97, 195
    and the Holy Ghost, 96
    ascension of, 169–70
    blood of, 94, 108, 125
    death of, 61
    as King, 56, 69, 70, 95
    Lord's Prayer, 78–79
    as mediator, 48, 63, 74, 95, 103, 169, 172
    as physician, 93, 98, 101, 102
    as Priest, 69, 70, 170, 171–73
    as Prophet, 69, 70, 74, 83
    resurrection of, 104
    as Shepherd, 193–97

INDEX OF SERMON TOPICS AND NAMES 213

Jews, 79, 129, 132, 171, 190, 191, 194–94, 197
Job, 53, 59, 65, 73, 147, 155, 173, 174, 176–77, 179, 193
John the Baptist, 77, 138
Joseph, 55, 58, 73, 150, 174, 190
Judah, 174
Judas, 125, 167, 177–78

law, 56, 58, 59, 118, 119–20, 121–22, 123–24, 125, 144, 151, 160–61, 173, 174, 181, 182
lust, 84, 95, 96, 103, 106, 107, 110, 112, 119, 124, 125, 173, 175, 183, 194 (see also unchastity)

Mary, 73
means of grace—in general, 46–47, 51, 56, 61, 72–73, 81–82, 84, 85, 88, 92, 102, 103, 110–11, 114, 118, 120, 125, 130, 135, 138, 141, 145, 148, 154, 157, 160, 162, 165, 167, 188, 191, 196, 198–99
means of grace—ordinances, 77, 104, 106, 110, 112, 121, 130, 131, 133, 135, 136, 141, 183, 186–88, 190, 194, 195
Melchizedek, 170–72
memory, 50, 58
mercy, 51, 55, 61, 68, 81, 91, 123, 124, 125, 135, 144, 147, 148, 149, 159, 191, 192, 196
ministers, ministry, 45, 64, 67, 76, 84, 128, 133, 136, 182, 194–95, 196
Moses, 55–56, 129

Nathan, 58, 61, 132
neighborliness, 54, 78–79
New England way, 81, 83
Nicodemus, 83, 130
Noah, 129, 177
oaths, 66, 150–52, 153, 157, 160
obedience, 65, 67, 87, 120, 178, 184, 198
ordinances—see means of grace—ordinances

pardon, 59, 60–63, 64, 72, 91, 93, 94, 104, 152, 156, 158, 162, 163
parents, parenting, 52–53, 81, 83, 98, 106, 120, 163–64, 190–92
patience, 63–64, 73, 99, 142, 143, 146–49, 198
Paul (Apostle), 46, 52, 53, 56, 58, 63–65, 66, 78, 79, 80, 81, 83, 85, 86, 95, 100, 101, 105, 120, 121, 124, 126, 129, 132, 136, 139, 143, 145, 146, 151, 152, 163, 194, 197–98
Peter, 77, 82, 105, 194
Pharaoh, 150, 182
Philemon, 65
popery, 81, 83
poverty, 48–49, 50, 54, 141
prayer, 47, 48–49, 53, 56, 61, 63, 73, 74, 78–79, 92, 99, 100–101, 102–3, 109, 112, 119, 125, 137, 140–41, 146, 162, 172–73, 176, 183, 184, 186, 188, 192, 198, 199
punishment, 62, 125, 150, 177–78, 182

questioning, 63, 76–77, 111, 131, 152, 179, 186

rejoicing, 64, 65, 66, 73, 75, 135, 158, 159, 164, 170
reform, 75, 107, 111, 134, 135
refuge, 157, 160–63, 168
repentance, 50, 62, 80, 83, 93–94, 103, 119, 121, 124, 126, 154, 168, 183, 184, 185, 187, 188, 196
rest, 123, 126–28, 134–35
righteousness, 63, 108, 170, 179, 194

salvation, 60, 81, 111, 113, 134, 135, 138, 140, 154–56, 162, 168, 169–70
sanctification, 94, 95, 97, 99–100, 104, 106, 172
Satan, the devil, 49, 69, 70, 77, 94, 96, 101, 103, 104, 107, 119, 122, 123, 124, 125, 127, 128, 131, 134, 138–39, 142, 145, 147, 149, 151, 158–59, 161, 163, 165, 167, 168, 170, 178, 187, 192–93, 199

Saul, 73, 77, 147, 168, 185
scandal, scandalous, 79, 88, 121, 138–39
self-righteousness, 68, 71
servants, 106, 120, 159
Shechem, 174
sheep, 110, 193–96
Shem, 171
sin, 117–26
    conviction of, 58–59, 87–88, 93, 131, 135, 182, 183
sloth, 139–42
Solomon, 46, 56, 104, 124, 140, 141
sorrow, 46, 49, 57, 66, 118–19, 123, 125, 127, 155–56, 190–91
suffering—see affliction
Tamar, 174
temptation, 45, 46, 49, 50, 56, 58, 62, 76, 77, 78, 82, 86–88, 94, 95, 98, 99, 100, 101, 102, 103, 104, 108, 113, 120, 127, 131, 138, 142, 147, 148, 149, 159, 165–66, 174, 175–76, 180, 185–86, 187, 193, 199
Titus, 65
trials, 65, 84, 86, 147, 149, 166, 170, 176, 184, 198
truth, 80–84, 130, 131, 180–81

uncertainty, 71, 76–77, 156, 168
unchastity, 173–78, 187
ungodly, 59, 67–68, 70, 71, 78, 106, 112, 114, 172

weakness, 91, 102, 148, 156, 165, 183, 186, 199
wickedness, 120, 124, 172, 174, 178, 180

youth—see children—youth

www.ingramcontent.com/pod-product-compliance
Lightning Source LLC
Chambersburg PA
CBHW052339230426
43664CB00041B/2491